THE PICNIC

The Meals Series
as part of the Rowman & Littlefield Studies in Food and Gastronomy

General Editor: Ken Albala, Professor of History, University of the Pacific (kalbala@pacific.edu)
Rowman & Littlefield Executive Editor: Suzanne Staszak-Silva (sstaszak-silva @rowman.com)

The Meals series examines our daily meals—breakfast, lunch, dinner, tea—as well as special meals such as the picnic and barbeque, both as historical construct and global phenomena. We take these meals for granted, but the series volumes provide surprising information that will change the way you think about eating. A single meal in each volume is anatomized, its social and cultural meaning brought into sharp focus, and the customs and manners of various peoples are explained in context. Each volume also looks closely at the foods we commonly include and why.

Breakfast: A History, by Heather Arndt Anderson (2013)

The Picnic: A History, by Walter Levy (2013)

THE PICNIC

A HISTORY

Walter Levy

ROWMAN & LITTLEFIELD
Lanham • Boulder • New York • Toronto • Plymouth, UK

Published by AltaMira Press
A division of Rowman & Littlefield
4501 Forbes Boulevard, Suite 200, Lanham, Maryland 20706
www.rowman.com

10 Thornbury Road, Plymouth PL6 7PP, United Kingdom

Copyright © 2014 by AltaMira Press

British Library Cataloguing in Publication Information Available

Library of Congress Cataloging-in-Publication Data
Levy, Walter.
  The picnic : a history / Walter Levy.
    pages cm. — (Altamira studies in food and gastronomy)
  Includes bibliographical references and index.
  ISBN 978-0-7591-2180-5 (cloth : alk. paper) — ISBN 978-0-7591-2182-9 (ebook)
  1. Picnics—History. 2. Picnics—Social aspects. I. Title.
  GT2955.L48 2014
  642'.3—dc23
                                                                2013027411

♾™ The paper used in this publication meets the minimum requirements of American National Standard for Information Sciences—Permanence of Paper for Printed Library Materials, ANSI/NISO Z39.48-1992.

Printed in the United States of America

CONTENTS

SERIES FOREWORD

Custom becomes second nature, and this is especially true of meals. We expect to eat them at a certain time and place, and we have a set of scripted foods considered appropriate for each. Bacon, eggs, and toast are breakfast; sandwiches are lunch; meat, potatoes, and vegetables are dinner, followed by dessert. Breakfast for dinner is so much fun precisely because it's out of the ordinary and transgressive. But meal patterns were not always this way. In the Middle Ages people ate two meals, the larger in the morning. Today the idea of a heavy meal with meat and wine at 11 A.M. strikes us as strange and decidedly unpleasant. Likewise when abroad, the food that people eat, at what seems to us the wrong time of day, can be shocking. Again, our customs have become so ingrained that we assume they are natural, correct, and biologically sound.

The Meals series will demonstrate exactly the opposite. Not only have meal times changed but the menu as well, both through history and around the globe. Only a simple bowl of soup with a crust of bread for supper? That's where the name comes from. Our dinner, coming from *disner* in Old French, *disjejeunare* in Latin, actually means to break fast and was eaten in the morning. Each meal also has its own unique characteristics that evolve over time. We will see the invention of the picnic and barbecue, the gradual adoption of lunch as a new midday meal, and even certain meals practiced as hallowed institutions in some places but scarcely at all elsewhere, such as tea—the meal, not the drink. Often food items suddenly appear in a meal as quintessential, such as cold breakfast cereal, the invention of men like Kellogg and Post. Or they disappear, like oysters for breakfast. Sometimes an entire meal springs from nowhere under unique social conditions, like brunch.

Of course, the decay of the family meal is a topic that deeply concerns us, as people catch a quick bite at their desk or on the go, or eat with their eyes glued to the television set. If eating is one of the greatest pleasures in life, one has to wonder what it says about us when we wolf down a meal in a few minutes flat or when no one talks at the dinner table. Still, meal-time traditions persist for special occasions. They are the time we remind ourselves of who we are and where we come from, when grandma's special lasagne comes to the table for a Sunday dinner, or a Passover Seder is set exactly the same way it has been for thousands of years. We treasure these food rituals precisely because they keep us rooted in a rapidly changing world.

The Meals series examines the meal both as a historical construct and a global phenomenon. A single meal in each volume is anatomized, its social and cultural meaning brought into sharp focus, and the customs and manners of various people are explained in context. Each volume also looks closely at the foods we commonly include and why. In the end I hope you will never take your meal-time customs for granted again.

Ken Albala
University of the Pacific

ACKNOWLEDGMENTS

This has been a long book-a-coming to print, and I thank everyone who offered ideas, advice, and encouragement. Foremost, it was Gene L. Moncrief who steadfastly kept me focused, stimulated, and well edited. (Love, etc.) For patiently listening to my chatter with enduring interest, I have untold gratitude to Alexander Levy and Meg Thompson, Matthew Levy and Amy (Amos) Yan, Katherine and Tony Roos, Kristina and Matthew Stark

At key moments, Andrew F. Smith provided choice advice, encouraged me. Chris and Gail Bones listened and took me to the Thames where Lewis Carroll picnicked with Alice and her sisters. Jill and Michael Todd listened and almost got me to picnic on the grass at the Glyndebourne opera. Robert and Karin Getting listened patiently at many picnics on the Saunders Kill. At a time when I was just starting out, John Julius Norwich surprised me with *The Picnic Papers*, Mark Hussey pointed me to Virginia Woolf's *The Voyage Out*, Tina Erickson got me a copy of the Strugatskys' *Roadside Picnic*, Dean Baldwin let me speak at the College English conference, and Krishnendu Ray told me about family picnics on the beach at Orissa. Thanks to colleagues in the Association for the Study of Food and Society and the Oxford Symposium of Food and Cookery. Thanks to everyone who graciously responded to my queries. Many libraries and museums provided assistance: the New York Public Library, the British Library, British Museum, Brooklyn Museum of Art, Metropolitan Museum of Art, Museum of London, Museum of Modern Art, National Gallery of Ireland, Tate Gallery, and the Victoria and Albert Museum. At Pace University, the staff at the Birnbaum library was extraordinary. Elisabeth Birnbaum, Amernel Valarie Denton, and Chloe Pinera were always helpful and got me materials from everywhere that an interlibrary loan might be arranged. Jonathan Blair helped with images and scanning. John Weedy provided the marvelous image of a picnic on the battlefield June 14, 1919. So many of you have given me leads, content, and contexts: Ken Albala, Karen Allen, Cricket Azima, Harold Brown. David Castronovo, William A. Clary, Bill Denheld, Cara da Silva, Jennifer Doyle, Katherine Dunbabin, Sara Dunne, John T. Edge, Rebecca Epstein, Brendan Flynn, Paul Fieldhouse, Steven Goldleaf, Jacqueline Goldsby, Barbara Haber, Michael Harden, Nina Harrison, Richard Hosking, Jenny Huston, Tijen Inaltong, Hiroshi Hasaguchi, Alice P. Julier, Karen Karp, Joni Kinsey, Beth Kushner, Diana Lachatanere. Helane Levine-Keating, Janet Marqusee Dewitt and Bebe Meaders, Anne Mendelson, Eileen Morales, Elbert Moore, Jr., Anne Murcott, James L. Myers, Alice McLean, Lynne Oliver, Judith O'Toole, Carol Padgett, Howell W. Perkins, Diana Redwood, Eugene Richie, Michael Russell, Martha R. Severens Emma Shepley, Abraham Silverstein, Henry D. Smith II, Jeff Sobal, Bes Spangler, Rosanne Wasserstein, William Whit, Psyche A. Williams-Forson, and Jean Fagin Yellin. I offer a *mea culpa* if I have forgotten that you helped. Because all of you helped me with the best parts, I confess that the errors are mine.

INTRODUCTION

This is a history of picnics and picnicking in England, Europe, and the United States. Selectivity has been required because people picnic world-wide and the custom is ubiquitous. There are thousands of picnics recorded in every genre in real life and the arts. For every item discussed or mentioned here, scores of others, alas, have been omitted.

Though picnicking ranges freely across real and fictional boundaries, they are relatively hard to find, particularly because they are not usually indexed. There are only a few who have tried to make sense of the history, and they deserve great credit for their efforts. Georgina Battiscombe's *English Picnics* (1949) has led the way and serves as a standard.[1] She is often the cited, and more often the uncited, source for picnic lore. Others who deserve acknowledgment are Osbert Sitwell, Carter W. Craigie, Mary Ellen Hearn, Karen Eyre and Mireille Galinou, Jeanne-Marie Darblay and Caroline Mame de Beaurepaire, Julia Csergo, and Francine Barthe-Deloizy.[2]

Robert Louis Stevenson called the aesthetic feeling based on being in a good place "the spirit of picnic."[3] Gertrude Stein agreed and tried to capture its essence in a prose composition "France" (1922), writing, "An excursion, what is an excursion, an excursion is a picnic, if it recurrent, it is a picnic, if there is no absence, it is a picnic, and necessarily, it is a picnic." She is clearer about expectations in the poem "Every Afternoon":

> We will picnic,
> Oh yes.
> We are very happy.

Very happy.
And content.
And content.[4]

A year later, composer Erik Satie published "Picnic," a musical joke twenty-five seconds long![5]

Feelings aside, others will add that the feeling requires food and drink, and that it is not a "true" picnic without these. Whether there is really a distinction between the real and the faux picnic remains moot. Stein and her partner Alice B. Toklas, frequently packed sandwiches in a basket, stowed them in their Ford, and set out to picnic. Toklas recorded this in her *Cook Book*,[6] but her writings comingle more on feeling than food.

No two picnics are alike. They are similar because they share common patterns. But not everyone leaves home, dines outdoors, and has fun. This history sets out to prove otherwise, but the reality is that picnics are all variations on a theme, and happy people tend to have happy picnics, while unhappy people tend to have unhappy picnics. Writers and artists having all the imaginative room can make a picnic any which way they choose, and as you will notice, they do so with bravado.

The picnic in real life has the advantage of being palpable, fresh, and festive. The real picnic combines preparation, expectation, and actuality. At a real picnic you can taste the food. Figurative picnics offer other pleasures and intellectual stimulation. They are the creative work of writers, painters, and musicians who suggest that where there is pleasure there is also conflict and tension. For every aspect of a picnic in real life, there is an opposite. The extensive range and frequency of figurative picnics attest to its enduring values for creativity. This is another surprise, but as picnics have succeeded in providing diversion in a busy world, so creative imaginations twist its expectations, providing new sources of pleasure and intellectual stimulation.

Picnickers seeking the ideal will be satisfied only with "a perfect day for a picnic." Spring or summer is preferred, but any season will do. They prefer the outdoors to the indoors, anywhere—on land or at sea, in backyards or parks, on beaches or rooftops—wherever a space can be found to spread a blanket or set a table and chairs. The perfect day is summery and clement; there is a light breeze to mitigate heat and rustle leaves, and the sky is clear with a scattering of clouds. The picnic blanket is set on grass beneath the shade of a large tree beside a stream or nearby water. Birds sing; a breeze moves the foliage. Incredibly, perfect picnics happen often enough so that they are expected—rain, cold, or ants to the contrary.

THE CLASSIC CONTEMPORARY PICNIC

1. Picnics are dependent on leisure, whether planned or spontaneous.
2. Destinations are invariably away from home (town or city), and typical destinations are sites in the country, beach, park, or forest. Mostly picnickers travel by car and seldom walk.
3. Preparations are usually gender specific: women prepare the food and pack the baskets; men manage transportation.
4. The common saying "a day in the country" conveys that a picnicker's preferred site is most frequently a grassy lawn beneath a shady tree beside a stream anywhere.
5. Picnickers prefer to sit on the ground on a blanket or cloth, sometimes with cushions, less frequently with tables and chairs.
6. Before the dining, picnickers may go off to play or find mild adventure or make love.
7. Food is usually prepared beforehand but may be cooked on-site. It is served all at a single course.
8. Etiquette ranges from informal to formal; some prefer disposable plates and utensils, others prefer porcelain, silver flatware, and crystal stemware.
9. The return home is within twenty-four hours.

1

THE HISTORY
OF PICNICS

Yet nobody, I think, would pretend that it was other than an ugly word, picnic, verging on chit-chat, or snip-snap.

—Osbert Sitwell, "Picnics and Pavilions,"
Sing High! Sing Low! (1944)

Have a picnic at the slightest excuse.

—James Beard, *Menus for Entertaining* (1965)

A picnic is an outdoor meal distinguished from other meals because it requires the leisure to get away from home. It is the antithesis of established social routine and work, for it is only by breaking out of the workaday world to play, party, eat, and drink that one can picnic.

A picnic immediately conjures powerful imagery suffused with pleasurable social associations with food and drink. Unlike breakfast, lunch, or dinner meals that are relatively time bound and consumed at specific times of day, a picnic is free of time restraints, and it may be consumed any time of day or night. Breakfast, lunch, and dinner are routine because people must eat, but a picnic is a reward of leisure that gets people out of work and out of the home. If necessary meals are consumed indoors in homes and restaurants, picnics are usually consumed away from home and often in a natural setting. They are recreational feasts and, either hosted or potluck, picnics are supplied with prodigious amounts of food and drinks. Whether gourmet or gourmand, it is presumed that no picnicker will leave hungry or thirsty.

The picnic pleasure principle suggests that picnics are simple, idyllic, and entirely without stress. This has generated expressions suggesting that something is an easy task or feat, or more likely its opposite. The most commonly used paradoxical expressions are "Life is not a picnic," and "War is not a picnic." *Harry Potter and the Deathly Hallows*, J. K. Rowling's final Harry Potter novel, has Ron Weasley, fresh from battling Lord Voldemort, tersely reply to Neville Longbottom, "It hasn't exactly been a picnic, mate."[1] In rural America, Allan Pinkerton, the original "private eye," suspected that a campfire in a deserted wood meant trouble. "There was no picnicking in those days," Pinkerton contentiously writes, "people had more serious matters to attend to— and it required no great keenness to conclude that no honest men were in the habit of occupying the place."[2] A picnic is effusively convivial, communal, and radiating good will. Only picnic haters such as author Robertson Davies ever complain that picnics are too much of a good thing. "Personally," he writes. "I have always greatly liked dinner-parties, and hated picnics. But then I am a classicist, by temperament, and I think the formality and pattern, either in love or in entertaining, is half the fun."[3] Colloquially, hipsters have taken a new slant, and it is a sharp slur is say that someone is "two sandwiches short of a picnic."

Effectively, what we now think of a picnic can be traced back about five hundred years. Although people have been dining outdoors forever, the picnic is specialized and has a relative historical start date but has no proper name. Appearing around the 1500s and 1600s, it was just an outdoor meal or party without a name. An outdoor meal was named by the Spanish a *merienda* and the Italians a *merenda*, but the name did not catch on elsewhere in Europe. In 1694 the French named an indoor meal a *pique-nique*, but they did not link it with dining alfresco. They resisted doing so and pervasively influenced other Europeans. The English were aware of the custom of a *pique-nique* dinner but did not publically engage in them until 1802, by which time they Anglicized the spelling as *picnic*. Four years later, the picnic dinner turned topsy-turvy, from indoors to outdoors. This linguistic adaptation was disregarded by the French but embraced by the English and then the Americans, so that by the mid-nineteenth century the only picnic is an outdoor picnic. Even the reluctant French concurred.

Historically, picnicking coincides with modern history; the shift from pastoral to urban living, the decline of villages and the rise of modern cities, and changes in work conditions that are the result of improved technology, industrialization, and modes of travel. Importantly, as people begin working more indoors in cities, there are new attitudes toward the need for leisure. There is an urge to leave the workaday and reverse patterns by leaving home and city for the country, or even some facsimile of country, a lawn or a grove of trees.

Because work is so important and cannot be left for long, the picnic is short. Usually, it is the time it takes to get away and return conveniently the same day. So when the opportunity for leisure arises a picnicker seizes the day, stocks a basket, gathers dining gear, a blanket, and perhaps an umbrella, and heads for somewhere where there is no work—a park, the country, the beach, or a forest.

If you think about it, the more urbanizing and industrialization create barriers to the country to keep people in towns and cities, the more people are apt to picnic. This is what is so striking about *Picnic* (2005), the street artist Banksy's beach scene depicting a group of indigenous African hunter-gatherers looking at a contemporary white, middle-class, urban family at leisure picnicking.[4] Conspicuously, while picnickers are smiling and convivial, the hunter-gatherers are incredulous, if not bewildered. The picnickers are eating and drinking and relaxing; the hunter-gatherers are standing like statues. The picnickers' children have come with toys, the hunter-gatherers with their hunting gear. The family is away from home; the hunter-gatherers are not. Their routine is constant, and they have neither the understanding of what it means to picnic in our sense. We recognize Banksy's joke because we have immediate knowledge and constant memories of our own picnics.

ORIGINS

Pique-nique is a French word of unknown origin. It is Parisian and appears first in 1649 in an anonymous broadside published in Paris titled *Durable Friendship of the Brothers of Bacchic Picnic* [*Les Charmans effects des barricades, ou l'amitie durable de la compagnie des freres Bachiques de Pique-Nique, en vers Burlesque*].[5] It is a satirical joke about the gourmandism and prodigious drinking of Brother Pique-Nique, a hero at the barricades during a period of unrest and civil war known as the Frond. It was also a period of food scarcity, and part of the satire was to redirect thoughts to a new era symbolized by Pique-Nique's gourmandism. Because there is no joke without a reference, the *Bacchic Picnic* must be satirizing an already established dining custom, or of some outlandish personality given the name *Pique-Nique*. Nothing tells us what or who might be the butt of the joke.

Whatever else was intended, sharing food and drink is what Pique-Nique and his brethren were about, and as their custom evolved in Parisian society, it became more genteel and prevalent enough so that the erudite linguist Gilles Ménage included it, for the first time, in *Dictionnaire du Etymologique de la Langue François* (1694) as a trendy dinner to which each guest contributed a share to the table, *chacun paye son* écot. He suggests this is a Flemish custom, but no evidence yet supports this. Significantly, he leaves plain that the word and the custom are urban, Parisian, because it is a unknown in the provinces, *il est inconnu dans la pluspart de provinces*. Even more importantly, Ménage implicitly suggests that it is a meal eaten indoors in the comfort of one's salon or dining room.

With hindsight, you may wonder how Ménage's *repas a pique-nique* changed from indoors to the outdoor picnic. The short answer is that this linguistic process took its time while two parallel meals competed for dominance—the French *pique-nique* and the English cognate *picnic*. The competition reflects France and England's political reality for one hundred years as robust linguistic exchanges mingle with war. Steadfastly, the French insisted that Ménage's definition of *pique-nique* is the only definition. When the word was admitted officially to the language in the *Dictionnaire de l'Académie Française* (1740), Ménage's definition was repeated unchallenged, and it continued unchanged for more than a hundred years. Being more linguistically flexible, the English sorted through variations until settling on *pic-nic* or *pic nic*, but most importantly it was also considered to be an indoor meal until 1806 when John Harris, a publisher of children's books, called an alfresco wedding party a *pic-nic dinner*.[6] Because the shift aroused no argument in England, we can assume that Harris's usage was already in linguistic play and that other outdoor picnic dinners were common but not reported privately or publically. The tempo of accepting the outdoor picnic was rapid, and within fifty years the indoor picnic was passé. It was replaced with the English potluck dinner, a century older than *pique-nique*, now familiar as a meal to which guests bring a share of something to eat. In fact, it was an Elizabethan custom mentioned first in author/playwright Thomas Nash's essay *Strange News* (1592) and play *Summer's Last Will and Testament* (1592).[7]

MERENDA AND MERIENDA

Overall, the French ignored adaptations and variations and stuck to the notion that a *pique-nique* must be indoors. They ignored the English shift from indoors to outdoors, just as they had long ignored the Italian *merenda* and the Spanish *merienda* because neither was an indoor meal. The stumbling block to linking *pique-nique* and the Spanish *merienda* was that at a French meal contributions must be shared for the provisions or the cost for an indoor meal, but at a Spanish meal, the meal was hosted outdoors. So, for example, Ménage was probably familiar with alfresco *meriendas* in Miguel de Cervantes's novel *Don Quixote* (1606), especially lunch with the Curate (chapter XLIX), and poet and author Francisco de Quevedo's *The Swindler* (1626) that takes place in the Casa de Campo—still one of Madrid's favorite parks. However, being outdoors, Ménage would not consider them because these were not in the *pique-nique* style.[8]

Because the Latin word *merenda* meant a light afternoon meal or snack, the French ignored it. *Pique-nique* was a meal, and diners shared by contribution or cost. It was not a snack. Ménage, who was an important etymologist and a Greek and Latin scholar, found no historical referents and connections. In *The Etymologies*, Isidore of Seville's authoritative encyclopedia of knowledge (ca. 615–630), a *merienda* is a meal taken late in the day between midday lunch and dinner. John Florio's influential English-Italian dictionary, *A World of Words* (1611), defines *merénda* as a "repast between dinner and supper," but he does not mention where it was served, or if it was even a shared meal. Though the concept of *merienda* had changed over the succeeding millennium, Ménage ignores it, and he infers that *pique-nique* is a Parisian word.

Others sometimes make illogical linguistic and alliterative connections and assumptions. Mr. Arthur Wilson, a well-meaning Englishman, was sure that *pic-nic* was a Swedish word because he found it in a Swedish dictionary, even though the Swedes never claimed the word. Editors of the *Columbian Cyclopedia* (1897) were adamant that "the picnic is pre-eminently an English institution: the F. *pique-nique* is derived from Eng. *picnic*, and not *vice versa*."[9] Patience Gray, a food writer, speculates that *merenda* derives from *merum*, Latin for "pure." In her Italian cookbook *Honey from a Weed* (1987), she reasons that because Italians drink wine at picnics, it must be pure; hence a picnic is a *merenda*.[10] Of course, this is not the case. From another angle, James Beard's *Menus for Entertaining* (1965) and M. F. K. Fisher's "The Pleasures of Picnics" make the case that "true" picnics must be outdoors. Fisher is implacable: a "true" picnic must be outdoors, away from home.[11] By 1953 when Fisher wrote the essay, only a crackpot might picnic indoors. Importantly, neither Beard nor Fisher considers that a picnicker must contribute or pay for the cost of the meal—an oversight that demolishes the cliché that everybody brings something to a picnic.

ANACHRONISMS AND VARIATIONS

So powerfully evocative is the concept of an outdoor picnic, it is taken for granted that almost any picniclike gathering without regard for historical time or place context *is* a picnic. This suggests many anachronisms, some of which may actually be relative to *picnic*'s linguistic evolution. Ancient Babylonians might be surprised to know they were picnicking on the ninth day of their New Year celebration when following their king and priests to a temple in the fields. But the historian of ancient Middle Eastern civilizations, Jeremy Black, suggests that leaving the city for the fields makes this something special, a "cultic picnic."[12] Granted, this is an anachronism, but it is also an attempt to find the right word to explain something to an audience already familiar with picnics.

There is no word for picnic among the classical Greeks. But for want of a better word, contemporary translators of the Attic playwright in Menander's comedy, *The Bad-Tempered Man* (316 BCE), make a ritual meal a picnic. The joke involves satirizing the preparation of a meal and sacrifice offered by a family seeking a marriage blessing to the god, Pan, at his temple above Athens. Because the meal is eaten away from home, modern translators call it a picnic. Some translators of *The Bad-Tempered Man*, E. W. Handley, Maurice Balme, and Robert Lloyd, call the meal a picnic, but this may be due to contemporary linguistic familiarity with picnicking. Balme makes the offering a scornful object of the bad-tempered man, Knemon: "The sacrifices these devils make! / They bring their picnic hampers and their jars / Of wine not for the gods but for themselves."[13]

Katherine Dunbabin, the prominent historian of Roman civilization, discusses picnics in her survey of Roman dining customs, *The Roman Banquet* (2003).[14] She is aware of the anachronism, but she states that *picnic* best suits meals that Romans enjoyed while sitting at the stone benches and tables outside the tombs of their dead or feasting at the end of a successful hunt. The center medallion in the fourth-century Sevso Hunting Plate shows an arbor, under which four men and a woman recline on a thick bolster, or *stibidium*, placed beside a dining table. While these hunters party, servants butcher, prepare, and cook the food, some fresh killed: elk, deer, bear, boar, and fish—a picnic.

Other picniclike events are found in the works of writers such as Ovid, Plutarch, Seneca, and Athenaeus. Ovid's *Fasti* contributes a description of Anna Perenna, a Roman New Year celebration in a sacred grove on the outskirts of Rome where "the common folk come, and scattered here and there over the green grass they drink, every lad reclining beside his lass."[15] Plutarch's *Table Talk* mentions the festival of Nones Caprotinae (July 7) and an outdoor banquet on the beach. Seneca's *Moral Letters to Lucilius* (65 CE) describes a luncheon in the country as one of the great, simple joys of life at which a man can eat figs and talk and write about the good life.

Searching for the right word and labeling an outdoor meal a picnic is common (and understandable). Scottish historian Thomas Carlyle reports that on
a clement evening in October 1654, Oliver Cromwell, the Lord Protector of
England, picnicked in Hyde Park. While it is true that Cromwell *did* dine on
the grass in Hyde Park, there was no English word for it in 1654. Cromwell's
secretary of state reported, "His highness, only accompanied with secretary
Thurloe and some few of his gentlemen and servants, went to take the air in
Hyde-park where he caused some dishes of meat to be brought; where he made
his dinner."[16] Since it was a pleasant outdoor meal, even with an unhappy ending, Carlyle's take was that it must be a picnic. Writing in 1868, Carlyle knew
that when dining outdoors in a leisurely way, it is a picnic, because that was
now the custom.

PARSING *PICNIC*

Picnic etymology is twisty and needs parsing. Why the French joined *pique* and
nique is a mystery that Osbert Sitwell, for one, chose to ignore. *Picnic* is an ugly
word, he writes, "a busy, self-assertive mediocre word, that has sacrificed all
dignity, but without attaining any compensatory sense of ease."[17] Ugly or not,
combining *pique* and *nique* ought to make linguistic sense. But attempts to do
so resulted in etymological obfuscation and frustration. The 1911 edition of the
Encyclopedia Britannica suggests that in French *pique-nique* may be a rhyming
word or a small, old, French coin, a *pique, or* related to the verb *piquer,* as in
"to prick." The *Random House Dictionary* reiterates that *picnic* is probably a
rhyming word of an indeterminate source but omits *nique;* so do Britannica,
Webster's *The Revised and Unabridged Dictionary, Merriam-Webster's New
International Dictionary,* and Larousse's *Gastronomique.* Eric Partridge's
Origins: A Short Etymological Dictionary of Modern English (1958) makes only
slight attempts to explain *pique,* but it offers no explanation for *nique.* Partridge
suggests *pique* is derived from *piquant,* meaning "sharp or pungent," but he
ignores *nique.* The *Oxford English Dictionary* provides the most definitive
entry. It stresses history but ignores the origin of the word—a tacit admission
of its obscurity.

When E. C. Brewer edited the durable *Brewer's Dictionary of Phrase and
Fable* (1870), he helpfully wrote that *picnic* and *pique-nique* are derivatives of
the Italian phrase *piccola nicchia* (a small task). But his source was muddled and
wrong. John Anthony had erroneously explained that when *piccola nicchia* is

shortened to *picc'* and *nicc'*, it is an easy transition to *pique* and *nique*.[18] Neither Anthony nor Brewer considered that Italians were not using *picnic* but expressions such as *colazione sull'erba, scampagnata*, or *merenda* for their picnics. Both are either unaware of the Spanish custom of *merienda* or chose to neglect a connection with *picnic*. Brewer's helpful suggestion is that *picnic* may be linked to *eranos*, the Greek custom of a meal to which guests bring a contribution. This reference is to Homer's *The Odyssey*, Book I, when Telemachus angrily complains that Penelope's suitors ought to be contributing a share to the meals she provides them. Ostensibly, this custom of sharing seems picnicky, but *eranos* did not survive. By the third century, it is already a quaint custom according to Athenaeus, in his book of commentaries *The Deipnosophists* (third century). By the end of the seventeenth century *eranos* is known only as a banking term signifying a loan. This is probably a reason for disregarding it and overlooking its original meaning. Modern picnicking also changed, and sharing by contribution was no longer a factor when Brewer was compiling his etymology.

PIQUE-NIQUE AFTER MÉNAGE

By 1750, the *repas de pique-nique* was socially à la mode in Paris—and it is always presumed to be an aristocratic custom. According to Philibert-Joseph Le Roux's *Dictionnaire comique, satyrique, critique, burlesque*, it is primarily fashionable among people of quality where wit is enjoyed at home or in a cabaret. The new twist is that picnickers are *required* to bring food or drinks or pay a share of the cost. But while the custom of *un repas de pique-nique* was a rising social trend, it was unappealing to writers and painters. Le Roux does not link *pique-niques* to anything but social dining indoors, although outdoor scenes of the genteel dining in parks and gardens were extremely popular and extensively painted by Jean-Antoine Watteau and his contemporaries, Jean François de Troy, François Le Moyne, and Cárle-André Van Loo, all of whom refrain from using *pique-nique* to reference an outdoor meal. Instead, these painters used Watteau's descriptors *fête champêtre* and *fête galante* for social and romantic entertainments and the hunters' repast during or after the hunt. From 1713 to 1723, Watteau's paintings such as *The Foursome, Assembly in a Park, Fête in a Park, and Fête Champêtre* demonstrate these scenes. Watteau comes closest to a *pique-nique* in the small painting *The Collation*, aka *Imbiss Im Freien* (ca. 1721), in which two couples eat lunch on the grass. The couples are intimate without being sexual, and they pose on the grass as at a picnic in our sense,[19] but this is not what the artist calls it. Likewise, Watteau's large *Rendezvous de*

Chasse is retitled in English as *The Halt during the Hunt* (ca. 1717–1720).[20] It is a scene typical of the genre, illustrating hunters who have stopped for lunch in a field being met by their wives or companions. Watteau, however, skips food, an omission that suggests this may be an excuse for an amorous tryst.

Overall, there is implicit agreement among painters that a *pique-nique* is not an alfresco lunch. The word, however, was circulating, and it was used for contrasting the intimacy of a *pique-nique* with a public feast in a Parisian street song (ca. 1748–1750):

> What is this public banquet?
> Is it a picnic?
> No,
> It is a blast
> Given, they say,
> To celebrate the peace.
> And all these fancy preparations
> Are being charged to the city.[21]

About the same time Parisians sang about picnics and public banquets, when Jean-Jacques Rousseau dined at home with friends in what he called the picnic style, he might enjoy *un repas de pique-nique*, but when he took a lunch along on a walk it was a *petite goûter* eaten on an excursion. *The Confessions* (1782) shows off Rousseau's use of the two patterns, one indoors and the other outdoors, that never properly converged. Though Rousseau was writing in 1767, he remembered that sometime about 1745 to 1747, he and the philosopher Abbé Étienne Condillac dined privately at home: *il venait quelquefois dîner avec moil tête à tête en piquenique.*[22] But he does not *pique-nique* on a walk in Chambéry with his mentor (and lover) Françoise-Louise *de Warens*.[23] Nor does his lunch with acquaintances Mlles. Graffenried and Galley count as a *pique-nique*.[24] Anachronistically, these are picnics, and this is how J. M. Cohen treats them in his translation of *The Confessions* (1954). Of the *petite goûter* episode, Cohen sensibly has Rousseau explain: "We carried a picnic with us to Chapeaux, which we heartily enjoyed."[25] It is a translation because it appropriately characterizes the event and the associations are correct, but Rousseau writes, *Nous portâmes aux Champeaux un petit goûter, que nous mangeâmes de grand appétit.*[26]

As restaurants became popular in Paris after the 1750s, it was sometimes the custom to share expenses in the *pique-nique* style. Le Roux hints at this in his *Dictionnaire* by mentioning that Parisians might picnic in a cabaret. Abel Broyer is more direct, and his *Le Dictionnaire Royal François-Anglois et Anglois-François* (1756) explains that *picnic* means sharing the cost of a meal, as in the euphemism "clubbing at a reckoning." Rebecca Spang's *The Invention of the Restaurant* documents the rise of the restaurant and dining out in Paris and takes the notion of each diner paying a share at a restaurant as *pique-nique*, "everybody owed something."[27] This was Rousseau's custom, and he mentions this in his memoir *Reveries of a Solitary Walker* (1776–1778), where he dined at Chez Vaccasin, an established restaurant, *en manière de pique-nique*. The shift from dining at home to sharing the cost at a restaurant is easy and practical. Rousseau might have preferred it, since he was usually short on funds. Eventually, this custom evolved, and in 1887, it was called *Dutch treat*, a term purported to originate in the United States.

PIQUE-NIQUE IN ENGLAND

By 1748 *assemblées* or salon gatherings among the aristocracy were sometimes referred to as a *pique-nique*, but not in England. It was a social feature in Leipzig, at the time Lord Chesterfield questioned his son, Philip, about how he spent his time. "I know that you go sometimes to Madame Valentin's assembly," Chesterfield asked. "What do you do there? Do you play, or sup, or is it only la belle conversation?" While Philip's reply is lost, Chesterfield responded on October 29, 1748: "I like the description of your picnic, where, I take it for granted, that your cards are only to break the formality of a circle, and your symposium intended more to promote conversation than drinking."[28] Whether Chesterfield knew about *picnic* before his son's reply is unknown. It seems not to have been circulating in London, or else Chesterfield might have made a connection. Nathan Bailey's *An Etymological Dictionary* (1721, 1756) and Samuel Johnson's *A Dictionary of the English Language* (1755) both omit *picnic*. (Johnson preferred adding as few French words as possible to the English lexicon.)

Fifteen years later, when Lady Mary Coke was in Hanover, Germany, during the social season of 1763, she wrote to her sister, "I was last night at a Subscription Ball which is called here Picquenic."[29] Though the ball is socially familiar, the name was not. A decade later, comedic playwright Samuel Foote joked about a meal called a "nick-nack" in *The Nabob* (1772). The tortured alliteration adds to the joke, but it would only have been successful if the audience knew *nick-nack* meant *un repas en pique-nique*.[30] It is not easy to surmise if Englishwoman Cornelia Knight, a novelist, knew about picnics before she attended one in 1777 during a layover in Toulouse on her way to Italy. She writes in her diary that she was entertained at a "pique-nique" dinner and dance, but she drops the subject.[31]

During a hiatus during Britain's war with France in 1802, a group of over two hundred aristocrats formed the Pic Nic Society. Their name Anglicized *pique-nique*, and their intent was to produce theatrical entertainments followed by lavish dinners and then gambling. William Combe, editor of the *Pic Nic* journal, explained, for those not in the know, that *pic nic* signified "a repast supplied by contribution," but he is skittish and barely mentioned its French roots.[32] Ironically, it was not the French context that ruined the Pic Nics but the greed of William Brinsley Sheridan, who operated a professional theater at Drury Lane and feared a loss of income. As the Pic Nic spat tumbled into the local newspapers, Londoners eager for scandal rejoiced when caricaturists, especially James Gillray, savaged everybody involved. The most enduring is Gillray's "Blowing up the Pic Nic's:—or—Harlequin Quixote attacking the Puppets. Vide Tottenham Street Pantomime (April 2, 1802)," which is particularly mean to Sheridan and Lady Albina Buckinghamshire. He is in a torn harlequin suit, and she is bare breasted.[33] The Pic Nic caricature was aimed at personalities and not at a picnic dinner. However, its notoriety worked a linguistic charm for *pic nic*, by which you might laugh at excesses of gluttony. In a flash, Gillray lifted *picnic* from obscurity into the light of English parlance. Even if people had never before heard of a picnic or dined at a picnic, they could still snicker at the outlandish behavior of the aristocrats. Even sixteen years later John Keats used *pic nic* in a letter to George and Georgiana Keats (1818): "Perhaps as you were fond of giving me sketches of character you may like a little pic nic of scandal even across the Atlantic—."[34]

As the Pic Nics sank from sight, *pic nic dinners* reappeared in two children's books, John Harris's *The Courtship, Merry Marriage, and Pic-Nic Dinner of Cock Robin and Jenny Wren* (1806) and Mary Belson Elliot's *The Mice, and Their Pic Nic: A Good Moral Tale* (1809). There was confusion about what a "pic nic dinner" was, however, because Harris made it an outdoor party, while Elliot set it in the pantry of a London townhouse. Eventually the public agreed with Harris, who deserves credit for being the first to call an outdoor party a picnic. This is a fortuitous linguistic leap that, at last, unites the two parallel customs, the indoor *pique-nique* dinner with the previously unnamed outdoor meal. No one, either English or French, seems to have noticed. The change was implicitly accepted, tucked away, and slowly applied as the English, but not the French, realized that outdoor meals now had a name.

A PICNIC BY ANOTHER NAME

In the early 1800s there is a disinclination among the French artists and writers to use *pique-nique* for an outdoor gathering, and it is not the word of choice.

Figure 1.1. James Gillray, "Blowing up the Pic Nic's:—or—Harlequin Quixote attacking the Puppets" (1802), engraving.

This is symptomatic in Jean-Anthelme Brillat-Savarin's *The Physiology of Taste, or Meditations on Transcendental Gastronomy* (1825), where it is called a *haltes de chasse*; in Gustave Flaubert's *November* (1842), where it is *une partie*; and Gustave Courbet's *The Hunt Picnic* (1858) where it is *le repas de chasse*. Édouard Manet's and Claude Monet's *Luncheon on the Grass* (1863 and 1865) are *dejeuners sur l'herbe*. Neither Émile Zola nor Marcel Proust uses *pique-nique* in their novels, though they describe picnic scenes: the former in *Madeleine Férat* (1886), and the latter in *Within a Budding Grove [À l'ombre des jeunes filles en fleurs]* (1919). Proust says that Marcel and his friends sat on the grass and opened their packets of sandwiches and cakes. For one of his most important series of lithographs, Fernand Leger used the colloquial expression *Partie de campagne* (1952–1953), and for his satirical sci-fi comedy, Jean Renoir named his film *Le déjeuner sur l'herbe* (1959).

Among the English, Jane Austen is among the first namers of picnic. There are two outdoor picnics in the novel *Emma* (1816), the first in George Knightley's strawberry garden at Donwell Abbey, and the second, at Box Hill, Surrey. But William Wordsworth never uses the word *picnic*. His sister, Dorothy Wordsworth, uses it in passing in 1808, but in 1818 her travel essay is titled "Excursion Up Scawfell Pike, October 7th, 1818," and the picnic at the summit is just another meal: "We ate our dinner in summer warmth; and the stillness seemed to be not of this world."[35]

There are two picnic episodes in Charles Dickens's *Pickwick Papers* (1835) that are not designated picnics—one in an open carriage, and the other in a field during a hunting outing. Ditto a meal on the prairie outside of St. Louis, Missouri, in *American Notes* (1842), that Dickens thought was among his best outdoor meals: "We encamped near a solitary log-house, for the sake of its water, and dined upon the plain."[36] Surely this is a picnic, but Dickens refrains from naming it so. It is also a feast and a typical example of picnickers' tendency toward gluttony.

Sometimes English picnics were known by the euphemisms *vagabonding, ruralizing,* or *gypsying*. Food, coffee, and tea were made over a gypsy fire. William Wordsworth, not a namer of picnics, describes an evening visit to Lake Grasmere in *The Excursion* (1814), in which a group sits in a circle around a "gypsy-fire." They have dinner, relax, and linger as a young girl sings a "simple song."[37] Andrew Hubbell suggests that a scene like this indicates that Wordsworth invented picnicking. But this is an exaggeration, and otherwise Hubbell is on target when he says that a picnic "is leisure time well spent."

Jane Austen suggested gypsying as a matter of simplicity in *Emma* (1816). At first Mrs. Elton, a busybody, wants informality: "There is to be no form or parade—a sort of gypsy party." Later she has other ideas that include a "picnic parade." Outwardly, Emma is submissive, but inwardly she is offended, because she disagrees with Elton's statement, "One cannot have too large a party."[38] Charles Robert Leslie's painting *Londoners Gypsying* (1820) shows a family ruralizing, though this might be Hampstead Heath. Dickens's *David Copperfield* (1850) makes the open fire the means to boil water for tea in "the gipsy-fashion." David's romantic affection for Dora Spenlow is displayed at her picnic birthday party, an event narrated in the chapter "Blissful."

CHILDREN'S PICNIC LITERATURE

The lasting influence of Harris's and Elliot's stories is due to the pattern they created for future writers of children's books. Even a partial list of these stories with picnic episodes is impressive. Picnics show up in *Tom Sawyer*, *The Wizard of Oz*, *The Wind in the Willows*, *The Secret Garden*, *Winnie-the-Pooh*, *Babar's Picnic*, *Chitty Chitty Bang Bang*, and several Mickey Mouse stories. Most indelible is "The Teddy Bears' Picnic," a classic song that suggests a picnic without ever getting to one. According to Jimmy Kennedy's lyrics, the bears play games, sing, and dance. There is neither food nor drink; it is neither a joke nor a satire. Questions about origins and history fade away, until all that matters is the surprise and that "today's the day the teddy bears have their picnic."[39]

PICNIC IN THE UNITED STATES

Picnic meant a New York joke when it first appeared in the journal *Salmagundi; or, The Whim-Whams and Opinions of Launcelot Langstaff, Esq., and Others* (1807). Whether it was Washington Irving or his collaborator Fitz-Greene Halleck who wrote the satire, *picnic* meant something silly. Under the heading "Fashions by Anthony Evergreen," they write: "Picnic silk stockings, with lace clocks, flesh-coloured are most fashionable, as they have the appearance of bare legs—. The stockings are carelessly bespattered with mud, to agree with the gown, which should be bordered about three inches deep with the most fashionable colored mud that can be found."[40] As an Anglophile, Irving probably picked up the term in the aftermath of the Pic Nic Society scandal during his tour of Europe from 1804 to 1806. *Salmagundi*, the name chosen for Irving's magazine, is a picnicky, all-in-one dish (cold salad, meats, and hard-boiled eggs) that's easily served and as transportable as any picnic food. The next year, *picnic* appeared in a Charles Williams's pirated version of Harris's children's book *The Courtship, Merry Marriage, and Pic-Nic Dinner of Cock Robin and Jenny Wren* in Philadelphia (1808), but it went unnoticed. Fifteen years later, James Fenimore Cooper used *picnic* as a nonsense word in his historical novel *The Pioneers* (1823). It is spoken by a drunk, uneducated character, Benny Pump, who spews a series of non sequiturs—"monkey," "parrot," "picnic," "tar pot," and "linguisters."[41] The effect of this alliterative string of words suggests that not only is a picnic nonsensical but also somehow vulgar. Cooper probably knew better, but his novel was set in 1797 when *picnic* was not a word used in American parlance. Eventually, Cooper got around to a genteel picnic in the novel *Home as Found* (1838), but he called the "repast on the grass" a *rustic fête*.[42] Disdaining affectation, Thomas Cole chose a picnic for the subject of the painting *The Pic-Nic Party* (1846). It is important because it is a recognizable outdoor party and immediately establishes the picnic as a serious theme for American artists.

By 1869, Americans were claiming picnicking as a birthright. "Picnic Excursions" (1869), an anonymous essay in *Appleton's Journal*, declares, "It is a cardinal belief with every man, woman, and child that a picnic includes pretty nearly the most perfect form of human enjoyment," then goes on, "but the great charm of this social device is undoubtedly the freedom it affords. It is to eat, to chat, to lie, to talk, to walk, with something of the unconstraint of primitive life. We find a fascination in carrying back our civilization to the wilderness."[43] The implication is that picnics are irrefutably American because Americans work hard and deserve leisure. Winslow Homer provided an illustration *The Picnic Excursion*, depicting a group of about eleven young women and two men stopping by the side of the road for a small refreshment. As two women watch, a man uncorks a wine bottle, and a small, wiry terrier looks askance, his eyes showing disapproval.[44]

INDOORS OR OUTDOORS

Until picnics shifted from indoors to outdoors, Americans, English, or indeed any picnickers enjoyed the comfort of their salons, dining rooms, or restaurants. Once picnics got out of the house, they maintained the same expectations but engendered a whole new set of attributes, one of which is to enjoy leisure in nature. This is not really new, but commentators accentuate the return to nature and play in its many variations, but they go picnicking as sightseers.

Osbert Sitwell first suggested that outdoor picnicking brings out a savage quality in people, stating that dining in nature is elementally savage in otherwise ordinary people: "You are savage once more," he supposes tongue-in-cheek, "a noble

Figure 1.2. Winslow Homer, *The Picnic Excursion*, wood block engraving. *Appleton's Journal of Literature, Science, and Art*, August 14, 1869.

savage who has descended from his mountainous retreat, or a mariner wrecked for an hour or two upon a desert island."[45] The hyperbole was not lost on Georgina Battiscombe, who was inspired by Sitwell and comes to the same conclusion in her excellent history, *English Picnics* (1949). With typical English sangfroid, she writes: The English picnicker "is a devotee of the simple life; for a brief moment he apes the noble savage. Before the Romantics had made nature fashionable no one connected the idea of pleasure with the notion of a meal eaten anywhere except under a roof."[46] Both she and Sitwell exaggerate though it is probable that Battiscombe's hyperbole is tongue-in-cheek. Eventually she disproves of the genteel savage notion by her own civilized examples, but nothing is about to rain, evidence to the contrary, on Battiscombe's English picnic.

2

CLASSIC PICNIC FARE IN THE UNITED STATES AND ABROAD

Picnic dinners are much the same in all parts of the world,
and chickens and salad are devoured at Jerusalem very much
in the same way as they are at other places.

—Anthony Trollope, *The Bertrams* (1858)

You can make it as simple or elaborate as you want.

—Laurie Colwin, "Picnics" (1993)

What do people bring to a picnic besides good spirits? The short answer is
that baskets, wickers, bento boxes, or paper sacks are usually crammed
full with anything portable. It's a regular social trait that picnickers all over the
world are careful about what is packed and served, care less about ingredients
than how much there is, and serve it all at once in one course. Food writer
Laurie Colwin suggested that a picnic might be as simple or as elaborate as
you want. The choice is a matter of appetite, style, and means.[1] However, most
picnic trend toward being elaborate, most baskets are overstuffed, and most
picnickers play the role of gourmand, even the dieters. What is striking is that
picnics and food scarcity do not mix. When it comes to picnic food, having
more, not less, of everything is normal, even if spur of the moment or carefully
planned.

In America, hot dogs and apple pie seem important, because they are ubiquitous. But picnic culinary history indicates otherwise. There is a very notable
exception. In 1939, when King George VI and Queen Elizabeth were hosted by

President Franklin and Eleanor Roosevelt at their country home in Hyde Park, New York, everyone gasped when the menu included hot dogs. If the royals were surprised, they kept their cool, since the real business was diplomacy. The picnic was just a subterfuge that enabled Roosevelt a chance to assure the king that he would support Britain in the inevitable war with the Nazis. No one sweated over an open grill, except the Roosevelts' cook, who worked the kitchen and grill about a mile away at Mrs. Roosevelt's Val-Kill cottage. There are claims that the Roosevelt/royals' picnic "made" hot dogs popular in America, but food writer Bruce Kraig's *Hot Dog* (2009) sets the record straight.[2] In fact, the menu was more than hot dogs, and the buffet luncheon included iconic American foods such as Virginia ham, smoked turkey, cranberry jelly, green salad, rolls, strawberry shortcake, hot coffee and tea, local draft beer, and orange and lime sodas. (There was no apple pie.) Of course, newspaper headlines seized the day, and even without verification, a reporter claimed that the

Figure 2.1. John Sloan, *South Beach Bathers* (1907–1908), oil on canvas. Collection of Walker Art Center, Minneapolis. Gift of the T. B. Walker Foundation. Gilbert M. Walker Fund, 1948.

king particularly liked the hot dogs, and the *New York Times* ran the headline
"King Tries Hot Dog and Asks for More and He Drinks Beer with Them."[3]
There are no photographs, and for the fun of it, you might imagine the royals
eating hot dogs with the same delight as the people in John Sloan's painting
South Beach Bathers.

Classic picnic fare is overwhelmingly not about hot dogs, and American food
and cookbook writers seldom make the effort to comment on them. More likely,
a picnic menu might include cold fried chicken, deviled eggs, sandwiches,
cakes and sweets, cold sodas, and hot coffee. Food author James Beard's *Cook
It Outdoors* (1941) makes it plain that "the food should be as much of a contrast
to your daily menu as the surroundings in which you eat are to your own dining room." Because "picnic appetites are usually stupendous," he insists that
there needs to be "oceans of food."[4] Alice Waters concurs, and *Chez Panisse
Menu Cookbook* (1982) suggests roasted red peppers with anchovies, potato and
truffle salad, hard-cooked quail eggs, marinated cheese with olives and whole
garlic, roast pigeon and purple grapes, sourdough bread with parsley butter,
Lindsay's almond tart, and nectarines.[5] English food writer Isabella Beeton's
"Bill of Fare for a Picnic of 40 Persons" designs a feast that must have taken the
cook staff days to plan, prepare, and pack. Beeton's picnic menu appears in her
monumental *Mrs. Beeton's Book of Household Management* (1859–1861) and is
the epitome of picnic fare, including: a cold roast beef, a cold boiled beef, two
ribs of lamb, two shoulders of lamb, four roast fowls, two roast ducks, one ham,
one tongue, two veal-and-ham pies, two pigeon pies, six medium-sized lobsters,
one piece of collared calf's head, eighteen lettuces, six baskets of salad, six cu-
cumbers, stewed fruit well sweetened, three or four dozen plain pastry biscuits,
two dozen fruit turnovers, four dozen cheesecakes, two cold cabinet puddings,
two blancmanges, a few jam puffs, one large, cold plum pudding, a few baskets
of fresh fruit, three dozen plain biscuits, a piece of cheese, six pounds of butter,
four quartern [*sic*] loaves of household broad, three dozen rolls, six loaves of tin
bread for tea, two plain plum cakes, two pound cakes, two sponge cakes, a tin
of mixed biscuits, one-half pounds of tea, a stick of horseradish, a bottle of mint
sauce, salad dressing, vinegar, made mustard, pepper, salt, good oil, pounded
sugar, three dozen quart bottles of ale, packed in hampers, ginger beer, soda water, and lemonade, of each two dozen bottles, six bottles of sherry, six bottles of
claret, champagne à discrétion, and any other light wine that may be preferred,
and two bottles of brandy. "Water," Mrs. Beeton offers without any apparent
humor, "can usually be obtained so it is useless to take it." This certainly light-
ens the load, immeasurably.[6]

Worldwide menus generally prove the point that more is better. Madhur Jaffrey's *Climbing the Mango Trees: A Memoir* (2005) describes picnicking in Delhi in the 1940s when the entire family, about thirty people including servants, would pile into cars and then set out for some garden or palace open to the public, such as Qutb Minar, a thirteenth-century tower.[7] The picnic began at dawn when the food was prepared at home: potatoes in ginger tomato sauce, *pooris*, meatballs with wetted palms, pickles, and fruits, all stuffed into baskets. Utensils would be packed, charcoal braziers, or *ungeethis*, pots, pans, and tea pots were collected and readied for use—what Jaffrey calls *batterie de cuisine pique-nique*. Once the site for the picnic was chosen, servants spread a blue-and-white-striped dhurrie over which a white cloth was spread. Picnickers sat cross-legged and picked food from serving platters with their hands. Jaffrey says that they rarely used plates or cutlery; instead, *pooris* were used as plates. Tea was poured into disposable terra cotta cups, *mutkainas*. Among Jaffrey's favorites for picnic lunches are meatball curry, koftas, eaten with *pooris*; lamb with spinach; mung bean fritters and *phulka*, bread—all foods she describes in her cookbooks, *An Invitation to Indian Cooking* (1973) and *A Taste of India* (1988).

By contrast, the style of a Bengali family at a *choruibhati, picnic*, on the beach at Orissa, Chandipur, seems informal but is traditional. According to Krishnendu Ray, a food historian, such a picnic is the culmination of a Hindu holiday where the meal is prepared on-site at an open-hearth fire called *chullah*.[8] Ray remembers that everything was packed to cook on-site—the raw ingredients, the pots and pans and such—a considerable undertaking. It is among the rare occasions when men do the cooking and the women do the prepping for the meal. One of the favorite dishes is a vegetable stew of potatoes, pumpkins and cauliflower, turmeric, fresh ginger, *kalonji* (caraway), fenugreek, fennel, cumin, and coriander. There is rice, *dal* (dried beans stripped of their outer hulls and split), stewed vegetables, and tomato chutney with dates, raisins, and *jaggery* (unrefined sugar).

Favorite times to picnic among the Japanese are in the spring and fall when picnikers view cherry blossoms (Hanami) or red maple leaves (Momojiri). For both occasions, the Japanese bring ample food in a bento box—a lunch box divided into compartments and stacked one on the other. A traditional bento might be filled with *hanami dango* (a three-colored rice dumpling on a skewer), *onigiri* (a rice ball, formed into triangular or oval shapes and often wrapped in seaweed), *norimaki* (sushi rolls), chicken or shrimp tempura, karaage chicken fried with sesame seeds, *kamaboko* (fishcake), and raw, cooked, or pickled vegetables.[9] Beverages packaged separately include water, wine, and *Nihonshu*, Japanese sake.

Far from ocean beaches, Tibetans prefer to picnic in gaily colored tents of golds, blues, and reds. But in Barbara Banks's memoir, "A Tibetan Picnic," they dine on grass warmed by the sun on a plateau about sixteen thousand feet high.[10] Lunch is sliced, dried mutton dipped in ground red pepper, roasted barley dough called *tsampsa*, cooked over an open fire, and black tea laced with *sö cha*, yak butter. There are no forks, no napkins, and no plates. Diners eat with their fingers, but carry along cups for the tea, of course.

During World War II in Italy, a local farmer prepared Eric Newby, then an escaped prisoner of war, a typical *merenda* of thick vegetable and pasta soup, polenta, hard pasta dura (white bread), and thin-cut culatello, which is unsmoked ham, served with Lambrusco wine swilled from the bottle.[11] Later Newby developed a more international palate as a travel writer, but in 1943, Italian foods were still not well known to him.

In South Africa, novelist Nadine Gordimer remembers a simple lunch for Sunday picnics as "a banquet of jellied tongue, sliced chicken, an ice cream," and spontaneous picnics with her friends who would rush to the local Jewish deli, not sure what they would purchase.[12]

The French picnic for author Peter Mayle's birthday was a four-hour feast that began with peach champagne and then moved on to melon, quails' eggs, creamy *brandade* of cod [cod and potato puree, a province dish], game *pate* stuffed tomatoes, marinated mushrooms, birthday cake, and *gâteau*. More formal than the ordinary luncheon on the grass, this picnic was served at a table for ten set in the shade with a white cloth and napkins, ice buckets, bowls of fresh flowers, dishes, cutlery, and chairs.[13]

Among international picnic cookbooks is Claudia Roden's *Everything Tastes Better Outdoors* (1984), which includes wonderful lists of "take out" foods and themed picnics. Foods packed for transport are the usual sandwiches, pâtés, terrines, eggs, cold meats and poultry, deserts, and drinks (sangria, yogurt, coffee and tea), and more. Themed picnics include menus for English, Japanese, Himalayan, Chinese, Southeast Asian, and Indian meals. The menu, "A Middle Eastern Affair," expresses Roden's picnic philosophy and is deeply rooted in her family history. Having grown up in Alexandria, Egypt, Roden remembers that the family's favorite picnic spot was in the dunes of Agami in Alexandria on Sham el-Nessim, an Egyptian national holiday that celebrates the arrival of spring. Even without knowing the size of her family, she proposes an elaborate and time-consuming menu: *Blehat Samak* / fish rissoles, *Qras Samak* /Arab fish cake with *burghul*, Brains Moroccan Style, *Sanbusak* / pies filled with meat and pine nuts, meat *Ajja* / omelet, *Kukye Gusht* / Iranian omelette, *Kibbeh Naye* / raw lamb and cracked wheat paste, Bazargan / burghul salad, *Tabbouleh* / cracked wheat salad, stuffed vegetables, *Lahma bil Karaz* / meatballs with cherries, *Salq bi loubia* / spinach with black-eyed beans, lentil tomato salad, and *Lubia bi Zeit* / green beans in olive oil.[14] Thankfully, it is not necessary to eat the whole lot.

Half a world away in Newark, New Jersey, restaurateurs Norma Jean Darden and Carole Darden have memories of picnics with their father, Bud, who loved American southern cooking. They celebrate an African American Fourth of July in *Spoonbread & Strawberry Wine* (1994) that includes Bud Darden's menu of roast suckling pig, fried chicken, barbecued spareribs, charcoal-broiled flank or shell steak, corn on the cob, greens (collard or mixed), string beans, potatoes, macaroni and shrimp salad, jubilee salad, deviled eggs, garlic French bread, ice-cold watermelon, strawberry wine punch, assorted sodas, and cold beer.[15]

A three-day picnic binge was comedian W. C. Fields's gourmand ideal. According to Fields's biographer, Robert Lewis Taylor, the picnic began when Fields ordered staff to fill wicker hampers with watercress; chopped olives and nuts; tongue; sandwiches of peanut butter and strawberry preserves; deviled eggs and spiced ham; celery stuffed with Roquefort cheese; black caviar; pâté de foie gras; anchovies; smoked oysters; baby shrimps and crabmeat; tinned lobster; potted chicken and turkey; Swiss, Liederkranz, and Camembert cheeses; a bottle of olives; three or four jars of glazed fruit; angel food and devil's food cakes; and a variety of combination sandwiches. There was a case of Lanson 1928, several bottles of gin, six bottles of fine, dry sauterne, and a case of beer. On their departure, Fields is purported to have said, "What we've missed, we'll pick up on the way."[16]

For his "Banquet at Calanques," on the Mediterranean in France, Ford Madox Ford says about twenty hungry picnickers sitting around tables made from the bottoms of boats consumed sixty-one bottles of wine and ate "half a hundred weight of bouillabaisse," "twelve cocks stewed in wine with innumerable savoury herbs," "a salad as big as a cart-wheel," and "sweet-cream cheese with a sauce made of marc and sweetherbs, apples, peaches, figs, and grapes."[17] It was not an easy task to deliver the food and wine, which had to be lowered by ropes from the top of the cliff. Guests had an easier time and came by boat.

Beard says in *Menus for Entertaining* (1997), "Wherever it is done, picnicking can be one of the supreme pleasures of outdoor life. At its most elegant, it calls for the accompaniment of the best linens and crystal and china; at its simplest it needs only a bottle of wine and items purchased from the local delicatessen as one passes through town. I recall a recent picnic in France where we bought *rillettes de Tours* (in Tours), and elsewhere some excellent *salade museau*, good bread, ripe tomatoes and cheese. A bottle of local wine and glasses and plates from the Monoprix helped to make this picnic in a heather field near Le Mans a particularly memorable one."[18]

M. F. K. Fisher is equally as adamant about "true" picnics. Her memory of picnicking on the beach while at school, recalled in "The First Oyster" (1942), impressed on her that a picnic must have sandwiches, hot fried chicken, deviled eggs, fruits, plates, knives, and forks.[19] But her mature words in the essay "The Pleasures of Picnics" (1957) argues that it must be a simple feast, and the food, the best obtainable, should be prepared to be eaten with fingers. The "true" picnic must be eaten outdoors and away from home, at twilight in midsummer, in April, May, or October.[20] Whatever else is served, there must be sandwiches. The company must be jolly, and people who do not like picnics must be "dismissed immediately." Despite her seeming intransigence, Fisher prefers not to cook outdoors, and the prepared meals she totes along include baked beans, cold roast "bird," caviar, cold champagne, still wine, and a chilled mousse.

Other dedicated picnickers care very much about on-site preparation and go to extremes, such as American tailgaters, who care enough to transport kitchens to sports stadium parking lots where smoking barbecued meats (pork, beef, and sausages) mix with exhaust fumes. Whether the sandwiches are simple or elaborate, anything that can be reasonably placed between two slices of bread is recommended. Sandwich lovers simply wrap up their bread and fillings, stuff it into a bag, and get on to the picnic. It is a recurring picnic favorite.

Contrasting the simple with the elaborate without fear of contradiction, the French gourmand Jean Anthelme Brillat-Savarin in "The Halte de Chasse," aka "Halt on the Hunt," in *Physiology of Taste* (1825) describes two picnics in the same afternoon without making it seem outré. The first is a "snack" of cold chicken, Gruyere, Roquefort, bread, and cold white wine, while for the second the hunters sit on the grass and wait for their ladies to arrive with an an elaborately catered feast of turkey in aspic, delicacies from Perigord and Strasburg, and supplemented with cold champagne that infuses the meal with "a vivacity foreign to the drawing-room, however well decorated it may be."[21] The deliberate contrast of the hunters' snack and the catered luncheon is characteristic of Brillat-Savarin's irony and his delight in mixing the ordinary and the elaborate. The incongruity shows off his food knowledge, hunting skills, ability to socialize in the rough, and his French gourmandizing.

Among moderns, Constance Spry wishes to picnic simply and eat elaborately, and in the *Constance Spry Cookery Book* (1957) she has it both ways. First, she complains that some picnics had gotten "far too grand" so that the food, the champagne, the plate, and the host of servers preempt the notion that a picnic was fun: "This is not the best way to enjoy a picnic." Then she candidly admits, "But alas, time is often our enemy, and much outdoor food must be carried ready prepared." Spry's suggestions range from a triple-decker sandwich to grilled hamburger, lobster salad or omelet on a roll.[22]

Spry's criticism of grand picnicking fell on Craig Claiborne's deaf ears. If anyone enjoyed largesse and over-the-top food dining, Claiborne compares with the best of our time, especially for the staged beach picnic that was expensed by the *New York Times* and was the subject of a feature in *Life* magazine (1965), and ran under the title "Magnificent Pique-Nique." It was planned by five "four-star rated New York chefs" who scanted cold chicken, deviled eggs, and sandwiches. Instead, twenty-five guests might choose from Mussels Ravigote; pâté; bluefish au vin blanc; beef salad; seviche; poached striped bass with sauce Rouille; grilled squab; cold, stuffed lobster; fruits; brie, Camembert, and chevre; and French bread. Though the wine was vin ordinaire, it was swilled from Baccarat crystal. When it was pointed out to Claiborne that his picnic was very French, his next endeavor was a traditional beach clambake on the Fourth of July: lobster, clams, and corn on the cob.[23]

When elaborate menus trump simple menus, look no further than English cookbook author Nika Hazelton's *The Picnic Book* (1969). To begin, Hazelton is against cooking on-site. "After all," Nika Hazelton explains, "I am perfectly willing to provide any amount of nice food for my guests, so why must I cook under the most inconvenient circumstances?"[24] Hazelton like to prepare themed meals for selected occasions, such "A Boat-Launching Picnic, A Winter Picnic, A West Indian Island Picnic," and even "A Paying-Back-an-Obligation Picnic." She is also persnickety about technique: "Many picnic suggestions, even good ones," Hazelton explains, "give recipes for a given number of people. I do not find this practical, but I've never set out to give a picnic for six or twenty. I invite the people I want, then figure out the food." A typical menu for what she serves at a "Picnic on the Grass at Ely Cathedral" includes: the colonel's clear Indian soup, potted salmon sandwiches, potted veal sandwiches, mustard butter, radishes, pickled walnuts, celery sticks, Atholl Brose [whisky, light cream, and honey], and potato starch sponge cake.[25] What kind of bread is preferred for the sandwich is left unsaid.

Admittedly self-indulgent, English cookbook author Mrs. C. F. Leyel's picnic includes what *she* likes, and *Picnics for Motorists, The Lure of Cookery Series* (1936) describes cold boiled bacon, Russian croquettes, hard-boiled eggs, French plums, and cold deviled mutton served, of course, on a bed of nasturtium sauce.[26] Osbert Sitwell supposes that the food for a perfect English outdoor picnic ought to be "food of the earth" such as bread, goat cheese, apples, celery, and bilberries, but "nothing lethal or botulistic."[27] If Sitwell is not joking, William B. Jerrold is. His satire on the English, upper-class social style of the 1860s, "Picnic Reform" (1869), is based on his epiphany that picnic food does not have be cooked at home but bought at posh, West End London stores (like Harrods). This haute cuisine he calls "potted luck," a pun, and includes such elaborate choices as *pâté de gibier de Yorck* [York], a raised French game pie, and *gigot d'agneau* [roast lamb], *poulet aux truffes* [chicken with truffles], *patisseries*, Gruyere, Roquefort, café, *estratto di tamarindo* [grappa], Bordeaux wine, champagne, and Carlowitz [Hungarian riesling], and Rudesheimer [German riesling].[28] Shifting notions about menus are still current. Joan Hemingway and Connie Maricich's cookbook, *The Picnic Gourmet* (1977), makes picnics seem simple until it is necessary to prepare a "A Roadside Picnic" of cold, green-pepper soup, French omelette picnic loaf, *pâté maison*, pickled mushrooms, fig, fresh fruit and walnut plate with cookies and chocolate, and café au lait.[29]

Summer Cooking (1955) is studded with Elizabeth David's simple and elaborate picnics between which she oscillates. "Picnic addicts," she writes "seem to be roughly divided between those who frankly make elaborate preparations and leave nothing to chance, and those others whose organization is no less complicated but who are more deceitful and pretend that everything will be obtained on the spot and cooked over a woodcutter's fire conveniently at hand."[30] At a childhood picnic, David remembers being led through a formal garden, across the lane and over a fence into a wood, followed close behind by a butler, chauffeur, and footman carrying fine china, silver flatware, tablecloths, and prepared dishes of cold chicken, jellies, and trifles. But the children did not dine with the adults; instead, there was an open fire, already stocked by the gardener, at which the children grilled quantities of sausages and bacon. For picnics in France just after the end of World War II, David shopped at local stores: olives, anchovies, salami sausages, pâtés, yards of bread, smoked fish, fruit, cheese, and "cheap red wine." Nevertheless, David's favorite picnic food is *tian*, a "simple" dish, not for the casual chef since it requires first buying a *tian*, a ceramic pot from which the dish takes its name. The recipe requires a gratin of green vegetables, spinach, and chard, marrows, cloves of garlic, olive oil, and salt cod, or fresh sardines or anchovies. It may be enriched with rice or chickpeas, thickened with eggs, and topped with breadcrumbs and Parmesan cheese.[31] Even at David's memorial service (1992), friends hosted an elaborate picnic of cornmeal and rosemary bread, lentil and goat cheese salad, spinach and Gruyere tart, baby beetroots with chutney, spiced aubergines, Piedmontese peppers, grilled tuna with red onions and beans, fruit and marzipan panforte, and white wine.

The privilege of choice is a great motivator, and rather than go easy, some prefer to be profligate. The elaborate display of food for Revival Sunday, or

Dinner on the Grounds, is an American southern custom among Methodists and Baptists. Since it is a church-related picnic, it might be that some sort of food restraint should prevail. But the food is prepared in mounds, and the eating is prodigious. In Virginia, the Lewis family's contribution to an African American Revival Sunday is typical southern hospitality. And Edna Lewis proudly describes it in her food memoir cookbook *A Taste of Country Cooking* (1976):

> My mother would spread out a white linen tablecloth before setting out the baked ham, the half-dozen or more chickens she had fried, a large baking pan of her light, delicate corn pudding, a casserole of sweet potatoes, fresh green beans flavored with crisp bits of pork, and biscuits that had been baked at the last minute and were still warm. The main dishes were surrounded by smaller dishes of pickled watermelon rind, beets and cucumbers and spiced peaches. The dozen or so apple and sweet potato pies she had made were stacked in tiers of three, and the caramel and jelly layer cakes were placed next to them. Plates, forks, and white damask napkins and gallon jars of lemonade and iced tea were the last things to be unpacked. All along the sixty-foot length of tables, neighbors were busy in the same way. There were roasts and casseroles, cole slaw and potato salads, lemon meringue, custard, and Tyler pies, chocolate and coconut layer, lemon cream, and pound cakes.[32]

Lewis's abundance and variety testifies to picnic gourmandism, though she clearly thinks of this as a result of God's bounty. The degree of extravagance also seems to signal a family's social standing in the community. The contribution to the picnic is a measure of worth. Photographers working for the U.S. Farm Security Administration documented scenes of Revival Sunday and Dinner on the Grounds in the 1940s.

Linda Hull Larned's *One Hundred Picnic Suggestions* (1915) puts forward the argument that motorcars might have led to improved picnic fare.[33] Larned's cookbook, which offers no discussion, is organized in two broad headings, "For the Picnic Basket," and for the "Motor Hamper," the former for ordinary picnickers and the latter for motorists.

The class distinction is more overt in *Kitchen Essays* (1922), Agnes Jekyll's collection of her *Times of London* food columns. "The travellers' food basket, equipped in some such ways as are here suggested," she smugly asserts, "will render its owners independent of time and place, fortified against hunger and thirst, immune to the extortions and insolence of officials, and they will be fresh and ready on arrival to enjoy the lovely sights and gay adventures awaiting them."[34] Her "Luncheon for a Motor Excursion in Winter" includes *Portage à*

Figure 2.2. Ben Shahn, *Sunday School Picnic,* Ponderosa Homesteads, North Carolina (1937). Courtesy of the Library of Congress.

la Écossaise [meat and vegetable soup in the Scottish style], stuffed salmon rolls, and lots of mulled claret and hot coffee.

In America, sandwiches are a premier picnic food, and there is much evidence in cookbooks for sandwich ingredients and combinations. Name it and serve it on or under bread, and it is a sandwich. It is transportable and easy to make. Bee Wilson's *Sandwich: A Global History* (2011) covers its comprehensive history by skillfully weaving its simplicity and variety.[35] Alan Davidson and Tom Jaine suggest in *The Oxford Companion to Food* that the sandwich is the supreme picnic food since it can be made of anything, transported easily, and eaten anywhere.[36] Sandwich supremacy is uncontested by M. F. K. Fisher, who does "not like to cope with open-air hearths and spitting casseroles and frying pans on a picnic," and who prefers her squished "Railroad sandwich." It is described in "The Pleasures of Picnics" (1957) and so named because it is made from a hollowed baguette spread with butter and slices of ham that is wrapped in a towel and sat upon until it is crushed flat.[37] In the great scheme, this is only slightly more sophisticated than Ernest Mickler's sandwich of white bread, mayonnaise, and chips in *White Trash Cooking* (1986).[38] Sandwiches were among Ernest Hemingway's favorite foods, especially when served with raw onions. His raw onion and peanut butter sandwich is described in his novel *Islands in the Stream* (1970), where it ought to have been forgotten. A. E. Hotchner, his biographer, however, has a great sense of humor and provides the recipe in *Papa Hemingway* (1955): bread, peanut butter, and raw onion.[39] To be fair, Hemingway liked many kinds of sandwiches, but they almost always include raw onion, and he never seems to drink water. Hemingway's best picnics, without sandwiches and with much wine, are described in his other posthumous novel *The Garden of Eden* (1986).

Not to be outdone, American food writer Laurie Colwin's favorites for picnics, or any time, are cream cheese and salami sandwiches, garnished with potato chips. Colwin makes no excuses for such fare, and in her essay "Picnics" (1993) she writes: "The idea was (and still is) that a picnic can be anything. It can resemble the Mad Hatter's tea party if you want it to. Its heart and soul is breeziness, invention, and enough to eat for people made ravenous by fresh air."[40] Laura Cunningham, in the memoir *A Place in the Country* (2000), shares gauzy recollections of being about five years old when her mother took her to a Manhattan park where they ate Wonder Bread sandwiches and fruit.[41] Anyone who has ever eaten Wonder Bread knows that it is the softest white bread that turns mushy with any filling, even butter.

Predictably, sandwiches coincide with the rising popularity of outdoor picnics, and the two are probably symbiotic. Like the definition of the word *pique-nique*, there is ambiguity concerning the sandwich's origin and name, and why it is associated with the Earl of Sandwich is a mystery. Englishman Edward Gibbon mentions the first sandwich in 1762 in his diary, and Frenchman Pierre-Jean Grosley remarks on sandwiches à la mode in London in *A Tour of London* (1770), but neither Gibbon nor Grosley associates the sandwich with alfresco dining.[42] There is, however, a tenuous picnic link between sandwiches and the food, originating in England, known as a "cold loaf," which is sandwichlike because it is made by stuffing bread with meat. There is a recipe for *pain de jambon à la mayence* in Menon's French cookbook *Les Soupers de la Cour* [*The Professed Cook*] (1755), later translated into English by Bernard Clermont (1812): "Cut thin slices of ready-boiled or roasted Westphalia ham; make a little farce with some of the fat and chopped sweet herbs; have such kind of paste as is made for French foils, beat a bit flat with the hand, according to bigness required, put some farce upon a few slices of ham, then the paste, and continue this two or three times over, finishing with the paste, which you form as a small loaf that nothing else may appear; bake it upon a baking-plate in a middling oven: serve cold."[43] Clermont added that because the cold loaf is portable, it is excellent for traveling, but he does not suggest picnicking.

It might be that English aristocrat Lady Mary Wortley Montagu carried a sandwich on a sightseeing picnic in 1752. Writing in 1906, Montagu's biographer, Emily Climenson, is sure that a "cold loaf" is a picnic, but this is an anachronism.[44] In West Westmorland, England, the thumbers or thumb-pieces serve as a sandwich euphemism which the gourmand, Edward Spencer, known for his humor and sports writing, links to sporting picnic lunches at Newmarket Downs. In *Cakes & Ale: A Memory of Many Meals* (1897), Spencer writes that these sandwiches, sold at food booths, "were rough, but satisfying, and consisted of thick sandwiches, cheese, and bread, with 'thumb-pieces' (or 'thumbers') of beef, mutton, and pork, which the luncher was privileged to cut with his own clasp-knife."[45] However, because the thumbers were messy (the meat juices and gravy leaked through the paper wrappers), they never gained favor. It is still a rule of picnic decorum among fastidious picnickers such as Miss Manners that if it is done at all, licking one's fingers is acceptable if "they are done with grace."[46] Frances Trollope, English travel writer (and mother of the novelist Anthony Trollope), liked sandwiches but never divulged what she put between the bread slices. She took her family on a memorable picnic in a hot, mosquito-infested forest on the outskirts of Cincinnati, Ohio. She describes the picnic unflatteringly and with humor in her travel memoir, *Domestic Manners of the Americans* (1832), and she vowed never to picnic in an American forest again. She also avoids picnicking in her other travel books.[47]

Gertrude Stein and Alice B. Toklas immensely enjoyed picnic sandwiches. For thirty years from 1916 to 1946, when Stein died, they selected between two choices. Toklas labeled these "First Picnic Lunch" or "Second Picnic Lunch,"[48] and in *The Alice B. Toklas Cook Book* (1954) recipes are given: First is chicken salad with mushrooms and hard-boiled eggs; and Second is chopped, rare roast beef with shallots, parsley, sour cream, and dry mustard. Being in charge of the kitchen, Toklas supervised making the sandwiches, but Stein was always in charge of the motorcars, always Fords, one called "Aunt Pauline" and the other "Lady Godiva." When not eating sandwiches, Stein and Toklas did their picnicking in country restaurants, splurging on such elaborate fare as steamed chicken *Mère Fillioux*, roasted saddle of young boar, and *Perpignan* lobster. Their propensity for such elaborate meals is an indicator that picnickers tend to pile it on and eat and drink believing that more is better than just having enough. This is a quirky characteristic of picnickers.

There is some debate over the convenience and messiness of cooking outdoors, a matter that will never be resolved. The last words belong to Miss Manners, aka Judith Martin, arbiter of social decorum and good taste, in *Miss*

Manners' Guide to Excruciatingly Correct Behavior (2005). Take or leave it, Miss Manners writes that whatever picnic food is selected, it "should be chosen (so) that (it) can be served at its proper temperature, and should be repackaged so that it may be served with no commercial containers appearing on the table or grass. If food is cooked at the picnic area, no more allowances are made for the chef's ruining it than would be made at a dinner party indoors."[49] Miss Manners' deadpan humor does not mask her concern that it is not what is served, but how it is served, and on that she speaks for the world.

3

PICNICS INDOORS

In a pic-nic supper, one supplies the fowls, another the fish,
another the wine and fruit, &c.; and they all sit down together
and enjoy it.

—Letitia Barbauld, *A Legacy for Young Ladies* (1826)

Pique-nique originally meant dining indoors, but today, we think of a picnic
only as being outdoors. The French had been picnicking indoors since
1649, when the Brothers of the Bacchic Pique-Nique, the society of gourmands,
gathered to share mounds of food and barrels of drink. About the same time,
Paul Scarron, a well-known satirist, was reputed to have dined *en pique-nique*
because he was financially broke and it was the only way to entertain without
embarrassment. Two hundred years later, the rumor still floated, and in 1774,
Oliver Goldsmith all but names a picnic in his satiric poem "Retaliation" that
begins with a reference to Paul Scarron's practice of hosting *pique-nique* dinners
in his home in Paris: "Of old, when Scarron his companions invited, / Each
guest brought his dish, and the feast was united."[1] Though Goldsmith seemed
comfortable that his English audience knew what a French picnic was, he did
not use the word or allude to Samuel Foote's joke in which *nick-nack* is substi-
tuted for *picnic*. Foote's *The Nabob* (1772), a comedy at the expense of country
gentry, presumes that everyone knows that you contribute to a "nick-nack."
Though it had a successful run in London, the word *nick-nack* (for picnic) did
not survive the play.

Whether Goldsmith knew it or not, the word *picnic* was actually published in
the voluminous *Lord Chesterfield's Letters* in 1774. It is the first public mention

of *picnic* in private English correspondence, but no one noticed at the time.[2] Actually, it is the second mention, because his son, Philip, told him about the picnic and may very well have given the Anglicized spelling, though that letter is lost. Contextually, Chesterfield used the word in 1748 when referring to an assembly or salon gathering in Leipzig where Philip was living. The custom of salons and assemblies is prevalent throughout Europe, including England, but it is only on the Continent that they were called *picnics*. Satisfied that Philip was not wasting his time, Chesterfield dropped the word and never used *picnic* again.

Another mild surprise is that the custom of sharing, though most evident among the aristocrats and intellectuals, crossed social boundaries. Thomas Wright's *A History of Domestic Manners and Sentiments in England during the Middle Ages* (1862) suggests that among the lower classes, sharing food and entertainment at a local inn or tavern or at home is common—a sign of a picnic—*Ech of them brought forth ther dysch; / Sum brought flesh, some fysh.* Wright also cites a song "Le Banquet des Chambrières fait aux Estuves" ["The Feast of the Bathhouse Chambermaids"] (1541) that even itemizes contributions to a gathering as one Andouille, four sausages, a cutlet, and hot sauce.[3] He points out these are not picnic suppers, per se, because the "word seems not to be clearly known"; he calls them picnics because it is convenient. "The pic-nics, which had formerly taken place at the tavern, were now transferred to the hotbath, each of a party of bathers carrying some contribution to the feast, which they shared in common."[4]

During the Middle Ages, bathhouses provided opportunities for indoor recreation at which food and sexuality were inextricably linked, and fifteenth-century illustrations make these look suspiciously picnicky, even if they are not. Several variations show lascivious bathers engaging in mild sexual activities and enjoying light meals purported to be sourced from Valerius Maximus's *Memorable Deeds and Sayings* (31CE), a history of gossip about Roman life composed around 31 CE. However, historian Scot McKendrick explains that these bathhouse scenes are not Roman but bathhouse dining circa 1470, where couples engaged in pleasure, "wine, meats, prostitutes, gaming, and doing nothing."[5] (The epitome of leisure for some.)

As the custom of sharing the cost of meal at a tavern or inn evolved, it shifted to restaurants. By the 1770s, Parisians dining *en manière pique-nique* would agreeably split the bill. Rebecca Spang discusses this in *The Invention of the Restaurant* (2002), particularly with regard to Jean-Jacques Rousseau's *Reveries of a Solitary Walker* (1776–1777).[6] Rousseau's remembrance of dining *en manière pique-nique* at Chez Vacossin is a logical carryover from dining *tête à tête en pique-nique* at home that he described in *The Confessions*. Then both customs proved convenient but contexts change, and you do not now think of sharing a bill as a picnic. In the 1830s, sharing the expenses suited writer George Sand, who recalls dining in a restaurant with a lover *a seize heures en piquenique* (1839).[7] Émile Zola reported it as being ordinary among the struggling working class, and in the novel *L'Assommoir* (1877), Gervaise Macquart and Coupeau's wedding party is *un pique-nique* celebrated at a local restaurant, the Moulin d'Argent.[8] This is a socially acceptable working-class custom, for without sharing the cost, the party would have been impossible. Even the bride and groom chip in, and for the cost of five francs there is a wedding dinner of several courses, including sliced ham, Brie, bread, then a vermicelli soup, and a rabbit ragout, that someone suggests is still mewing. There is a scrawny roast chicken, and it ends with desserts of cheese, fruits, floating island pudding, coffee, and brandy. When they drink too much wine, and the cost is more than expected, everyone faces the embarrassment of having to scrabble to pay more than expected. The point here, however, is that in 1877, the French were still picnicking indoors. Even elsewhere in his writings, Zola refrains from naming an outdoor luncheon or dinner a *pique-nique*.

The English more or less followed the French indoor custom until the beginning of the nineteenth century, when the Pic Nic Society was established in London. Approximately set during a lull of the wars with France in 1801 and ending with the abrogation of the peace of Amiens in 1830, the Pic Nics might flaunt their Francophilia. So gathering a select society of about 200 hundred "dilettanti" or "fashionables," they aimed at producing amateur theatricals, lavish dinners, and entertainments including gambling. Their motto was "excess," and their favorite poem was Catullus's "Carmina, Carmen, 13," which begins with inviting a friend (Fabullus) to dinner and requesting that he bring the goods and drink:

> My Fabullus, my table.
> Like your name, is a fable,
> But may furnish a splendid repast.
> If you come, do not fail
> To bring bread, beef, an ale,
> Or, Egad! My dear friend, you will fast.[9]

At time when the British nobility and aristocracy were spending lavishly, the Pic Nics were noted for verve, gourmandism, and notoriety, all of which gave a new meaning for dining *en manière pique-nique*, and it inadvertently made *picnic* a common word.

For most Britons, the Pic Nics' dinners were a novelty because it was not hosted but called for supplying the food and drink by subscription. These dinners were served in hired rooms in fashionable Tottenham Street, where there were no catering facilities and everything had to be prepared elsewhere, then transported, stored, arranged, and served. For each supper a Pic Nic was required to contribute six bottles of wine and a dish. According to the London *Times*, a newspaper friendly with the Pic Nics,

> A Pic-Nic Supper consists of a variety of dishes. The Subscribers to the entertainment have a bill of fare presented to them, with a number against each dish. The lot, which he draws, obliges him to furnish the dish marked against it, which he either takes with him in his carriage, or sends by servant. The proper variety is preserved by the Maître d'Hotel, who forms the bill of fare. As the cookery is furnished by so many people of fashion, each strives to excel. And thus a Pic-Nic Supper not only gives rise to much pleasant mirth, but generally can boast of the refinement of the art.[10]

Henry Angelo's firsthand account *Reminiscences* (1830) is both comical and serious about how contributions might have affected some subscribers of small means as they faced the anxiety of the draw.

> Nothing could exceed the amusement which this lottery gastronomic produced; for that hoodwinked duchess, Fortune, played her tricks with her wonted ill-nature. Those who had the least to spare were the first to draw the most expensive lots; and those, on the contrary, to who money was of little import, drew the cheapest. Some luckless fair, whose beauty was her sole dowry, drew a Perigord pie, [game pie flavored with truffles] value three guineas at least, whilst her rich neighbor drew a pound cake, value half a crown. Then some needy sprig of fashion a younger brother, drew his lot of misery in a ticket for a dozen of champagne; and a wealthy nabob, another half a dozen China oranges [from Portugal or Spain].[11]

Dinner and gambling aside, the Pic Nics aroused the ire of Richard Brinsley Sheridan, playwright and member of Parliament, who owned the Drury Lane Theatre, because he thought that amateur theatricals would diminish his audience and receipts. Spitefully, he tried to shut them down, and succeeded, but not before *pic nic* became a common word meaning an indoor meal by contribution of the guests. The word, too, was the subject of derision. As public brawling mounted, James Gillray, among the greatest caricaturists, pilloried them all, suggesting that they are *all* nitwits. The caricatures so adversely ridiculed the Pic Nics that they could not go on, and in 1803, disheartened, they disbanded. Particularly, Gillray's "Blowing up the Pic Nics:—or—Harlequin Quixote attacking the Puppets. Vide Tottenham Street Pantomime (April 2, 1802)" helped make *picnic* a familiar if notoriously silly word.[12]

The net result was that as the Pic Nics evaporated, the word *pic nic* became commonly known as an indoor party. But if others emulated the new fashion they remain to this day unknown. Inexplicably, however, three years later *pic nic* appears as an outdoor wedding dinner in John Harris's children's story *The Courtship, Merry Marriage, and Pic-Nic Dinner of Cock Robin and Jenny Wren*, and then three years after that as an townhouse dinner party in Mary Belson Elliot's *The Mice, and Their Pic Nic: A Moral Tale*.

Because Harris and Elliot spell *pic nic* as two words, it is obvious that they are alluding to the Pic Nic society. But each takes the word and embellishes its context. Harris presumes the outdoor "pic nic dinner" is something appropriate and socially acceptable, as everyone knows; while Elliot attacks the concept as sinful, an example of gluttony and false pride. This is what happens at awful dinners in London townhouses of the rich.

Elliot's is not just another mouse story, for it has important roots in Aesop's fable "The Country Mouse and the City Mouse" and Horace's "De Mure Urbano et Mure Rustico." Aesop and Horace contrasted simplicity and sophistication, but what Elliot preaches is that life in the country is good and life in the city is evil. For her, "pic nic dinners" in London will bring retribution, which she provides by having the tabby cat storm the pantry and eat all but a few of the scrambling mice. By her rigid standard, London or Pic Nic Mice are representative of the upper classes that ought to know better but spend their time frivolously. What makes it worse is that their name is Anglicized French, a poor choice since Britain was at war with Napoleon in Spain. Like the real society of Pic Nics, the London Mice's picnic ends ignominiously when the tabby cat puts an awful, gruesome end to the feast. "Further Disasters" captures the moment as the cat lands and the mice flee. The mice are appalled, and "their ears assail'd with their friends' dying groans, / And the noise which the enemy made with their bones."[13] Those Devonshire country mice who survive will return home to tell their story and be content with their place on the barn floor eating grains.

Despite this merciless moralism, Elliot was unable to deter its increasing widespread usage of *picnic*. In 1812, it appears in Maria Edgeworth's bestselling novel *The Absentee*, in which a group of prim young women bring their own food to a luncheon rather than dine in the company of men of which they are wary. Edgeworth refers to this as a "PICNICK lunch," and to make sure its silliness does not go unnoticed, it is spelled in capital letters.[14] Jane Austen deftly weaves two picnics into the novel *Emma* (1816). The first is a strawberry-picking picnic at Donwell Abbey, about which George Knightley, the host, deadpans his disapproval: "My idea of the simple and the natural will be to have the table spread in the dining-room. The nature and the simplicity of gentlemen and ladies, with their servants and furniture, I think is best observed by meals within doors. When you are tired of eating strawberries in the garden, there shall be cold meat in the house."[15] The second picnic at Box Hill is entirely outdoors, and Knightley is compliant, a capitulation that suggests Austen's preference for the spontaneity and informality of the outdoor picnics as contrasted with the routine etiquette of the dining room.

Indoor picnic dinners were approved by poet and social advocate Anna Letitia Barbauld. Included in the collection of her advice to the rising generation, *A Legacy for Young Ladies; Consisting of Miscellaneous Pieces, in Prose and Verse* (1826), she recommends that pic-nics be at home because it is socially proper. "In a pic-nic supper," she writes, "one supplies the fowls, another the fish, another the wine and fruit, &c.; and they all sit down together and enjoy it."[16] It is a "feast" of conviviality and conversation at which guests contribute according to their talent, like a potluck dinner, though Barbauld shows no interest in potluck dinners, then percolating in English society. These works conveyed the meaning of dining by happenstance, something the genteel Barbauld would disapprove of. Charles Dickens, being more fluid, differentiates *potluck* and *picnic*. In the novel *The Mystery of Edwin Drood* (1863), the dinner Mr. Grewgious orders from a local hotel is potluck: "For dinner we'll have a tureen of the hottest and strongest soup available, and we'll have the best made-dish that can be recommended, and we'll have a joint (such as a haunch of mutton), and we'll have a goose, or a turkey, or any little stuffed thing of that sort that may happen to be in the bill of fare—in short, we'll have whatever there is on hand."[17] But when Miss Twinkleton bring two contributions: a veal pie and her inimitable gossipy self to the party, it is a picnic.

At midcentury, indoor picnicking is the butt of a joke in *Harper's* magazine. The caricature "A Capital Idea for Rainy Weather in Winter—Make Believe That the Drawing Room Is a Shady Spot in the Woods and Give a Picnic in It" (1858) is crammed with oppressively bored people.[18] At the turn of the twentieth century, G. K. Chesterton's joke in "The Wildness of Domesticity" (1910) is that a picnic indoors is safe, convenient, and private. "When a man spends every night staggering from bar to bar or from music-hall to music-hall," Chesterton argues, "we say that he is living an irregular life. But he is not; he is living a highly regular life, under the dull, and often oppressive, laws of such places. Sometimes he is not allowed even to sit down in the bars; and frequently he is not allowed to sing in the music-halls. Hotels may be defined as places where you are forced to dress; and

Figure 3.1. "A Capital Idea for Rainy Weather in Winter—Make Believe That the Drawing Room Is a Shady Spot in the Woods and Give a Picnic in It," *Harper's Weekly*, December 4, 1858.

theaters may be defined as places where you are forbidden to smoke. A man can only picnic at home."[19] Two decades after, Margaret Mitchell's heroine Scarlett O'Hara puts indoor picnicking to the test and fails it. "I hope it doesn't rain tomorrow," Scarlett O'Hara pouts. "It's rained nearly every day for a week. There's nothing worse than a barbecue turned into an indoor picnic."[20]

At this point, because food writers do not recommended them and artists and writers find them sterile and without interest, the indoor picnic ought to be dead. Yet the life of indoor picnicking in the twenty-first century thrives on the Internet. Fourteen million listings supply an endless collection of indoor picnics eaten on the floor, a bed, kitchen, dorm room, or garage. The prevailing sense is that this is goofy and jokey. Images show picnickers with smiling faces and relaxed bodies, children safe on a carpeted floor, and lovers snug on a rug before a fireplace. Mostly, what these picnics lack in creative inspiration, they make up in kitsch and fun.

There are some standouts, especially picnics on trains, that do not fit into a standard picnic repertoire. The most appealing is probably Augustus Egg's painting *Travelling Companions* (1862), a scene set in a French or Italian first-class railway compartment in which two women, nearly identically dressed, sit opposite one another so that they look like a mirror image, but one sleeps while the other reads. Next to one is a bouquet of flowers; next to the other is a picnic basket with fruit. Though art critics suggest that the basket is a symbol of domesticity, a picnic lunch on a train is convenient.[21] Whether it is tasty food is moot, though Egg's friend Charles Dickens considered English train food insipid and later satirized it in "The Boy at Mugby" (1866).

A picnic in a railway passenger car is D. H. Lawrence's joke in the novel *Aaron's Rod* (1922), when Aaron and friends briefly layover in a small Italian town, and while waiting to go on, they impulsively decide on a picnic:

> Everybody who passed the doorway stood to contemplate the scene with pleasure. Officials came and studied the situation with appreciation. Then Francis and Aaron returned with a large supply of roast chestnuts, piping hot, and hard dried plums, and good dried figs, and rather stale rusks. They found the water just boiling, Angus just throwing in the tea-egg, and the fellow-passenger just poking his nose right in, he was so thrilled. Nothing pleased Angus so much as thus pitching camp in the midst of civilisation. The scrubby newspaper packets of chestnuts, plums, figs and rusks were spread out: Francis flew for salt to the man at the bar, and came back with a little paper of rock-salt: the brown tea was dispensed in the silver-fitted glasses from the immortal luncheon-case: and the picnic was in full swing.[22]

Lawrence's humor depends on turning expectation of a picnic on the grass topsy-turvy. And everyone, the picnickers, the other passengers, and the conductor, loves the novelty.

The food writer Constance Spry opens a discussion of picnics with a train compartment picnic in *The Constance Spry Cookery Book* (1957). It is so memorable that even fifty years later, she recalls being comforted on her way to her first house party by train with a purchased picnic basket lunch: a wing of chicken, roll, butter, biscuits, cheese, celery, a sweet cake of some kind, and an apple. She says it was inexpensive and ordered ahead. As an adult, she recalls with equal enthusiasm a more upscale luncheon basket: a "neat cardboard box containing two little screw-top cartons and other small packages. In one carton was a perfect freshly made lobster salad in a delicious dressing, the second carton contained fresh fruit salad of peaches, strawberries, and orange. Crisp poppy-seed sprinkled rolls were quartered and buttered, and a Porosan bag [a porous material used for straining jelly] held the crisp heart of a cos lettuce."[23]

Perhaps the most significant train picnic is in Jacob Lawrence's set of historical paintings *The Migration Series* (1941), documenting African Americans' relocation from the agrarian South to the industrial North. The migration began after 1919 and accelerated in the late 1930s when millions sought to relocate to industrial centers where they hoped for new jobs. *The Migrants Arrived in Pittsburgh* (1941) captures the moment when a family sees the great smokestacks through their railway compartment window and knows that they have arrived in what might be the promised land.[24] Their optimism is symbolized by the image of the glowing yellow picnic basket set on an open table so that it looks like an offering on an altar. The family is excited, and as the man in red gesticulates at the stacks, they are hopeful about a successful future. At this moment, Lawrence suggests they are not mindful of the significance of the factory stacks belching smoke or of the struggles these portend. As he shows the family, they are safely indoors and viewing the world protected by the glass window of the railcar. With hindsight, of course, Lawrence implicitly makes it unmistakable that once outdoors, their lives will *not* be a picnic.

The indoor picnic comes full circle in two episodes that are exemplary of the highs and lows in contemporary history. A low point is *O-Zone* (1986), Paul Theroux's sci-fi ecological novel, and it takes place in a disaster zone where picnickers in spacesuits sit in a ruined apartment around a makeshift wooden dining table. The menu seems appetizing: noodle gluten, hollandaise whitefish, shrimp paste, oyster pellets, textured lobster, crab strings, meat butter, spinach sauce, and nonalcoholic wine. But since all are served in tubes, the contents must be sucked. "You don't squirt it," one of them says, "you squeeze it—pressure means everything with space food."[25] The high point of indoor picnicking happens in 1965 when the first *Gemini 3* mission astronauts struggled with a corned beef and cold slaw sandwich that John Young smuggled onto their spacecraft cabin. It was an attempt at maintaining their connection with Earth food, but when Virgil Grissom began to eat it, the sandwich bread fell apart and floated through the zero-gravity cabin. NASA controllers in Houston laconically suggested that next time the astronauts might try a chicken leg.[26] It is an amusing moment and the first picnic in space.

4

PICNICS OUTDOORS

> Wherever it done, picnicking can be one of the supreme plea-
> sures of outdoor life.
>
> —Elizabeth David, *Summer Cooking* (1955)

Picnics are thought of as typically eaten on a blanket on a fine patch of grass. Yet the possibilities for places to picnic outdoors are endless and choices sometimes idiosyncratic. No place and no means of transportation are impossible, if a picnicker has a mind for it. What a picnicker needs is means and attitude. Where to picnic is variable, and often neither cold nor heat is an impediment, though they may be inconveniences. What is suitable for one set of picnickers is out of bounds for someone else. Name a place and someone has probably picnicked there to get away and out from under the roof: backyards, roof tops, parks, seashores, by rivers, sand dunes, deserts, forests, mountains, jet planes, the North Pole, and even Earth's orbit. How they get there is part of the fun, and every means of transportation is used—on foot, horse, carriage, motorcar, train, boat, ship, airplane, and rocket ship.

By the mid-twentieth century, the indoor picnic might never have existed, and the outdoor one was ubiquitous. The outdoor picnic thrives because it gets people away from their routine and workaday living. We idealize a picnic as being always available and easily accomplished on some "perfect day" in spring or summer under a clear sky with a scattering of clouds, cooled by a light breeze that rustles the leaves in trees in which birds sing cheerfully. This is Henri Matisse's sense of the picnic in the painting Luxury, Calm, and Pleasure (1904–1905). Where the air

Figure 4.1. Henri Matisse, *Luxury, Calm, and Pleasure [Luxe, Calme et Volupté]* (1904–1905), oil on canvas. Musée D'Orsay. Courtesy of the Granger Collection, New York.

vibrates with glowing reds, golds, and blues, the sea shines evanescently, and the picnickers are indolent.

Not really caring much for how a picnicker travels, food writers seized the day, and books about food and instructive cookbooks proliferated and flooded the marketplace. All that matters to them is that a picnicker get there, and "there" is outdoors. As styles, tastes, locations, and distances vary, so do foods and drinks. But the unifying caveat is that the picnic must be outdoors. This is a matter of faith for such as James Beard's *Cook It Outdoors* (1941), Yvonne Young Tarr's *The Complete Outdoor Cookbook* (1973), and Claudia Roden's *Everything Tastes Better Outdoors* (1984), and many others.[1] The unshakable belief that people must leave home to picnic, however, is an English contribution to picnic history. The phrase *we go outdoors for picnics* is so ordinary that until 1806, to be precise, *picnic* was a noun used to describe an indoor meal. It was John Harris, an Englishman, who broke the linguistic, if not the environmental, barrier and named an outdoor meal a *pic nic dinner*. The shift was unheralded and aroused no comment. *The Courtship, Merry Marriage, and Pic-Nic Dinner of Cock Robin and Jenny Wren* resituated an ordinary wedding feast outdoors under a bunting, and it seemed so ordinary that no one resisted the linguistic gaff. Within the decade, subsequent editions of *The Courtship* explicitly place the "pic nic dinner" under a leafy arbor. Why and no one before Harris had made the connection is a wonder, and he is to be thanked for the obvious.[2]

Of course, outdoor meals are historical, and dining alfresco had no specific name. Depending on the time of day, it might be breakfast, lunch, or dinner. The Roman *merenda* was a snack. Other times, such alfresco meals and entertainments are given names or a convenient synonym or figurative phrase such as *taking the air*, which suggests that we need to escape from being confined in habitations and cities and get outdoors. Sometimes "taking the air" is as simple as going to a park, and this was not something uncommon for Oliver Cromwell, Lord Protector of England, who with "a few of his gentlemen and servants" removed to Hyde Park "where he caused some dishes of meat to be brought; where he made his dinner."[3] Samuel Pepys, the English diarist, engaged in a *frolique* (a variant spelling of *frolic*), meaning an occasion of gaiety or merry making—and it might as well be a picnic. For the "frolique" on Sunday, June 26, 1664, Pepys, his wife, Hope, and friends packed "good victuals and drink" and set out for some leisure boating on the Thames (toward Gravesend).[4] As with many others in the history of picnics, the rain cut it short, and they returned damp. Though the *Diary* was not published until long after Pepys's death, it suggests that such an outing was common.

A century and a half later after *frolique* faded, Harris's *pic nic dinner* began a steady trend, first stuttering, and then gaining fluency as it firmly entered common usage. It had a distinctive sound, and it was easily understood. It was suitable for alliteration—a powerful means for popularity, especially in phases that just skirt cliché, such as *perfect picnic, pleasure party picnic, perfect picnic party, perfect day for a picnic, perfect day for a picnic on the grass or in the country*, and so on. Because the meaning of the word conjured good times and fun, it was comfortable to use for almost any outdoor meal and gathering. As the enthusiasm for escaping urbanized communities increased, picnicking became associated with the leisure of getting away for a convenient lunch, a motoring to the country, and sightseeing—anywhere! Had the French been more linguistically agile, they might have considered broadening their concept of *pique-nique* and outdoor picnics. But they resisted, preferring instead expressions *partie de campagne, partie de plaisir*, and *déjeuner sur l'herbe* when they meant to go outdoors for what the English called a *picnic*. With unmitigated enthusiasm, the English captured the word, and though they also frequently used the synonyms such as *outing, excursion, gypsying, vagabonding,* and *ruralizing, picnic* inexorably became the word of choice.

In 1808, Dorothy Wordsworth was uncertain about the origin of the word *picnic,* but she knew it was an outdoor party. A letter to her friend Catherine Clarkson captures her pleasure and intellectual curiosity.

> What do you think of a picnic upon Grasmere Island? she writes, Nineteen of us were to have dined there, and were all caught in a thunder shower, and all wet to the skin on our way to the lake side. The Wilson's were of the party. Mr. Wilson said to me, "I would not for the world that the shower had not come. For the world I would not have nineteen persons racketing, and walking about the whole day upon that island, disturbing those poor sheep." By the bye what is the origin of the word picnic? Our Windermere gentlemen have a picnic almost every day.[5]

Clarkson's reply is unknown, but many to this day still ask about the origin of *picnic,* and as you have read, there is only a fuzzy answer—that no one really knows.

Essayist and food writer M. F. K. Fisher's "The Pleasures of Picnics" (1957) is categorical and argues, "A true picnic must be carried away from human dwellings, and it must be kept simple. It can consist of a piece of bread and an apple, eaten anywhere in the outdoors that will make it taste good, but it is not strictly speaking, a *picnic* if it is on a terrace, or in a patio, or under the linden tree in the backyard."[6] Fisher insists the meal must be a feast, jolly, and that people who do not like them must be "dismissed immediately." Surely she jests, for if taken literally, Fisher's advice incalculably eliminates more picnics than can be imagined. However, being inventive and arbitrary, picnickers select any place suitable. Usually a picnic in a green place reinforces the cathartic desire to be in a natural setting, and picnics on grass or a lawn, in a park grove or a forest are the prevailing environments. But any place is a place for picnics, and whether one is as categorical as Fisher, food writer or not, must picnickers have their say. Some might quibble that a house garden or yard is suitable. But picnickers are known for their preferences and individual likes and dislikes. All picnics may be structurally similar, but the preferences are idiosyncratic.

At first, author and food writer Laurie Colwin hated outdoor picnics; then she changed her mind. In "How to Avoid Grilling" (1988), she announced, "I do not like to eat alfresco. No sane person does, I feel."[7] Her idea for dining out is a screened porch "without the bother of mosquitoes, horse and deer flies, as well as wasps and yellowjacks." "When it is nice enough for people to eat outdoors," she writes, "it is also nice enough for mosquitoes, horse and deer flies, as well as wasps and yellowjackets. I don't much like sand in my food and thus while I endure a beach picnic I never look forward to them."[8] Five years later, she had a sea change, and in "Picnics" (1993), during a vacation on the Balearic island of Minorca, she states that the "heart and soul" of a picnic is "breeziness, invention, and enough to eat for people made ravenous by fresh air."[9]

The word *picnic* so convenient and pervasive that it is applied anachronistically to any outdoor gathering with food and drink regardless of time and place—especially for meals associated with hunting, and so linking sport with feasting outdoors but without calling the feast a picnic. Inherently what makes outdoor picnics unique is that it has a cathartic effect of being on the grass or in the country. The renewed physical and spiritual interest in nature that had been evolving from the early eighteenth century finally blossomed. The Romantic affinity for nature broke down walls both literally and figuratively, and people went outdoors specifically to be entertained—at a picnic. This shift is historian Georgina Battiscombe's claim in *English Picnics* (1949) that picnickers are "noble savages." Battiscombe's point is that an "English" picnicker "is a devotee of the simple life that coincides with the appreciation of nature and sightseeing that began at the turn of the 19th Century." Battiscombe's apt phrase *anywhere except under a roof* perfectly describes "the unsettled desire for picnickers to find the right place wherever it might be or wherever it might lead them."[10]

Anyone can picnic on the grass, but going to extremes helps make the case for picnic individuality or idiosyncratic choices. Ray Bradbury hypothesized a picnic on Mars in his "Million Year Picnic" (1946), the final story in *The Martian Chronicles* (1958).[11] The crew of NASA's *Gemini-3* smuggled aboard corned beef sandwiches into the cabin, making this the first picnic in space.[12] Earthbound, you cannot go more to extremes than to picnic at the North or South Pole. For a Christmas joke the Santa Update website reported that for 2012 "Mrs. Claus leaves the Pole with a Picnic Basket." But it was no joke when French explorer Jean-Baptiste Charcot, whose ship the *Pourquoi-Pas?* was parked in Antarctic ice, picnicked on Mardi Gras 1909. Though it was Antarctic summer in February and the temperature was below freezing, Charcot and his crew playfully painted their noses red, dressed in outlandish costumes, and improvized music on pots and pans. It was a release of pent-up tension and deep anxiety that was necessary to get away from the dull routines of a hostile environment.[13] Robert Peary, on his trek to the North Pole, sarcastically joked "we did not enjoy picnicking" when the temperature was -30°F.[14]

For the pleasure of picnicking in the cold, even -20°F, the Siberians will drive in deep snow to a clearing in the Taiga, a great wilderness of pine forest, for an afternoon feast. Such a picnic is one of David Shipler's remarkable anecdotes that he collected while serving as bureau chief for the *New York Times* that begins "What do Siberians do when they are sitting around bored and it's 58 below outside? Go on a picnic, naturally."[15] The day began well when he and five companions piled into a Gazik, a Russian Jeep, and chugged over unpaved roads to a clearing where they spread out a copy of *Pravda* to serve as a picnic blanket. The abundant food included three kinds of local salmon, horsemeat, bread, apples, onions, salami, tea, mineral water, and vodka, sliced salami, smoked *omul* and *ryapushka*, black and brown bread cut into thick slices, and chunks of lightly smoked colt's meat. The day ended well, the festive meal was over, and the picnickers thoughtfully sprinkled vodka into the fire as an offering to the Taiga. They piled back into the Gazik that was left running the whole time.

Making the best of escaping desert heat, before the temperature got to a stifling 110°F in Baghdad, Gertrude Bell and a group including King Faisal picnicked early in the morning beside Aqar Quf, a ruined brick tower in the desert. As British Oriental Secretary to the High Commissioner (and spy) in Baghdad, Bell often picnicked with King Faisal. For this outing the party got out early and breakfasted at 6:30 a.m. so they could get back to the city before the heat rose. Sometimes Bell got tired of picnics: "We are having a very exhausting time, physically and politically. Physically because of the incredibly horrible weather. It's not very hot, never much over 110, but heavy and close beyond all belief."[16] Agatha Christie got ecstatic in the desert, too. Her desert picnic, called an *expedition*, was time off from an archeological dig in Syria with her husband, Max Mallowan. After scrambling to the top of al-Kawkab, about 1,640 feet, Christie's memoir *Come, Tell Me How You Live* (1946) gushes that it was so wonderfully peaceful and yet exciting as she was flooded with a "great wave of happiness."[17] Incidentally, the picnic did not transfer well to her fiction, and in *Appointment with Death* (1938), the day is "really stiflingly hot."

The extreme ranges from low to high or cold to hot reveals that picnickers are intrepid and determined for respite from the city. Sometimes this is confusing, as in the case of Charles Dickens, who left London to work while vacationing on the Isle of Wight where he was writing *David Copperfield* and enthusiastically picnicking. "We are going on another picnic," he writes, "with the materials for a fire, at my express stipulation; and a great iron pot to boil potatoes in. These things, and the eatables, go to the ground in a cart."[18] These picnics might have gone with small notice except that Dickens used a picnic setting for David's courtship of Dora. The picnic also got a great laugh when Dickens's friend, John Leech, satirical cartoonist for *Punch* magazine, made one a joke. "Awful Appearance of Wopps at a Picnic" (1851) is a mock tragedy of what can go wrong at a picnic when a gigantic wasp attacks and the picnickers panic. Everything is turned topsy-turvy, and as people scattered, a heroic figure of Charles Dickens stands with his left arm around his wife, Catherine, and his right hand brandishing a dinner knife.

In Great Barrington, Massachusetts, Herman Melville, Nathaniel Hawthorne, and friends picnicked in the rain on Monument Mountain, near Great Barrington, Massachusetts, in 1850. The trek was an easy 1,700 feet, because with some foresight, they took no food but brought only Heidsieck champagne and one silver cup from which they all drank. Loose informality lubricated by the champagne got them all a bit drunk by the time they reached the summit. The result was a curious mixture of conviviality, and true to their personalities, Melville leaned perilously over the edge, and Hawthorne mourned they were all going to hell. Afterward, Melville was effusive, and he dedicated his novel *Moby-Dick* to Hawthorne. But Hawthorne laconically entered in his journal: "Ascended the mountain—that is to say, Mrs. Fields & Miss Jenny Field—Messrs. Field & Fields—Dr. Holmes, Messrs. Duyckinck, Mathews, Melville, Mr. Henry Sedgewick, &.—and were caught in a shower."[19] Eventually Hawthorne used a masquerade picnic as the central episode in his novel *The Blithedale Romance* (1852), but Melville never used it to good purpose except in a Civil War poem, "The March into Virginia Ending in the First Manassas (July, 1861)," in which he contrasts war and a picnic party in May.

So from the grass to rivers, mountains, or battlefields there are outdoor picnics. Ordinary people prefer them, as do professional food and cookbook writers. As usual there are variations and preferences, especially about food, but the common thread is outdoors. So not only does James Beard title his cookbook *Cook It Outdoors* (1941) but also he (incredulously) includes plans for building stone fireplaces. "This is a fireplace you might build yourself," but he also says that it is fine to have portable stoves that you can "stow in your car for a picnic."[20] A more practical Beard suggests that for a relaxed, impromptu picnic, "throw anything at hand into a picnic basket," he urges picnickers, and then drive or walk to the wildest place imaginable" and "flop on the grass or the beach and be absolutely relaxed and carefree."[21] *Menus for Entertaining* (1965), his last cookbook, nails his preference to the countryside: "The color and charm of the countryside can make the most modest meal taste superb. Have a picnic at the slightest excuse. It is even fun to have a box lunch and a hot drink in the car on a wintry day, while you look out at a dazzling stretch of landscape."[22] "Lovely surroundings" are the keywords for Mrs. C. F. Leyel's *Picnics for Motorists* (1936). "No one is too young or too old to delight in such a simple pleasure as a picnic in lovely surroundings and there is no more perfect way of spending a hot day. Sea, river, hills, woods, or fields all make their appeal, and it is one of the best ways to get complete relaxation."[23] Of a like mind, Alice B.

Toklas and Gertrude Stein stopped to gather flowers while picnicking. Writing in her *The Alice B. Toklas Cook Book* (1954), Toklas is excited: "We gathered early wild flowers, violets at Versailles, daffodils at Fontainebleau, hyacinths (the bluebells of Scotland) in the forest of Saint-Germain," before settling down to a lunch of sandwiches made of chopped roast beef salad or chopped chicken salad or more complex fare at a nearby restaurant.[24]

Elizabeth David writes about outdoor picnics, which she considered herself addicted. She explains this in the last chapter of *Summer Cooking* (1955), which she aptly held for last because it captures her enthusiasm for the joy of outdoor dining and makes a good ending for a cookbook. Though she picnicked everywhere, France was a special place for her, and in *An Omelette and a Glass of Wine* (1984) she explains straight away that the best place to picnic is above Aurillac, where there is a "stretch of water, mysterious, still, full of plants and birds, away from the road, sheltered by silver and with a stone table waiting there especially for us."[25] At the start of her career, Elizabeth David walked with Norman Douglas in the hills above Antibes, where they shared a picnic: he carried cheese that he cut with a pocketknife, and they would stop for wine. It was a spontaneous lunch that David much appreciated and which she later preferred to the planners, "those who frankly make elaborate preparations and leave nothing to chance, and those others whose organization is no less complicated but who are more deceitful and pretend that everything will be obtained on the spot and cooked over a woodcutter's fire conveniently at hand."[26] As one inspired by David, food writer and restaurateur Alice Waters never considers anything but an outdoor picnic. The *Chez Panisse Menu Cookbook* (1982) even begins with a picnic menu that is an homage to David "because she loves to eat out-of-doors."[27]

Other food writers stay closely to established precedent. "My idea of a good picnic," Nika Hazelton writes *The Picnic Book* (1969), is "one that I can fix up at home and need only carry and unpack at the chosen spot. I loathe cooking out-of-doors, which I find an inconvenient bore. After all, I am perfectly willing to provide any amount of nice food for my guests, so why must I cook under the most inconvenient circumstances?"[28] The dunes of Agami on the Mediterranean just beyond Alexandria is where Claudia Roden remembers how, in the 1930s, "town dwellers go out in the country or in boats, generally northward, eating out in fields or on the riverbank."[29] *Everything Tastes Better Outdoors* (1984), Roden's contribution to the well-prepared picnic, alternates between the elaborate and informal picnic, but they are always outdoors. Her most ecstatic picnic in the Seychelles Islands was like being the Garden of Eden: the smells of pungent spices, chilies, and roasting pork in a primeval forest filled her "with sudden bursts of happiness."[30]

Not everyone likes a picnic outdoors. There are deficiencies: it rains, wasps sting, ants appear, wind disrupts a place setting, dogs incessantly bark, the company is dour, and so forth. Some think this is awful but inevitable, and that the ideal picnic is never quite achievable. Such is satirist Logan Pearsall Smith's view of a wet, chilled English picnic that failed to match any of the marvelous scenes in Watteau's *fête galantes* and *fête champêtres*.[31] Even less enthusiastic and truly without guile, Princess Margaret, Queen Elizabeth II's late sister, opined that outdoor picnics should all but be abolished. In "Picnic at Hampton Court" (1983), she writes, "Nearly all picnics in Britain end up in a layby by the road because, in desperation, no one can decide where to stop."[32] In order to avoid indecision, Princess Margaret prefers the comforts of picnicking indoors in the Banqueting House at Hampton Court. (Really?)

Historically, animal nuisances have the unintended effect of subtly affirming that picnics are outdoors. From our perspective, ants ruin a picnic, but from an ant's perspective, picnics are always outdoors. When we stop to think about it, there are never jokes about ants and other insects disrupting indoor picnics or potluck dinners. Endless cartoons of ants, wasps, bees, cows, bulls, barking dogs, and bears provide comedic balance to picnics, just pleasantly taking the edge off conviviality, but without getting serious enough as to be ruinous. Myth buster and ant etymologist Deborah M. Gordon's *Ants at Work* (1999) suggests that "the observation that where there is a picnic, there will be ants, rests on the notion that there is an ant lurking everywhere, all the time, ready to mobilize its nest mates when a picnic appears."[33] This is reassuring—and fun to know.

5

PICNICS IN THE ARTS
AND POPULAR MEDIA

Fictional picnics and their foods are variable enough to suit any purpose. Writers and artists presume that because everyone knows what a picnic is then *any* picnic can be reinvented and reimagined, portrayed realistically or symbolically, treated in a straightforward manner or turned topsy-turvy to serve the topic at hand.

The wonder is that picnics are so flexible and resilient. They are easily subjected to free association and may even be turned topsy-turvy, but their essence is strong and inherent, expectations undiminished. Elizabeth Bowen's essay "Out of a Book" (1946) construes the picnic as a metaphor removed from its origins and history. "No, it is not only our fate but our business to lose innocence," she writes, "and once we have lost that, it is futile to attempt a picnic in Eden."[1] This "lost innocence" sounds ominous and somehow sexually decadent, but Bowen is reflecting on the power of reading and its affect on imagination. Once we begin to read, Bowen is letting on, innocence is lost—and the picnic is over.

Creators may use the picnic theme in fiction, prose, poetry, a painting, music, and dance, or even sculpture. The genres and mediums may be transposed or exchanged. For almost twenty years, Pablo Picasso compulsively recreated versions of Édouard Manet's painting *Luncheon on the Grass* on canvas, paper, and clay, until, at last, Carl Nesjar cast his plan in cement for placement on the lawn of the Stockholm Museum of Art. Currently, the picnickers in the Picasso/ Nesjar Édouard Manet's *Luncheon on the Grass* sit stolidly on the grass without benefit of apples, cherries, and oysters, food or wine.[2]

Artists and writers seldom hesitate to cross borders and freely associate real and fictional picnics. Poet Alfred Tennyson's picnickers filled their basket with dark bread, cold game pie in aspic, and cider that they ate and drank while chatting, singing, and talking over old love affairs in the poem "Audley Court" (1838). It is so enthusiastic, and the opening lines so often quoted, that readers believe there is a real Audley Court. It is comical to think of searchers roaming the environs of Cambridge, reciting:

> The Bull, the Fleece are crammed, and not a room
> For love or money. Let us picnic there
> At Audley Court.[3]

It may be that Joan Lindsay's *Picnic at Hanging Rock* (1969) is fiction, but people want it to be otherwise and obsessively research Lindsay's narrative to solve the mystery. No doubt, more than one fan of the novel has searched the Hanging Rock for clues even though the picnic was in 1913.

Gustave Flaubert realized this irony of life and art eleven years after he described picnic detritus in his first novel, *November* (1842). Flaubert was amazed that his art had unwittingly imitated life and he explained to his mistress, Louise Colet, "The day before yesterday, in the woods near Touques, in a charming spot beside a spring, I found an old cigar butt and scraps of *pâté*. People had been there picnicking. I had described such a scene in *November*, eleven years ago: there it was entirely imagined, and the other day it was experienced. Everything one invents is true, you may be sure."[4] The picnic's detritus is important because it foreshadows the hero's suicide; the broken bottle and knife metaphorically suggest his very unpicnicky attributes of depression and unhappiness. Flaubert was pleased is that he invented the picnic scene and the metaphor long before he stumbled upon it in real life.

There is no telling how life imposes itself on fictional picnicking, but the relationship is sure, and the imagery is ubiquitous in all literature, all the arts, and other media. The irony is that sometimes you need to be made aware of it. Many people are familiar with the most famous picnics—Édouard Manet's painting *Luncheon on the Grass*, George Gershwin's opera *Porgy and Bess*, William Inge's play *Picnic*, Fernando Arrabal's one-act drama *Picnic on the Battlefield*, Kenneth Grahame's juvenile novel *The Wind in the Willows*. But there are many others, among them one of Walt Disney's first cartoons, Mickey Mouse's *The Picnic*, and Ian Fleming's last book, the juvenile novel *Chitty Chitty Bang Bang*. It takes thoughtful reconnoitering to name others, though picnics appear in every genre and medium: prose, poetry, drama, and music for adults and children; essay and fiction; painting, engraving, and sculpture; and film and photography. These figurative picnics are typically ordinary and purport any picnic you might attend. So many of them are filled with *joie de vivre*, such as Henri Cartier-Bresson's photograph, *Sunday on the Banks of the Marne*, where portly bourgeoisie eat. Their basket is chock-a-block with cold chicken and bread, and if anything seems to have motivated their day in the country, it is the food and the pleasure.

But sometimes, the sense of picnic is purposely superficial and meant to be misleading. It is especially the case when these fictional picnics are intended as symbols and metaphors that intentionally reverse expectations for dramatic effect. Manet's *Luncheon* is suffused with images of sexuality. Inge's *Picnic* is really about a young woman's sexual awakening and her seduction. Ernest Hemingway's picnic lunch on a fishing trip in the novel *The Sun Also Rises* (1926) signals a serious discussion of faith and religious belief. His motorcar trip with F. Scott Fitzgerald is comic. The picnic he endured in the rain and his self-control makes for a memorable episode in the posthumous memoir *A Moveable Feast* (1964).

Picnic fun is also the aim of William Gilbert and Arthur Sullivan's first opera *Thespis* (1871). They began their favorite trick of turning things topsy-turvy by staging a picnic on Mount Olympus that fails because "everybody contributes what he pleases."[5] The result is that while there is claret for the claret cup, there isn't any lobster for the lobster salad. Parody can only work if you are in on the joke.

FICTION AND ART

> "Now—they're goin' to have a picnic," he said, half audibly.
> "What?"
> "Now—they're goin' to have a picnic."
> "Who's goin' to have a picnic?" demanded the cook, loudly.
>
> —Stephen Crane, "Shame" (1900)

"Picnic dinners are much the same in all parts of the world," Anthony Trollope writes in the novel, *The Bertrams*, "and chickens and salad are devoured at Jerusalem very much in the same way as they are at other places."[6] Mostly, as Trollope humorously suggests, the English don't really care where they picnic as long as there is food. This, however, is only part of the story. What is served at fictional picnics is neither outrageous nor invented. It's not even exotic. The food and drink are familiar, usually supplied in excess, and almost always enhance the meaning or imagery of a fictional tale, poetry, painting, and other media.

Margaret Mitchell's novel *Gone with the Wind* (1936) contrasts two menus prepared simultaneously at the April party days before the start of the Civil War in Charleston, South Carolina. The first is for the local aristocrats in the Wilkeses' garden at Twelve Oaks plantation. The second is among the African American slaves also feasting, but only where they cannot be seen behind the barns. As an icon of southern civilization, the Wilkeses demonstrate their wealth and social graciousness. But hiding the African Americans' party out of sight and behind the barns is a deliberate slight to mark their perceived inferiority. The dual picnics seem intended by Mitchell to soften the existence of slavery, but in fact it highlights the problem which Sidney Howard's screenplay for the film *Gone with the Wind* (1939) glosses over. As Mitchell describes the scene, there are long, trestled tables covered in linen with backless benches and chairs and cushions spread out elsewhere in the shade. But what the ease and elegance of the table setting cannot do is eliminate the odors of the barbecuing pits for the guests, from which "succulent odors of barbecue sauce and Brunswick stew floated," or those from behind the barns where the African Americans cooked hoecakes and yams and chitterlings, a dish of hog entrails. Scarlett is greatly affected, and as "the smell of crisp fresh pork came to her, Scarlett wrinkled her nose appreciatively."[7]

When the Price family serves southern fried chicken to the African villagers of a town in the Belgian Congo on the Fourth of July circa 1959, it might have just been another picnic. But as told by Barbara Kingsolver in her novel *The Poisonwood Bible* (1998), it is the ornery brainstorm of the Reverend Nathan Price who decides to celebrate it as Easter Sunday. Because he needs a dinner, he requests that Orleanna and their five daughters prepare a church picnic dinner. Being a resourceful southern woman, Orleanna uses what is at hand: chickens, and being practical, she wrings their necks, plucks their feathers, and fries them as she might have in Georgia. But nothing goes according to plan except the fried chicken, and despite Reverend Nathan's urging, the villagers refuse baptism because there are crocodiles in the river. As remembered by Rachel, one of the daughters, "The picnic was festive, but not at all what he'd had in mind. It was nothing in terms of redemption."[8] The incongruity of a Easter Sunday/ Fourth of July picnic is totally lost on Reverend Nathan, revealing his missionary zeal and shaky hold on reality.

For a complete change of locale, Calvin Trillin's picnic in the essay, "Fly Frills to Miami," from *Alice, Let's Eat* (1978), is a joke about airplane food. The

Figure 5.1. Picnic scene in *Gone with the Wind* (1939). MGM/Photofest.

story is that when Trillin's wife, Alice, complains about travel expenses, Calvin decides to go cheap by purchasing food for his flight from New York to Miami. The result is an application of "Alice's Law of Compensatory Cashflow" that is intended to be economical but ends with an absurdly expensive and comic riff on gluttony. With gusto, Trillin spreads the contents of his carry-on: fresh caviar, smoked salmon, crudités with pesto, tomato-curry soup, butterfish with shrimp stuffing, gelée, spiced clams, lime and dill shrimp, tomatoes stuffed with guacamole, marinated mussels, assortment of pâtés, stuffed cold breast of veal, chocolate cakes, praline cheesecake, and Italian cheesecake with fresh strawberries, Grand Marnier, and Pouligny-Montrachet. When the woman sitting next to him leans over and says "You must be a gourmet eater," Trillin's joke comes full circle. Gourmet or gourmand, it's all the same at a picnic.[9]

Chiefly, what makes fictional picnic food different is attitude. You cannot always assume that food is merely food. Unbound by real-life food choices, regard for diet or fetishes, artists and writers can make their foods inform you about a story's meaning or a character's interior life. Food details may seem innocuous, but they are added for a purpose and may give depth of meaning and superficial luster to any work of art in any genre. Sometimes, what is intended is not evident, and you may have to scrutinize a picnic. What you see is sometimes a strange mixture designed to make things more pleasant than they are.

Imagine being on the grass in Big Sur, California, looking out at the sea. Then imagine that your hostess is a prudish crank, a *belle dame sans merci*, who wants the world to be rid of anything she thinks is messy, unclean, or sensual. This is science writer Philip K. Dick's picnic in the novel *Eye in the Sky* (1957), a novel about the consequences of living in a parallel reality in which a single person can play god and control life on Earth. So though the location for the picnic is a picturesque hillside in Big Sur, California, the parallel reality is governed by Edith Pritchett's deepest desire to make the world "nice," like getting rid of the Cold War, disease, and polluting factories. She serves good food, too—hard-boiled eggs, yogurt, cold cuts, smoked herring, potato salad, stewed apricots, and orange-blossom tea. But she is prudish enough to get rid of love and sex, and there is not enough orange-blossom tea to make good sense of that. The picnic ends when Pritchett, having turned the hillside into a wasteland, enthusiastically destroys "air," and at last herself.[10]

By contrast, Marcel Proust's picnic food seems ordinary and literal. We know the ordinary madeleine is a small, sweet cake, and from the novel *Swann's Way* (1913), we learn that it plays an important part as a symbol of memory. Similarly, in the sequel, *Within a Budding Grove* (1914), Proust serves ordinary food to help the reader understand the character of his protagonist, Marcel, the same boy who once dreamed of madeleines. Now sixteen, he still prefers sweets to sandwiches at a picnic. "Seated on the grass," Marcel says, he and his friends "would undo our parcel of sandwiches and cakes. My friends preferred the sandwiches, and were surprised to see me eat only a single chocolate cake, sugared with gothic tracery, or an apricot tart. This was because, with the sandwiches of cheese or of green-stuff, a form of food that was novel to me and knew nothing of the past, I had nothing in common."[11] It is unclear what the "green stuff" is, but what you can tell is that Marcel is still immature, both about food and mainly about how to flirt with young girls.

A routine sandwich takes on a different quality in Stephen Crane's story "Shame" (1990). It is a story about how Jimmie Prescott is shamed when the cook puts sandwiches into a worker's lunch pail instead of a genteel wicker basket. It is a humorous case of getting what you wish for. When Jimmie blubbers that he cannot go to the picnic without something to eat, the cook makes salmon sandwiches in record speed: "Well, then, stop it. I've got enough on my mind." It was by chance that she was making salmon croquettes for luncheon. A tin still half full of pink, prepared fish was beside her on the table. Still grumbling, "she seized a loaf of bread and, wielding a knife, she cut from this loaf four slices, each of which was as big as a six-shilling novel. She profligately spread them with butter, and jabbing the point of her knife into the salmon-tin, she brought up bits of salmon, which she flung and flattened upon the bread. Then she crashed the pieces of bread together in pairs, much as one would clash cymbals. There was no doubt in her own mind but that she had created two sandwiches."[12] From a food preparation point of view, it is admirable cookery. From Jimmie's point of view, the lunch pail is grief and the picnic is a disaster; from Crane's view, it is a perfect example of a boy learning to be a teenager.

In a broader historical context, there is ample evidence from the seventeenth century to the present that food imagery at a picnic is resourcefully embedded as a matter of interest, satire, or humor, to fill out a narrative, define a scene, enhance a character, or suggest an argument about issues such as love, war, or morality. The picnic pattern is applied everywhere and appears in "high and low" art and fiction. For example, in Miguel de Cervantes's novel, *Don Quixote de la Mancha* (1605), at a *merienda*, the alfresco lunch is purchased from a nearby inn. Though the food is ordinary—cold rabbit, pastries, and wine—the conversation is remarkable, for it is a moment when Don Quixote argues for the powers of imagination and creativity against the Canon, who affirms that imagination is pernicious.[13]

Less acclaimed, Mary Elizabeth Braddon's novel, *Mount Royal* (1882), has a picnic on the mound of what is the ruin of Tintagel castle, Cornwall. It is a place steeped in myth and history, for it is where Tristram and Isolde loved and were killed by the jealous King Mark, where King Arthur was conceived and born, and about which poets and writers tell its history in prose and verse. Though Braddon's picnickers are aware of where they are, they cannot help but talk while eating their prosaic cold chicken and salad and drink wine. Although they are sympathetic to Isolde, especially, no one suggests a toast.[14] Years after, when Frederick Ashton choreographed the ballet *Tintagel* (1952), he based the frame of his story on Braddon's novel. He even included a roast chicken and wine among the props. A George Platt Lynes photograph of the scene makes the allusion certain.[15]

ART

As a rule, the well-provisioned basket has more, not less, of everything. Full baskets are evident in such food-centric picnics as Francisco Goya's painting, *La merienda a orillas del Manzanares* (*The Picnic at the Edge of the Manzanares*

River) (1776), Charles Dickens's novel, *The Posthumous Papers of the Pickwick Club* (1835), Thomas Cole's painting, *The Pic-Nic Party* (1846), Édouard Manet's *Luncheon on the Grass* (1863), and Henri Cartier-Bresson's photograph, *Sunday on the Banks of the Marne* (1938). What this group has in common is ample food and drink to augment a day in the country that is the basis for leisure, social conviviality, and a sense of contentment. Goya and Dickens provide a sense of humor, while Cole and Cartier-Bresson stress the sense of contentment.

Goya's painting, *Merienda*, is a country feast of chicken, sardines, casseroles, bread, cheese, cake, and many bottles of wine.[16] Knowing the scene was intended to be installed in a formal palace dining room, Goya personally decided on the *merienda* since it was typical of alfresco pleasures. It was to be social, convivial, and tinged with a wry sense of humor. Other paintings involved in this project show people enjoying other country pleasures, such as dancing, but the *merienda* illustrates alfresco dining. It illustrates that part of the meal when the young men about town, called *mojos*, have eaten well and are probably tipsy. They are flirting with a *maja*, perhaps a prostitute carrying a basket

Figure 5.2. Francisco de Goya, *The Picnic at the Edge of the Manzanares River [La merienda a orillas del Manzanares]* (1776), oil on canvas. Museo del Prado. Photo by De Agostini/Getty Images.

of apples or oranges. The men lift their cups to toast her beauty, but the woman of their party, her eyes cast downwards, is unimpressed or embarrassed. (The sexual allusion, however, is not unusual, and lovers' picnics are more sexually metaphorical when it comes to foods. This is another category of picnic that will be discussed separately.)

Charles Dickens's novel, *The Pickwick Papers* (1835), treats the picnic as a joke, and the "eatables" is a satire of middle-class excess—the same audience that he aimed to attract and who immediately took his humor in stride and loved him for it. In the chapter, "Field Day and Bivouac," Samuel Pickwick and friends (Snodgrass, Winkle, and Trundle) are invited to join the Wardles' family luncheon in their open carriage. The comedy is that a carriage designed for four must seat eight, and it is so tight that everyone must sit knee to knee with the ladies on their laps, a situation that encourages flirting. There are so many "eatables" that you have the suspicion the Wardles might have expected to feed a regiment. Hampers are full of chicken pigeon pie, tongue, veal, ham, lobsters, salad with dressing, and wine, all to be consumed with standard dining gear (dishes, flatware, glassware, and more) that has to be juggled on their laps. Moreover, the booming cannons, musketry, and other sounds of the mock battle accompany the conversation. Mr. Wardles, a jolly, stout man, wonderfully keeps his equanimity throughout it all:

> "Now we must sit close," said the stout gentleman. After a great many jokes about squeezing the ladies' sleeves, and a vast quantity of blushing at sundry jocose proposals, that the ladies should sit in the gentlemen's laps, the whole party were stowed down in the barouche; and the stout gentleman proceeded to hand the things from [Joe] the fat boy (who had mounted up behind for the purpose) into the carriage.
>
> "Now, Joe, knives and forks." The knives and forks were handed in, and the ladies and gentlemen inside, and Mr. Winkle on the box, were each furnished with those useful instruments.
>
> "Plates, Joe, plates." A similar process employed in the distribution of the crockery.
>
> "Now, Joe, the fowls. Damn that boy; he's gone to sleep again. Joe! Joe!" (Sundry taps on the head with a stick, and the fat boy, with some difficulty, roused from his lethargy.) "Come, hand in the eatables."[17]

A second picnic in *The Pickwick Papers* includes Sam Weller's disputation on the ingredients of "weal pies." It takes place during a hunt picnic and is discussed within a discussion of hunt picnics.

Figure 5.3.   Thomas Cole, *The Pic-Nic Party* (1846), oil on canvas. © Brooklyn Museum/Corbis.

As with the Wardles who add four to the picnic without flinching, family picnics as a rule are provisioned with more "eatables" than necessary. The act of hosting and sharing inherently calls for abundance if not excess. Two picnics about a hundred years apart demonstrate this: Thomas Cole's painting *The Pic-Nic Party* (1846) and Henri Cartier-Bresson's photograph *Sunday on the Banks of the Marne* (1938).[18] Cole's picnic food is emblematic of American social cohesiveness and plenty, while Cartier-Bresson's is a snapshot of a typical French bourgeoisie day in the country. Cole's is a picnic of about twenty family, friends, and children, but Cartier-Bresson's is a picnic for two middle-aged couples. Both inform you that outdoor picnickers require lots of food and wine. For Cole, food and drink is scattered throughout the site. There are baskets of hams, roasts, chickens, bread, and an open fire with coffee or tea brewing, wines in the cooler, and a bucket of ice cream.

Once on his way to a real-life picnic to High Peak, in the Catskill Mountains of New York, Cole excitedly writes that they packed: "Sundry baskets, containing many good things, provided by the ladies, giving weighty promise that we should not die of famine among the mountains."[19] When this enthusiasm is transferred to *The Pic-Nic Party*, Cole demonstrates his certitude of the pleasant life. Cartier-Bresson's is less personal and produces a snapshot of French life that is a Sunday tradition: to escape work and eat cold chicken, bread, and wine outdoors on the grass. Cartier-Bresson captures the moment when their conviviality is restrained and these portly picnickers sit separately and comfortably, focused on eating and drinking.

Antonio Carracci's *Landscape with Bathers* (ca. 1616), a very early and recognizable beach picnic, suggests that wine and bread are sufficient. A basket of food and wine flasks sit next to a fully clothed woman, whose stare and beckoning wave suggest an invitation to share the picnic fare on her cloth.[20] Behind the picnic, nude, muscular men scamper like crabs on rugged, rocky outcroppings. The scene may have some deeper meaning, but what this is remains a mystery that is the very same quality in Édouard Manet's *Luncheon on the Grass* (1863).[21] A chief difference is that Manet delights in food, a jumbled assortment on a blue cloth, all of which have sexual connotations. Wine, cherries, peaches, figs, bread, cheese, and oysters have symbolic sexual associations. Oysters, especially, are regarded as aphrodisiacs, cherries and peaches have suggestive contours resembling the female torso, and the overturned basket may suggest loss of innocence. It has been purported that Manet referred to the *Luncheon* as a *partie carrée*, sexual tryst, but the only sure evidence in the painting is the food, which is suggestive enough for the nude woman to stare directly at the viewer and challenge him or her to think otherwise. Figs, cherries, oysters have

Figure 5.4. Édouard Manet, *Luncheon on the Grass* (1863), oil on canvas. Musée D'Orsay. © Corbis.

strong claims on aphrodisiacs, though these may be more metaphorical than real.

Nearly a year after Manet's *Luncheon*, Mary Elizabeth Braddon's novel *The Doctor's Wife* (1864) included two picnics at which exquisite foods and wines are intended to aide a sexual seduction. It is uncertain if Braddon knew Manet's *Luncheon*, but she surely knew Gustave Flaubert's novel *Madame Bovary* (1856), and Isabel Gilbert, like Emma Bovary, is unhappily married to a boring doctor and will be seduced by a rich aristocrat. Isabel's seduction begins at a picnic for orphan children with more elaborate food and drink that any child might ever dream of. The cumulative influence on the susceptible Isabel is successful and proves again that food and sexuality are a natural combination, but it has the effect of illuminating Isabel's shallow character. Believing that she is chosen for romance, Isabel imagines herself in a fairy tale where "the patriarchal oaks" shelter her from "the outer world," making it the "Ultima Thule of bliss in the way of a picnic."[22] The baskets of food contain a great pound cake, pastries, and biscuits for the children, but for the adults, the foods are rich and elaborate:

"a tongue, then a pair of fowls, a packet of anchovy sandwiches, stilton cheese and Madeira and sparkling Burgundy." Isabel is impressed. At a second picnic, Lansdell, Isabel's suitor, redoubles his effort to seduce Isabel with game pie with a highly glazed crust like a piece of modern Wedgewood, young fowls nestling in groves of parsley, tongue decorated with vegetable productions chiseled into the shapes of flowers, York ham in a high state of polish like Spanish mahogany, lobster salad, and cold chicken jellies and creams, hothouse grapes, peaches, and pineapple. In sum, the two picnics suggest that the road to Isabel's adultery is paved with elaborate foods that give her a sense that she is in a kind of paradise. A glass of wine might encourage a woman to become amorous, but this gourmandish feast is surely Braddon's idea of a sly joke at the expense of a young, immature housewife on the verge of being seduced.

Claude Monet's painting *Luncheon on the Grass* was meant to be a reinterpretation of Manet's picnic on a monumental scale of fifteen by twenty feet. He began the painting in 1864, but the project stalled and was abandoned in 1865.[23] The story of the painting, as told in Joel Isaacson's *Monet: Le déjeuner sur l'herbe* (1972), is that Monet intended his picnic to be a historical work depicting bourgeoisie society at the level of academic painting. Eventually, the incomplete painting was divided into three panels. Only the oil sketch shows the complete work. Monet hung only the central portion at Giverny. In the central panel, the figure of Camille, who was not then his wife, sits holding a plate and reaching forward as if to serve. The cloth is laden with food: a roasted chicken, a terrine, a loaf of bread, a jumble of fruits, and bottles of wine. The opulence of the scene belies the fact that in 1865 Monet, then twenty-five-years-old, was broke. The painting was cut in three, and the picnic food is shown in the central panel.

By 1883, when he settled at Giverny, Monet was fastidious about freshness, insistent on quality, and adamant on dining elegantly in the country style, as discussed in Claire Joyes's *Monet's Table* (1989).[24] At some picnics, the family sat on a picnic cloth; other times the family dined at a trestle table using benches and chairs. In either situation, the cloth was white and set with dishes, flatware, and glasses. Servants are unobtrusive. Monet's well-stocked kitchen at Giverny provided a picnic meal with stuffed eggs, pate en croute, duck or beef pie, cold beef a la mode, bread, grapes, apples, cakes, chestnut or honey cookies, Genoa cake, fruit cake, champagne or wine.

When Lewis Carroll took to the beach, he meant to upend picnic expectations with humor. Tweedledee's poem "The Walrus and the Carpenter" (1871) is a sardonic story about the silly young oysters that ignore an elder's advice and get duped into picnicking out of the water. What the oysters fail to notice is that the Walrus and the Carpenter are carrying bread, pepper, and vinegar, and so as they walk along the beach, they also miss the irony of the Walrus's (ambiguous) invitation to eat:

"The time has come," the Walrus said,
"To talk of many things:
Of shoes—and ships—and sealing-wax—
Of cabbages—and kings—
And why the sea is boiling hot—
And whether pigs have wings."

"But wait a bit," the Oysters cried,
"Before we have our chat;
For some of us are out of breath,
And all of us are fat!"
"No hurry!" said the Carpenter.
They thanked him much for that.

"A loaf of bread," the Walrus said,
"Is what we chiefly need:
Pepper and vinegar besides

Figure 5.5. John Tenniel, "'O Oysters,' said the Carpenter." *Through the Looking-Glass and What Alice Found There,* by Lewis Carroll (London: Macmillan, 1871).

> Are very good indeed—
> Now if you're ready, Oysters dear,
> We can begin to feed."[25]

Even those who do not like oysters get the joke. Among Carroll's picnics, this episode in *Though the Looking-Glass* is a favorite not least because of Alice's misplaced sympathy and childish confusion:

> "I like the Walrus best," said Alice, "because you see he was a little sorry for the poor oysters."
> "He ate more than the Carpenter, though," said Tweedledee. "You see he held his handkerchief in front, so that the Carpenter couldn't count how many he took: contrariwise."
> "That was mean!" Alice said indignantly. "Then I like the Carpenter best—if he didn't eat so many as the Walrus."
> "But he ate as many as he could get," said Tweedledum.
> This was a puzzler. After a pause, Alice began, "Well! They were both very unpleasant characters—."[26]

Other picnic food standouts appear across genres: James Jacques Joseph Tissot's painting, *Holyday* (1876), Guy de Maupassant's story, "Boule de Suif" ("Ball of Fat") (1880), Eudora Welty's story, "Asphodel," (1942), the William Styron novel *Sophie's Choice* (1979), and Maya Angelou's fictionalized memoir, *I Know Why the Caged Bird Sings* (1969). Each represents different social customs and contexts that are based on the essential architecture of a picnic.

James Tissot's *Holyday* is the epitome of an upper-class Victorian picnic in which a family and friends are gathered around a sparkling white cloth.[27] The family is near the end of their picnic lunch, so that they are now at that dreamy end stage of a picnic when all are sated, and there is still dessert. The cloth is filled with china, flatware, a cake, sliced cheese on a platter, a platter of grapes, tea served from a silver carafe, and bottles of fizz. When Oscar Wilde, then twenty-three-years-old, reviewed the painting in 1877, he snidely complained that Tissot's picnickers were overdressed and common looking and were seated beside an "ugly, painfully accurate representation of modern soda-water bottles!"[28] The woman holding the teacup and staring off into space may be Kathleen Newton, Tissot's mistress and favorite model. *Holyday* is an ambiguous title, perhaps a pun on *holy* and *holiday* and the languid joy of leisure.

Informally dressed picnickers eating hot dogs with mustard and whole steamed crabs from a beach vendor is the subject of John Sloan's painting *South Beach* (1907–1908).[29] Judging from the smiling faces, the hot dogs and crabs will be devoured happily, if not ravenously. The scene is a happy joke because it takes scrutiny to realize that some basic picnic gear is missing, like a blanket and towels. But what does strike home is that these are spontaneously happy people enjoying a simple lunch, probably coming to enjoy the beach on Staten Island, a short ferry ride from Manhattan.

Maupassant's "Boule de Suif" (1880) is a critique of French social hypocrisy and moral confusion. The story takes place during the French defeat by the Prussians in the War of 1872. It caricatures a group of travelers from all classes of society as they flee Rouen to escape the Prussians. At first, they ignore the fat prostitute, Boule de Suif, aka Elizabeth Rousset, who packs a basket for a three-day carriage journey, the aroma of which is inescapable:

> Boule de Suif stooped quickly, and drew from underneath the seat a large basket covered with a white napkin.
>
> From this she extracted first of all a small earthenware plate and a silver drinking cup, then an enormous dish containing two whole chickens cut into joints and imbedded in jelly. The basket was seen to contain other good things: pies, fruit, dainties of all sorts—provisions, in fine, for a three days' journey, rendering their owner independent of wayside inns. The *necks of four bottles* protruded from among the food. She took a chicken wing, and began to eat it daintily, together with one of those rolls called in Normandy "Regence."
>
> All looks were directed toward her. An odor of food filled the air, causing nostrils to dilate, mouths to water, and jaws to contract painfully. The scorn of the ladies for this disreputable female grew positively ferocious; they would have liked to kill her, or throw, her and her drinking cup, her basket, and her provisions, out of the coach into the snow of the road below.[30]

Despite her profession, of course, she has a good heart, and when she realizes "all eyes were fixed on her," she shares her feast. But when the basket is empty, and after Boule de Suif sacrifices herself for the benefit of the others to a predatory Prussian officer, she is ostracized. As they leave for their final stage of the journey to Le Havre, the selfish passengers refuse Boule any companionship or food. At this climax, the incivility and boorishness of the aristocrats and middle classes is smugly revealed and reviled. As Boule de Suif cries, Cornudet, a leftish thug, sarcastically sings the "Marseillaise," but he does not help her or offer any food.

However, there is nothing comic about Sophie Zawistowska, the pathetic heroine of William Styron's novel *Sophie's Choice* (1979). According to Stingo, the novel's narrator, picnics become a kind of ritual for Sophie as she tries to mitigate her tragic memories living in the Nazi concentration camp at Auschwitz. Now living in Brooklyn, New York, the privilege of eating as much as she can makes her feel alive and "achingly sensual." Stingo, the narrator, writes that these picnics were a "pleasant game," and Sophie would prepare by purchasing a picnic lunch at one of the "glorious delicatessens" on Flatbush Avenue, Brooklyn. Standing in front of the counter with "the privilege of choice" gives Sophie a feeling of sensuality mixed with deep memories of the past. Sometimes, Stingo says that her eyes teared as she selected a pickled egg, a slice of salami, a half a loaf of black pumpernickel, a bagel, bratwurst, braunschweiger, sardines, pastrami, or lox. When these were packed into a paper bag, she marched into Prospect Park and ate while she read a favorite passage from a novel. Stingo calls this "a fete champêtre for one."[31]

Excessive picnic eating is meant as a sign of social solidarity and community for Maya Angelou's fictionalized memoir, *I Know Why the Caged Bird Sings* (1969). The customary "summer picnic fish-fry" has a menu that "would have found approval on the menu of a Roman epicure."[32] The town of Stamp, Arkansas, holds the outdoor event of the year, and everyone brings mounds of food, assuming that more makes the outing better, friendlier, more memorable. The menu she provides includes everything—fried bass, chicken, ham, barbecued spare ribs and chickens, bologna, hard-boiled eggs, potato salad, pickles, chowchow [vegetable relish], chocolates, pound cake with icing, orange sponge cake, coconut and chocolate layer cake, candy bars, cold watermelon, Coca Colas, and White Lighting [gin or moonshine?]. All of this food, Angelou suggests, is a public display of happiness and resilience beneath which lies the deep anxiety and hurt that African Americans must suffer in an antagonistic southern white society in the 1940s. Superficially, excess masks pain, and the fish fry picnic is a metaphor suggesting why Angelou named her story *I Know Why the Caged Bird Sings*.

Conversely, it is this fish fry that stereotypes African Americans in Roark Bradford's novel *Ol' Man Adam an' His Chillun, Being the Tales They Tell about the Time When the Lord Walked the Earth Like a Natural Man* (1928).[33] Bradford's idea was to retell Old Testament stories reenacted in an African American dialect he invented. It begins in a segregated Heaven entirely populated with "angelic" African Americans with white, fluffy wings forever gathering for a fish fry picnic visited by "De Lawd," who finds the "b'iled custard" not to his taste. As a sign of the times, the novel was popular enough among white audiences to be dramatized as *Green Pastures* by Marc Connelly in 1930 and adapted for film by William Keighly and Marc Connelly in 1936. It was this kind of racism that Angelou's "summer fish-fry" sought to erase in *Caged Bird* and set the record straight. In 1936, white audiences accepted stereotyping and racial slurs as a matter of course, but now *Green Pastures* is a museum piece.

SIGHTSEEING

Dear Mrs. Ambrose—I am getting up a picnic for next Friday, when we propose to start at eleven-thirty if the weather is fine, and to make the ascent of Monte Rosa. It will take some time, but the view should be magnificent. It would give me great pleasure if you and Miss Vinrace would consent to be of the party.

—Yours sincerely, Terence Hewitt

—Virginia Woolf, *The Voyage Out* (1915)

When the urge to see new sights is enhanced with a picnic, pleasure is even more memorable. Alexander Pope, the poet, put the two together first, but he recorded it in a letter that got buried for two hundred and fifty years. Writing Martha Blount, his friend and lover, in August 1734, Pope describes a picnic lunch he and Charles Mordaunt, later Lord Peterborow, had in the ruins of Netley Abbey, Southampton. Accompanied by three mariners, one of whom served lunch, they sailed across to the island "well victualld with Cold Pye, Pigoons & turkiesd" gallons of brandy, Frontignac [muscat], and claret. They added a salad of alisander, or wild parsley, the roots of which might be eaten raw with oil and vinegar. They were very hungry, but they toured the ruins, Pope all the while looking "to chuse the best place to dine in." Pope wanted to eat in the ruins and so avoid snakes and toads, but Mordaunt insisted on eating alfresco. So they sat on broken capitals and used a fallen pillar as a table.[34] It is a forerunner of the typical English picnic, and it compares to the halt on the hunt picnics that French painters such as Jean Antoine Watteau and his ilk had popularized in France. Pope does not call this a picnic; it was just a luncheon during a sightseeing adventure. It is just that Pope was part of a slow trend that eventually flourished seventy years later. Especially in England during the first two decades of the nineteenth century, picnicking was noticed and incorporated into painting and prose. Painters J. M. W. Turner and Thomas Rowlandson saw the value in embellishing a landscape. Novelist Jane Austen recognized the novelty for socializing, and Percy and Mary Shelley (then Mary Godwin) and Dorothy Wordsworth made picnics a part of their personal essays on travel.

Turner began adding outdoor meals (which he never named picnics) to enliven landscape scenes in drawings and paintings around 1803. Turner saw possibilities beginning first with the watercolor *Lake Geneva & Mont Blanc* (1803) and then frequently throughout the 1830s. J. M. W. Turner is a master of atmospheric tumult, and his many picnic scenes on the grass are always out of sight of cities; sometimes they are just beyond London in Richmond or somewhere by a lake or waterway. Sometimes they are elegant and refined, as *England: Richmond Hill, on the Prince Regent's Birthday* (1819), or more merry, as *Dartmouth Cove, The Sailor's Wedding* (1824–1827), or casual, as *Childe Harold's Pilgrimage* (1832). Turner's interest in sightseeing and topographical art was a source of vacation, travel inspiration, and income. *Picturesque Views of the Southern Coast of England* (1826) or *Picturesque Views in England and Wales* (1838) include sightseeing picnics, which suggests Turner's delight for picnicking.

Throughout his career Turner showed that he was a man who liked happy picnics. Cyrus Redding, a friend accompanying Turner on a tour of Devonshire, writes an anecdote of a Turner picnic in "English Eden," at which Turner provided "an ample supply of cold meats, shell fish, and wines. In that delightful spot, we spent the better part of a delightful summer's day. Never was there more social pleasure partaken by any party in that English Eden. Turner was exceedingly agreeable for one whose language was more epigrammatic and terse than complimentary upon most occasions."[35]

The addition of picnics for lively visual interest begins as a sketch for two of Turner's early works, *Party of Men Picnicking* (1802) and a watercolor *Lake Geneva & Mont Blanc* (1803). These may be general interest or be partly attributed to the London Pic-Nic Society scandal of 1802 to 1803 that he could hardly escape knowing. Turner might have also read Oliver Goldsmith's novel *The Vicar of Wakefield* (everybody did) and have known Thomas Rowlandson's illustrations of the picnic scenes in that novel and more importantly his topographical painting *Richmond Bridge, London* (ca. 1808).[36]

Rowlandson's depiction of picnicking on the Thames sands at low tide suggests this was a popular sightseeing jaunt for Londoners, who would hire a boat to Richmond Bridge and when the tide was out, picnic on the wide, sandy shore. Rowlandson's people are always grotesques no matter their class, and his working-class picnickers sit close together, happily gorging themselves. Turner's version of the same scene, *Richmond Hill and Bridge, Surrey* (1828), includes the middle classes enjoying the day despite a brisk wind.[37]

In fact, that's the humor of the scene—the people running against the wind, a man chasing his hat, an unattended sun umbrella. The painting was a favorite of John Ruskin's, and it was the first painting by Turner that he owned. It was then titled *Richmond Hill and Bridge, with a Picnic Party* and represented leisure as opposed to work. At an exhibition of his paintings by Turner in 1878, Ruskin subtitled *Richmond Hill and Bridge* as *Play* and contrasted it with a

Figure 5.6. J. M. W. Turner, *Richmond Hill and Bridge, Surrey* (1828), engraving on paper.

painting of Dudley, a dull industrial town, that he subtitled *Work*. Implicitly Ruskin understood the value of leisure and, after all, what is a picnic except for play?[38] Turner's picnics are always happy. Turner's scenes *Plymouth Dock Seen from Mount Edgecumbe, Devonshire* (1816) and *Plymouth Devonshire [Mount Edgecumbe]* (1832) are ebullient and based on actual observation. Thornberry remembers Turner saying of them, "We shall see nothing finer than this if we stay till Sunday, because we can't." [39]

Among the major oil paintings, *England: Richmond Hill, on the Prince Regent's Birthday* (1819) is a garden party on a grassy knoll looking west down the Thames, a striking, shiny swath in a green landscape, beneath a glowing afternoon sky.[40] Turner appended a quote from James Thomson's "Summer," a section of *The Seasons*, leaving no doubt that the picnic in the landscape is intended as a symbol of a happy England in a golden age: "Happy Britannia!" The picnic in the painting *Childe Harold's Pilgrimage–Italy* (1832) connects to Canto IV of Byron's poem (1818) and the lines of verse, "and now, fair Italy! / Thou art the garden of the world, the home / Of all Art yields, and Nature can decree." Presumably Turner means you to think of Italy, but the landscape is the Thames Valley, the same used in *England: Richmond Hill*. Among Turner's antecedents is Claude Lorrain's *Landscape with Dancing* (ca. 1648), aka *The*

Marriage of Isaac and Rebecca, but while Lorrain is demonstrably in an idealized Italy, Turner usually liked to be specific. On the other hand, Jean-Baptiste Camille Corot's *View Near Naples* (1841) seems an allusion to both Lorrain and Turner.[41] Uniting all of these paintings is picnicky qualities—a happy, Eden-like landscape in which ordinary people dance, sing, eat, and drink at leisure.

Turner never left off, and picnics regularly appear, often for the sake of adding play to otherwise topographical scenes. One such happy scene that combines landscape and private memory is Turner's painting *Melrose Abbey* (1832), a record of a tour guided by Walter Scott.[42] The landscape is topographical where the ridge above the River Tweed makes a long *S* curve past the town and into the distant haze where the abbey is distantly visible. It was a place very dear to Scott, and Turner included him in the scene picnicking. Scott was ailing at the time, and the serenity of the landscape and the calm of the picnickers served as a *memento mori*. *Melrose Abbey* is among his topographical and atmospheric gems. Art critic Philip Gilbert Hamerton, however, complained that *Melrose Abbey* was ruined by a nasty picnic that obscured the view.[43]

Jane Austen's visit to Netley Abbey, Southampton, which she used for the setting of *Northanger Abbey* (composed in 1799), might have included a real picnic. Her first literary picnic, however, is referenced as a sightseeing "party of pleasure" in the novel *Sense and Sensibility* (1811) "to see a very fine place about twelve miles from Barton" for which it was convenient to bring a meal of "cold provisions."[44] Significantly, the "pic-nic parade" in the novel *Emma* (1816) is a day trip to Box Hill, Surrey, then a privately owned park popular as a sightseeing destination offering a panoramic view 564 feet above an extended valley in Surrey.[45]

Austen's characters were not the first to make such a picnic at Box Hill. In 1733 George Lambert painted *A View of Box Hill, Surrey* (1733) and enlivened the scene with a group of picnickers enjoying the view and watching farmworkers harvesting corn.[46] As is often the case, drinking is an important part of picnicking, and one of the men points toward an overturned jug of wine, which suggests that there was more interest in drinking and less in food. Emma Woodhouse's picnic to Box Hill is not unpleasant, but the day is hot and the conversation is unexpectedly dull in Jane Austin's *Emma*. It ends unexpectedly as a downer, and Emma is so embarrassed when she cannot resist being sarcastic and insults Miss Bates. Every Austenite can recite Emma's retort to the hapless Miss Bates. Emma later apologizes. Knightley, Emma's suitor, chastises her for the gaff, and she leaves Box Hill feeling so much social pain that you might think Emma had committed a murder—she is so mortified and grieved. On the other hand, the view from Box Hill may be a "fine prospect"; but it is never properly described and may as well not even be there at all. The food is a vague "cold collation," an information gap many have wondered about because Austen regularly mentions food in her letters. Maggie Black and Deirdre Le Faye's *The Jane Austen Cookbook* (1995) and Maggie Lane's *Jane Austen and Food* (1995) offer suggestions, but you wish Austen might have spoken for herself.[47]

Dorothy Wordsworth, the sister of the poet William, was an inveterate sightseer. It is known that she picnicked on Lake Grasmere in 1808, but when writing about a trip to the summit of Scawfell Pike, England's highest mountain, she calls it an excursion. "Excursion Up Scaw Fell Pike, October 7th, 1818," her only published work (1822), is a scenic description of a three-hour walk, supervised by a local guide, who arranged for provisions to be carried by packhorses. But what they dined on is unknown. Dorothy is much more interested in the view. At the summit, she says, "We ate our dinner in summer warmth. . . . We paused, and kept silence to listen, and not a sound of any kind was to be heard. We were far above the reach of the cataracts of Scaw Fell; and not an insect was there to hum in the air warmth; and the stillness seemed to be not of this world."[48] The moment is broken when the guide hurries them along to avoid a coming storm, which ironically fizzled out. Readers of Dorothy's essay in *Guide to the Lakes* (1822) would have understood that the meal on the summit was a picnic. But Dorothy decided not to use the word. As scenes in the Lake District became more popular, elements of picnicking appeared: Thomas Allom's *View from Langdale Pikes, Looking Towards Bowfell, Westmorland* (1832), an illustration for *The Northern Tourist: Seventy-Three Views of Lake and Mountain Scenery*, might have served as an illustration for Dorothy's "Excursion." Allom's picnickers are seen sightseeing on a grassy ledge at ease, though a tumultuous sky gathers in the distance.[49] In America, Nathaniel P. Willis and William H. Bartlett collaborated on *American Scenery, or Land, Lake, and River: Illustrations of Transatlantic Nature* (1840). Several scenes include picnics, particularly Bartlett's *View from Mount Holyoke* [Massachusetts] (1838).[50] The Americans' intention to publish a series of picturesque views is a response to popular English picture books, especially the picnic on Mount Holyoke, to compete with Turner's *Picturesque Views in England and Wales* (1824–1827), among others. In 1836, Thomas Cole painted the scene he titled *View from Mount Holyoke, Northampton, Massachusetts, after a Thunderstorm—The Oxbow*, but he rusticated the scene—leaving out the picnic ground, a small store selling refreshments, and picnickers.

Sometimes the union of sightseeing and picnics is creatively inspiring. The atmospheric clash of scenery gave a start to Percy Shelley and Mary Godwin, who thought they picnicked in "the most desolate place in the world."[51] Actually it was the Mer de Glace in the French Alps at Montanvert, a popular sightseeing destination. They wrote about it in *History of a Six Weeks' Tour* (1817), a hasty piece of travel writing that ought to have been forgotten except that it is the inspiration for Percy's poem "Mont Blanc" (1817) and Mary's *Frankenstein; or the Modern Prometheus* (1818). The cause for their dour experience is that the weather was mildly inclement and overcast, so when they reached the overlook, the Sea of Ice stunned them. For the record, Percy says, "On all sides precipitous mountains, the abodes of unrelenting frost, surround this vale: their sides are banked up with ice and snow, broken, heaped high, and exhibiting terrific chasms."[52] When at last they picnicked, Percy matter-of-factly says that they dined on the grass, "in the open air, surrounded by this scene. The air is piercing and clear. We returned down the mountain, sometimes encompassed by the driving vapours, sometimes cheered by the sunbeams, and arrived at our inn by seven o'clock."[53] Mary was impressed and repelled by the contrasts, but the scene made a lasting impression, and she used it in the novel *Frankenstein* in chapter IX, in which Victor writes, "The sight of the awful and majestic in nature had indeed always the effect of solemnizing my mind."[54] But the picnic is omitted. (Poor Victor Frankenstein seems never to have enjoyed a day of leisure.)

You might think that in the midst of this sublimity and tumult, Percy and Mary were at peril and risking their lives on this ascent of the mountain. But the trip was routine; guides, horses, and even a substantial hut for protection from the weather were available. Carl Ludwig Hackert's views of the Mer de Glace in 1781 shows a group of picnickers relaxing under an umbrella as they view the sublime scenery at their ease.[55] Hackert's scene is from a sunny day in August; luckily, and for the greater glory of poetry and fiction. Though Percy and Mary were there on a miserable day in July, their picnic was inspiring and charged them with imaginative power that transposed a real place and event into poetry and fiction.

More congenial sightseeing and soothing picnicking is Charles Dickens's tour of a prairie in southern Illinois that he described in *American Notes for General Circulation* (1842). He requested the excursion because it was an opportunity to see the vast plains of North America, but he was mildly disappointed because it was so vast and unremittingly flat; it clashed with his affinity for English landscape. "It is not a scene to be forgotten," he records, "but scarcely one I think (at all events, as I saw it), to remember." For Dickens, the view of the prairie was grand and not the most desolate place on Earth. He was not bored, and when he sat down to eat, the excursion assumed the Chekhovian solemnity of picnics. It was a "plain" picnic dinner that pleased him: "roast fowls, buffalo's tongue (usually boiled or smoked), ham, bread, cheese, and butter; biscuits,

champagne, sherry; lemons and sugar for punch; and abundance of rough ice."
With hindsight he remarked that "the meal was delicious, and the entertainers
were the soul of kindness and good humour. I have often recalled that cheerful
party to my pleasant recollection since, and shall not easily forget, in junketings
nearer home with friends of older date, my boon companions on the Prairie."[56]

Sometimes sightseeing is marred by trash. Isabella Lucy Bird complained
about rowdy picnickers and picnic junk. An intrepid traveler, Bird toured the
United States and wrote *The Englishwoman in America* (1856). It is mostly a
high-spirited adventure, except at Niagara Falls. At first, she is overpowered by
the American falls: "I left the cars, and walked down the slope to the verge of
the cliff; I forgot my friends, who had called me to the hotel lunch—I forgot everything—For I was looking at the Falls of Niagara." But on the Canadian side,
she calls it the British side, the glamour and exhilaration gives way to something
tawdry—she uses the word *disfigured*. "Not far from where I stood, the members of a picnic party were flirting and laughing hilariously, throwing chicken-
bones and peach-stones over the cliff, drinking champagne and soda-water."[57]
Bird is upset by how simple it is to disfigure the grandeur of Niagara with rowdy
picnickers. Bird's is an aesthetic judgment, but picnic detritus demonstrates
how picnickers' insensitivity can mar the beauty of a scene.

Knowing Anton Chekhov, you would expect that any picnic of his will
turn sour. There is no disappointment in the novella *The Duel* (1891). Even
the scenery is refuted, and when Laevsky is urged by his friend Samoylenko
to regard it, he replies, "Ach, the damned mountains!" . . . "How sick I am of
them!"[58] Later, however, in the dusk, the picnickers finally settle down at an
open campfire where they share fish soup, bread, and wine that is eaten "with
religious solemnity . . . only done at a picnic." Chekhov's characters are always
on the verge of happiness and then lose it. Nothing, not even a picnic, can be
happy for long in Chekhov's universe. Even in life, he complained, "We've
been having a warm spell with rain, but the evenings are delightful. A verst away
[about 2/3 of a mile] there is good swimming and picnic sites, but there's no
time to go swimming or picnicking. Either I gnash my teeth and write, or work
out picayune financial problems with carpenters and workers."[59] Chekhov's
contrast is comic but elicits a joyless Ha!

The great joy of picnicking and sightseeing is the supremely vivid winter
picnic of Elizabeth von Arnim in her autobiographical novel, *Elizabeth and
Her German Garden* (1898). It suggests an impressionistically colored joie de
vivre on a bluff overlooking the Baltic Sea. Though it is January, freezing, and
everything around is covered in sparkling snow, the heroine Elizabeth makes
this a birthday for herself so that she can enjoy the moment. Suddenly, a view

of the sea surprised her coming out from the mossy, pine-covered forest. The dazzling yellow shoreline borders a blue sea with boats afoot with orange sails. Elizabeth and friends admire the view from the sleigh and then set up for the meal: "I warmed the soup in a little apparatus I have for such occasions," she says, "which helped take the chilliness off the sandwiches,—this is the only unpleasant part of the winter picnic, the clammy quality of the provisions just when you most long for something very hot." There is humor as she confides, "It is the most difficult thing in the world to eat sandwiches with immense fur and woolen gloves on, and I think we ate almost as much fur as anything, and choked exceedingly during the process."[60] Some people will go to great lengths to find pleasure away from home, especially because her husband (called the Man of Wrath) hated picnics and never accompanied her on such a jaunt.

Forster's most serious and accomplished novel, *A Passage to India* (1924), contains probably one of the most important picnics in a serious story of social inequality. It is the story of a sightseeing expedition to the Hindu caves carved into the Marabar Hills. From the beginning it is a less than perfect day, one so fraught with errors of judgment, feeling, and thought that the net result is terror, clamor, and impulsive fear—pandemonium. At the same time it is a bore: Mrs. Moore yawns but praises Dr. Aziz, because "he has taken endless trouble to make a success of our picnic."[61] Ironically, her statement is two-edged; Aziz has taken trouble, and there will be trouble, the consequences of which are exceedingly unpleasant—unpicnicky.

The event begins badly when some guests miss the train. Then the train ride from Chandrapore to the Marabar Hills must be made long before sunrise to beat the heat of the day. A breakfast of poached eggs and tea cooked in the lavatory is eaten by Quested and Moore eat because they feel required to. At the Marabar train station, Aziz has arranged (at great expense) for an elephant to taxi them to the Hills. Everyone is frightened, and a servant slips and falls into the netting under the elephant. Quested and Moore are appalled. At a site selected for its shade, a picnic is prepared—a table set with plates, flatware, glasses, and cups, and an umbrella is opened. Utensils are unpacked. Inexplicably another breakfast of poached eggs, toast, porridge, mutton chops, and tea is served. Moore and Quested are puzzled, but Aziz erroneously believes that "English people never stop eating, and that he had better nourish them every two hours until a solid meal was ready." Despite not being hungry, the women are demur, and Aziz is conned into believing this is "how his hospitality is accepted." Entering the caves proves uncomfortable because it is dark and smells putrid. Aziz is a poor guide as he knows nothing about Hindu because he is a Muslim. Moore gets claustrophobic and leaves after lunch, Quested reluctantly returns to the cave with Aziz, and in a moment of confusion, when Aziz leaves her to smoke a cigarette, she runs from the cave and down the hillside in a panic. Inexplicably, Aziz does not follow her but returns to Moore. Mounting the elephant, they return to the station and board the train that resembles a string of coffins. Returned to Chandrapore, Aziz's troubles intensify when he accused of trying to rape Quested. He is arrested and led off to jail. Few picnics in life, literature, or art have such a depth of personal calamity. When Quested lies that she is the victim of attempted rape, Forster means this to suggest the opposite, that it is the English who are raping India. Aziz says, "This picnic is nothing to do with England or India; it is an expedition of friends." But he's got it wrong from the start, and as things go badly they never get righted and it is, after all, a horrible, senseless picnic.[62]

Virginia Woolf defuses conflict during a sightseeing picnic in the novel *The Voyage Out* (1915). Though the view is panoramic and the picnickers happy, Woolf was seriously depressed over her relationship with her prospective husband, Leonard Woolf, and her sexual preference for women. Trying to suppress her personal turmoil, Woolf turned to imagination; the tone in this work is positive, and the picnickers are happy and playful. There is even social bantering about ants. Miss Allan puts down her sandwich and blurts out, "I'm covered with little creatures." As it is, "The ants were pouring down a glacier of loose earth heaped between the stones of the ruin—large brown ants with polished bodies." The picnickers come to the rescue as if it was a battlefield, which it is: "The table-cloth represented the invaded country, and round it they built barricades of baskets, set up the wine bottles in a rampart, made fortifications of bread and dug fosses of salt. When an ant got through it was exposed to a fire of breadcrumbs, until Susan pronounced that that was cruel, and rewarded those brave spirits with spoil in the shape of tongue."[63] Battling the ants becomes a game that removes the veneer of decorum that usually inhibits good society. Mr. Perrott removes an ant from Evelyn's neck, and Mrs. Elliot remarks confidentially to Mrs. Thornbury that it would be no laughing matter "if an ant did get between the vest and the skin." There is an awkward moment when the picnickers voyeuristically peer at Susan Warrington and Arthur Venning happily embracing and kissing. Overall, good spirits prevail. At the summit of Monte Rosa, a tablecloth is spread in the lee of a ruined wall on which they picnic on cold chicken, sandwiches, wine, fruit, banana, and tea. Symbolically this represents a high point in the narrative, but the descent is a letdown. In real life, Woolf tried suicide at this point in writing the novel but was unsuccessful; life was not a picnic. Her fictional heroine, Rachel Vinrace, is not so lucky, and when Woolf resumed writing, Rachel dies of a fever.

MOTORISTS

The Ford gives you unlimited chance to get away into new surroundings every day—a picnic supper or a cool spin in the evening to enjoy the countryside or a visit with friends.

—Ford Motors (1925)

Bright shone the morning, and as I waited (they had promised to call for me in their motor) I made for myself an enchanting picture of the day before me, and our drive to that forest beyond the dove-blue hills, the ideal beings I should meet there, feasting with them exquisitely in the shade of immemorial trees.

—Logan Pearsall Smith, "The Ideal," *More Trivia* (1921)

As motorcars became the transportation of choice, picnics changed; first, because no other mode of transportation provided such easy access for travel; and second, because motorcars spawned picnic cookbooks. At a glance, this is a surprise because these connections are now implicit. Histories take the linkage for granted, even Julian Pettifer and Nigel Turner, whose *Automania: Man and the Motor Car* (1984) provides evidence for the interplay of picnics and motorcars, are only cursorily interested.[64] Not Walt Disney. In fact, from the very beginning of the Mickey Mouse cartoons, motorcars are the preferred and the *only* way to get to a picnic. *The Picnic* (1930) is typical: Mickey, Minnie, and Pluto drive a convertible to the country, spread a blanket, unpack food and a phonograph, and have a grand time. Even when it rains, they are happy, singing with gusto.[65]

Writing "The Motor Picnic" in 1905, Grace Margaret Gould, a fashionista of the period, announced the obvious: "Surely the influence of the motorcar is far reaching. Now it is the old-fashioned picnic which is caught up in its whirling way and given a new-fashioned touch."[66] Around the same time, Edith Wharton was motoring through the Berkshire Hills of western Massachusetts with a Pope-Hartford. She was having a love/hate relationship with her motorcar because it often broke down. She joked about it with her friend, Henry James, and they referred to the "motor" as "Alfred de Musset," after George Sand's lover whose illness was a cause for breaking off the affair. It apparently did not stop her picnics then or later. She picnicked in England and France in a reliable Mercedes that had room to strap on large food hampers, *panniers de voyages*, or *paniers à provisions*, as Samuel Beckett calls them in *Waiting for Godot (1952)*.

Sometime about 1909, food writer James Beard went on his "very first auto-mobile ride" to a picnic on the outskirts of Portland, Oregon. "We drove in a huge touring car," Beard recalls in his memoir, *Delights and Prejudices* (1964). "It was an exciting day for all of us, for picnicking in a car was relatively rare, and to drive out of town with a hamper of food was a great adventure. I remember this picnic especially, because it had been suggested at the spur of the moment, which added to the fun."[67] This delightful experience proved fortuitous because Beard became a food writer and eventually wrote four picnic cookbooks.

As motorcar production increased and prices declined, all classes of society took advantage of the motorcar's promise for daytripping and sightseeing, and it was not long before the first picnic cookbook appeared. This is surprising. Picnicking was now ubiquitous, and yet no one had thought to write a picnic cookbook, not the French, English, Spaniards, or Italians. It was the Americans who first exploited this hidden market, and soon the English caught on. But it took the appearance of the motorcar to stir the imagination. The first cookbook to aim at the motorcar market is Linda Hull Larned's *One Hundred Picnic Suggestions* (1915). Though the title does not mention motoring, the text is a hybrid composed of two parts, one for ordinary picnics anywhere, and the second for motorists: "For the Picnic Basket," and "For the Motor Hamper."[68] Inspired by the rising practicality and affordability of motorcars, Larned provides menus and suggestions but without detailed discussion, helpful hints, or in-depth instruction. Suggestions are arbitrary, but the inference is that whether you are a motorist or nonmotorist, your picnic will be outdoors. Larned's implicit assumption is that her cookbook is for the upper classes, which she expects are savvier about food.

More overtly upper class is Agnes Jekyll, whose chic and chatty food columns for the *Times* of London were published as *Kitchen Essays* (1922). "Luncheon for a Motor Excursion in Winter," one of her entries, suggests a "luncheon-basket" stuffed with portage à la écossaise, meat and vegetable soup in the Scottish style, stuffed salmon rolls, and lots of mulled claret and hot coffee. "The travellers' food basket," she writes, "equipped in some such ways as are here suggested, especially camp stools, waterproof rug and fur coats will render its owners independent of time and place, fortified against hunger and thirst, immune to the extortions and insolence of officials, and they will be fresh and ready on arrival to enjoy the lovely sights and gay adventures awaiting them."[69]

Around the same time Jekyll wrote about motoring picnics, the Jowett Car Company, located in Yorkshire, England, posted advertisements linking motorcars with the pleasure of picnicking. A 1920 advertisement pictures a family picnicking on the grass beside their Jowett convertible. The copy directly links the material and spiritual worlds—the Jowett, the picnic, and the "Freedom" to see and feel nature: "Have you spied the purple iris blossoming along the river bank? Have you glimpsed a bit of heaven whilst 'picnicking' [*sic*] by the scented pinewood?"[70] The powerful connection of freedom and picnicking proved appealing. Doing exactly as advertised, Katherine Mansfield, the author, visited Mentone in 1920, where she wrote to a friend, "We go for picnics up among the mountains and long day excursions by motor."[71] Mansfield's laconic but apt remark that these picnics are day excursions and are made possible by a motorcar seems ordinary, but it really confirms that of all modes of transportation, the motorcar made picnicking the most convenient.

Five years later, Ford Motors combined outdoor excursions and social entertainment. The advertising pitch for the 1925 Touring car, affordably priced at $295, claims that it will give drivers the "chance to get away into new surroundings every day—a picnic supper or a cool spin in the evening to enjoy the countryside or a visit with friends."[72] Ford makes no allusions to food and drink, and the price does not include a picnic basket, but the ad's visual scenery is of a country farm roadside market where baskets are laden with produce, including melons and pumpkins. Predictably, Ford's branding effort coincided with the publication of *The Motorist's Luncheon Book* (1923), May E. Southworth's cookbook, and it rides the trend that makes the connection explicit. She is so hyper that you get a sense she might be writing at the behest of the motorcar industry. "The love of the great outdoors grows with each new automobile," Southworth writes. "The friendly road beckons, the trusty motor champs at the brake, and the urge of taking to the open is irresistible, for anything from a few hours to a day or a week. . . ." The design of this little book is not recipes, but only an endeavor to lighten the burden of the one whose task it is to cater to these joy hampers and fill them full, for "who ever knew a motorist to arrive except in a starving condition?"[73] Joining the picnic motorists cue, food writer Mrs. C. F. Leyel jauntily admits in *Picnics for Motorists* (1936) that she prepared a cookbook with food she likes rather than foods specially selected for motorists. Because motoring is trendy, she feels that no one will mind her food choices; however, she does admonish motorists to clean up after themselves. "It is very distressing to see the countryside disfigured sometimes by paper bags and empty botttles," she writes, "and it spoils the enjoyment of all those to whom a picnic in the open air is a very real pleasure."[74]

Conjointly with the typical motor picnic, tailgating, a specialized variation, became increasing popular. It is based on picnicking beside your motorcar that is parked at a sporting event. Among the English, this might include horse races at Epsom or even a military reenactment. William Powell Frith's painting *The Derby Day* (1856) is probably among the greatest crowd scenes in art. By Frith's reckoning, the races at Epsom Downs hold less interest than the fun in the carriage parking area. Henry James, who pilgrimaged to Epsom on Derby Day, writes about this chaos in his travel essays *English Hours* (1905). With his customary acuity, James writes that the crowd was very animated, especially at lunchtime when the top of every carriage became

> the scene of a picnic. From this moment at the Derby, demoralisation begins. I was in a position to observe it, all around me, in the most characteristic forms. The whole affair, as regards the conventional rigidities I spoke of a while since, becomes a real *dégringolade* [French—"to tumble down"; English—"a rapid decline or deterioration in condition"]. The shabbier pedestrians bustle about the vehicles, staring up at the lucky mortals who are perched in a kind of tormentingly near empyrean a region in which dishes of lobster-salad are passed about and champagne-corks cleave the air like celestial meteors.[75]

There is more to picnicking in or near your carriage, of course, than lobster salad and champagne. The plain fact is that the carriage picnics were as ordinary to James and Dickens as the motorcars, trucks, and SUVs are to modern tailgaters who would rather settle on asphalt and concrete in the parking area of a sports stadium. In the TV cartoon series *The Simpsons* (2008), Homer Simpson calls tailgating "the pinnacle of human achievement." It is not the game, Homer tells his son Bart, "Since the dawn of parking lots man has sought to stuff his guts with food and alcohol in anticipation of watching others exercise."

The lure of parking-lot picnicking cuts across the grain of lunching on the grass. It nevertheless satisfies millions for whom the outdoors is seldom separated from a motor vehicle of some sort in which they have stuffed whole kitchens, including refrigerators, grills, smokers, and ovens. The foods reflect the masculine nature of the sports—football, horseracing, and motorcar racing. Meat reigns, and you cannot escape the smell. Ex-footballer John Madden is sure that the pork butt is the most preferred meat. "I have seen it in every parking lot that I have ever visited."[76] When Madden and food writer Peter Kaminsky joined to write *John Madden's Ultimate Tailgating* (1998), they filled the book with suggestions for meat menus that often require intensive preparation, long cooking times, and lots of cold beer. Chef Mario Batali's suggestions in *Mario Tailgates NASCAR Style* (2006) are more varied but require thoughtful, extensive preparation and careful cooking. Batali is mildly appalled that fans cook without the benefit of a professional kitchen such as he is used to, but his basics call for a charcoal grill and "a carefully selected toolbox full of pans, bowls, and utensils."[77] Because these foods require such care, tailgaters seldom get to the sporting event. Simply cooked hamburgers and hot dogs await hungry fans inside the arena actually watching the game.

Once Jowett and Ford got them started, other manufacturers touted pleasure picnicking by car: Chevrolet, Oldsmobile, Nash, Lincoln, Renault, and Sunbeam. Though many manufacturers are now defunct, the picnic thrives. Ford seems to have captured the loyalty of writers such as Alice B. Toklas and Gertrude Stein, who became lifelong boosters of motorcar picnics and Fords. After settling in Paris during World War I, a Ford was Stein and Toklas's means for getting out of Paris. Their scheme was to prepare a lunch, pack, and then drive without knowing where they might stop to eat. They never stopped picnicking, and on June 28, 1928, Stein wrote to a friend, "Here is a picture of me in my last of the Fords. It is one of my sorrows that Henry [Ford] won't make any but I do what I can to prove that America is the mother of modern civilization. It's nice here in a Ford car eating pleasantly."[78] As rigid as they were about their Fords, Stein and Toklas were rigid about their picnic routine. Stein was always the driver; the cars were given feminine names, "Aunt Pauline" and "Lady Godiva"; and their picnics were most often sandwiches, indicative of economy.

While Stein and Toklas motored through western France, Ernest Hemingway and Scott Fitzgerald motored from Lyon to Paris. Along the way, they had a moveable feast, the comic highlight of Ernest Hemingway's *A Moveable Feast* (1964). The trip happened in spring 1925 when Scott Fitzgerald asked Hemingway, whom he had only recently met, to accompany him in an open-top Renault on the three-hundred-mile trip. Fitzgerald would pay expenses, but Hemingway was on a tight budget. Fitzgerald's idea of a lunch was truffled roasted chicken, bread, and many bottles of Mâconnais wine, and Hemingway always felt cheap because he could not afford to order such fare. At first it was pleasant to ride in the open car, but it rained intermittently, so that they were soggy and out of sorts and had to eat under the shelter of trees or in local cafes. Hemingway wrote that the lunches were excellent, but he suggests that the wine saved the trip from total disaster. Long after, on reflection he was amused enough to write, "If we had waterproof coats, it would have been pleasant enough to drive in that spring rain." However, Hemingway was candid enough to admit that this was "not a trip designed for a man easy to anger."[80]

Happy motor picnics proliferated in the United States and were often documented during the Depression years by a government eager to prove that people still had good times. Russell Lee's photograph *A Family Picnic on the Fourth of July at Vale, Oregon* (1941) is a visual document of American life showing a middle-class family sitting beside their motorcar.

Figure 5.7. Russell Lee, *A Family Picnic on the Fourth of July at Vale, Oregon* (1941). Courtesy of the Library of Congress.

The family makes a neat unit and illustrates an iconic picnic. The father and mother sit on the running board while the four children sit on the grass around a small cloth holding prepared foods brought along in a Sanka instant coffee box. Utensils include durable, inexpensive agateware plates. About the same time, Marion Post Wolcott's photograph, *Guests of Sarasota Trailer Park, Sarasota, Florida, Picnicking at the Beach with Their Family and Neighbor's Children* (1941), records how people stay close to their 1938 Pontiac rather than venture out. Enduring a cold spell instead of the usual temperature in the low seventies, the picnickers are bundled in coats and hats. Undeterred, they have set up a table and chairs, set out a blanket on the sand, and unpacked their gear.[81]

Two decades later, Americans were still picnicking beside their motorcars. Robert Frank motored across the continent, and his series of photographs in *The Americans* (1959) show the deep integration of the motorcar and the picnic. *Picnic Ground, Glendale, California* (1959) features young couples casually picnicking in front of their cars. They wear bathing suits and sit on towels, suggesting that they are near a pool or lake, but there aren't any picnic baskets, food, or drinks. The picnickers have only each other in mind, and they sit huddled together or embracing, listening to the car radio blaring through the open door of the parked 1953 Packard. Thirty years after Jowett Motors advertised,

Frank shows us that the proximity of the picnickers to their parked cars unintentionally suggests that automobiles, picnics, and the parking lot are inseparable.

So strong is the bond between automobiles and the people who own them that there is a familiarity and ease that brings solace and pleasure. The picnicky feeling reappears in one of Agatha Christie's few poems, "Picnic 1960," where it is a metaphor for a life well lived and enjoyed. Though it was not published until Christie was seventy and in declining health, it is importantly placed as the final item of *Poems* (1973). What is unusual is that Christie, usually accustomed to luxury and the seclusion of the rich, selects a busy road for her "perfect picnic":

> Hundreds of cars rushing past all the time,
> Sunshine and clouds up above!
> Afternoon tea by the side of the road
> That is the meal that I love.[82]

There is more than a whiff of solace and pleasure—and it's the kind of motorcar picnic that is expected if you are happy.

On the other hand, for sheer whimsy and fun, Paul Bowles and James Schuyler's performance piece *A Picnic Cantata: For Four Women's Voices, Two Pianos, and Percussion* (1954) depicts motoring to the country as a playful series of picnicky discontinuities; images bounce off images and words repeat, until the picnic is finished and it is time to clean up and drive home, very contentedly:

> We can't go on a picnic
> without ketchup and a car.
> Have you a car?
> You are in my car.
> So we are.[83]

HUNTERS' PICNICS

> Amid all the circumstances in life, when eating is considered valuable, one of the most agreeable is, doubtless, when there is a pause in the chase. It alone may be prolonged the most without ennui.
>
> —Jean-Anthelme Brillat-Savarin, Meditation XV,
> "Haltes de Chasse" (1825), translated by Fayette Robinson

There is a remarkable trail of evidence linking Romans in the fourth century to English aristocrats in the twentieth century enjoying a hunter's meal or halt on the hunt, something the French usually call *un repas de chasse* or *halt de chasse*. Reasons not to call this a picnic are mixed. The English left the hunter's meal unnamed until after 1806, when they began calling almost any alfresco meal a picnic. The French refrained from calling anything outdoors a *pique-nique* until the English virtually made the word their own, and only afterward did they acknowledge that a picnic might be enjoyed outdoors instead of indoors.

The selective history of the hunter's picnic begins with the Roman hunting plates from the mid to late fourth century that are embellished with hunters dining in the field. Silver plates from Sevso and Cesna suggest that this was a flourishing custom.[84] Katherine Dunbabin refers to these as picnics, but there is no better word to describe such scenes. She writes that "open-air dining had of course been practiced since time immemorial," but in the fourth century wealthy Romans used the opportunity for hospitality and display.[85] The custom flourished, and hunt dinners appear elsewhere, most notably in the villa in the Sicilian town of Piazza Armerina, then eclipse until prominently reappearing in Gaston III, the Count de Foix's hunting treatise *The Book of the Hunt* (1389), where it is called an *assemblée*.[86] Illustrations of the *assemblée* and textual commentary make it clear that this is not a leisurely meal but a pragmatic business meeting discussing the day's hunt. The scene is so picnicky that if you are not aware of hunting protocols, you will presume it is a picnic. When the text was translated into English as *The Master of Game* (1413) by Edward of Norwich, second Duke of York, the meeting was described in a way that is easy to confuse it with a modern picnic:

> And the place where the gathering shall be made should be in fair mead well green, where fair trees grow all about, the one far from the other, and a clear well or beside some running brook. And it is called gathering because all the men and the hounds for hunting gather thither, for all they that go to the quest should all come again in a certain place that I have spoken of. And also they that come from home, and all the officers that come from home should bring thither all that they need, everyone in his office, well and plenteously, and should lay the towels and board clothes all about upon the green grass, and set divers meats upon a great platter after the lord's power. And some should eat sitting, and some standing, and some leaning upon their elbows, some should drink, some laugh, some jangle, some joke and some play. . . . And when they shall have eaten, the lord shall devise where the relays shall go and other things, which I shall say, more plainly, and then shall every man speed him to his place.

If Edward had set out to describe how to picnic, the matter would be indisputable. Yet it is not. Following Gaston, Edward knows that whatever the setting, the function of the *assemblée* is work, and a picnic requires leisure.

Despite its powerful and pervasive influence, in Gaston's *Hunting Book* the *assemblée* inadvertently became a precursor of a picnic of leisure. Morphing in

Figure 5.8.   George Gascoigne, "Of the place where and how an assembly should be made, in the preference of a Prince, or some honourable person," woodcut on paper. *The Noble Art of Venerie or Hunting* (London 1575). ©The Print Collector/Corbis.

1561, Jacques du Fouilloux's *La Venerie* retains Gaston's textual information but illustrates the *assemblée* as *un repas de chasse*, a distinct break in the hunt and a meal in the field as hunters relax, dine, and drink wine.[87] Fourteen years later, when the English poet and courtier George Gascoigne revised the Gaston and Fouilloux as *The Noble Art of Venerie or Hunting* (1575), the meal trumps the hunt.[88]

Gone is the old hunt protocol now replaced with a banquet presided over by Queen Elizabeth I, probably at Kenilworth, whose courtiers acknowledge her as the host. Gone is Gaston's business meeting, and in its place is a dedicated meal that has little to do with hunting other than as an excuse for a feast for the queen, her nobles, and courtiers, served by staff. Gillian Austen, Gascoigne's biographer, suggests that accentuating Elizabeth's presence increased her status, for she was an avid hunter, and hunting which was the national sport.[89] The afternoon feast adds to fashion currency, and Gascoigne's addition of a menu is excessive. Though meant for a queen, it is excessive in the tradition of picnics—including cold loins of veal, cold capon, beef, goose, cold mutton, neat's tongue, hog gambones [smoked ham or bacon], wigeon [duck] pie, sausages, savories, sweet wine, wine, and beer. If Gascoigne had another word for the *assemblée*, he might have called it a picnic, but the word was as yet unknown. Because hunting was essentially the national sport, Queen Elizabeth's presence greatly encouraged the *assemblée*. For another edition in 1611, Elizabeth I was rubbed out of the *assemblée* and replaced by James I. This, too, encouraged outdoor courtly feasts among the leisured classes. If the emerging middle classes and the peasantry dined outdoors during or after hunting, they covered their traces for these occasions.

Alfresco feasts attracted others to make such scenes subjects for painting or literature. Eventually, early eighteenth-century French painters and their patrons found the theme attractive. However, Jean-Antoine Watteau took up the *halte de chasse* and portrayed it as a moment of leisure when the hunt stopped and the hunters, their ladies, wives, and mistresses met in the field for social conviviality. The shift left little doubt that it is not the hunting but the entertainment that matters. Such meetings at a prearranged time and place, in hunting lingo, are "trysts," and they might be innocent or opportunities for sexual liaisons. In time, *tryst* took on the latter definition, but Watteau and his followers only hint at relationships and discreetly obscure real intentions. These trysts may or may not include food and drink, so that they scarcely resemble Gaston's or Gascoigne's *assemblée*. Style changed and new talented painters such as Watteau characterized his trysts as *fêtes champêtres* [country feasts] and *fêtes galantes* [rustic entertainments], and among these *The Halt during the Chase* (*Rendezvous de Chasse*) (1717–1718) is the closest he gets to hunting.[90]

Figure 5.9. Nicholas Lancret, *Picnic After the Hunt* (ca. 1735–1740), oil on canvas. Samuel H. Kress Collection, Courtesy National Gallery of Art, Washington, D.C.

Others, painting in Watteau's style, cared more about the *repas de chasse*. François LeMoyne's *Hunting Picnic*, aka *Le déjeuner de Chasse* (1723), shows a white cloth with wine, bread, and roast chicken. Nicholas Lancret's very decorative *Picnic After the Hunt* (1735–1740) is more a lovers' tryst than luncheon.

Jean-François de Troy's *A Hunt Breakfast*, aka *Le repas de chasse* (1737), is a meal catered on the terrace of a local inn. The ladies have come by coach and are seated at a table in the courtyard. Though foods are not significantly detailed, wine is plentiful. The Wallace Collection writes that this is "a picnic outside a cottage on the outskirts of a forest" but still refers to the title as a "breakfast," though it is a midday luncheon. However, Carle-André van Loo was a man with an appetite, and *A Halt during the Hunt* (1737) prominently displays the meal of prepared meats that symbolize the hunt.[91] Hunters and their ladies lounge casually around a large, white cloth, a statement of wealth, that is littered with roast beef, roast rabbit, breads, and wines.

A century later, Charles Dickens parodied the aristocratic swank of the *repas de chasse* in the novel *The Posthumous Papers of the Pickwick Club*, aka *The Pick-*

wick Papers (1837). The episode is without swank or deep regard for the manly aspects of hunting. Dickens's chapter title "A Pleasant Day with an Unpleasant Termination" is a satiric jab at the erstwhile aristocratic sport and stylish dining in the rough now reduced to an excuse for a convivial lunching and drinking. It is a hunt that is just an excuse to get drunk. It goes badly from the start, especially at the expense of the short, balding, pot-bellied Mr. Samuel Pickwick, Esq. All elegance and high style are replaced with satiric humor. Watteau's panache and courtly dalliances vanish. Pickwick gets so tired by the heat of the day, and suffers so severely from his rheumatism, that he has to be carried in a farmer's wheelbarrow. The *piece de resistance* of the meal is ordinary veal pie, but Sam Weller, Mr. Pickwick's Cockney valet, ruins it by suggesting it is made with cat meat. "Wery good thing is weal pie, when you know the lady as made it," Weller says, "and is quite sure it ain't kittens; and arter all though, where's the odds, when they're so like weal that the wery piemen themselves don't know the difference?"[92] For these hungry hunters the contents of the pies are meaningless, and when they are devoured with "a capital cold punch," Pickwick gets drunk and falls dead asleep, during which time he is arrested for trespassing and poaching and is carted off to jail in a wheelbarrow.

If people laughed at Dickens's devilish satire and Pickwick's misadventure, Gustave Courbet's dedication to hunting makes amends. A man without humor when it came to hunting, he was undeterred by someone else's satire. Hunting was his favorite sport, and the painting *Hunt Picnic*, aka *Le repas de chasse* (1858) is not only very large (81½″ ⎰ 128″) but also depicts a real meal in the field, roast beef, bread, and cold white wine.[93] Courbet also dispels the aristocratic theatricality of Watteau and van Loo. Gone are the silks and fashionable costumes. Though there are ladies present, there is no aura of a sexual tryst. Courbet's real knowledge of hunting and its rituals prevails, and he gives us something more like what a hunter's lunch might be. He even includes himself dressed in hunting gear seated in the center of the scene, forming the apex of a triangle of the food in front of him: the wine to the left and the day's kill on the right. Emphasis is on the hunt, and there is a pile of trophies. The subject is the beginning of a celebratory hunters' lunch signaled by the master of the hunt, dressed in red coat, yellow jodhpurs, and black cap, blowing his horn, calling the hunters and letting them know that the ladies have arrived and that they must all come in from the field and join the meal. While Giovanni Bellini had painted the *Feast of the Gods*, a ribald story sourced from Ovid, Courbet painted *Le repas de chasse* based on his real-life experiences as a hunter and a man who liked food, especially game.

Courbet's feast suggests familiarity with Jean Anthelme Brillat-Savarin's food meditation on "Halt on the Hunt" (1825) and shares its joie de vivre. However,

Courbet's style is more appropriate to a hunt and is rugged. In the chapter "Haltes de Chasse," Brillat-Savarin suggested that the luncheon be situated in some predetermined agreeable place, cool and sheltered, where the tired hunters might dine and even engage in amorous play. Courbet's ladies are at the center of the assembly, and it gives them status equal to the men. To make the contrast between the wildness and violence of the hunt, Courbet's main entre is purposely a large roast, a symbolic food that proves the hunter's prowess. It contrasts with Brillat-Savarin's preference for Perigord pie and Strasburg pâtés. Courbet takes Brillat-Savarin at his word, and a hunter eating the food that he kills gives him strength and superiority. Other foods are as yet uncovered in the picnic hampers, but there is ample white wine cooling in the stream and fresh game piles beside the picnic baskets, which have not yet been opened. Courbet's *repas de chasse* affirms his love of hunting, food, and women, just as Brillat-Savarin described:

> I have hunted in the centre of France, and in the very depths of the departments. I have seen at the resting places carriage loads of women of radiant beauty, and others mounted on a modest ass, such as composes the fortunes of the people of Montmorency. I have seen them first laugh at the inconveniences of the mode of transportation, and then spread on the lawn a turkey, with transparent jelly, and a salad ready prepared. I have seen them dance around a fire lighted for the occasion, and have participated in the pleasures of this gypsy sport. I am sure so much attraction with so little luxury is never met with elsewhere.[94]

The hunt meal is mocked in Robert Altman's film, *Gosford Park* (2002) and then suffused with nostalgia in Julian Fellowes's "A Journey to the Highlands" episode in *Downton Abbey* (2013).[95] Altman's view of English country life is hostile, and he portrays it as a being so cold and damp one wonders how the diners manage to hold on to their knives and forks. What little enthusiasm there is suddenly turns edgy when a guest drops a glass of Bloody Mary on the stone floor. Everyone cringes. From Altman's view the hunter's lunch is just another meal in the open without swank, joy, or conviviality. But as a metaphor, the red splotch on the floor, like blood, foreshadows the murder of the host Sir William McCorlde, a cruel and bad man. The hunt picnic in *Downton Abbey* portrays the Crawleys' and their ilk enjoying the high style, glowing with a sense of well-being and their fervor for the picnicky aspects of aristocratic life. Surprisingly, in "A Journey to the Highlands," it is Lord Grantham and the Marquess of Flintshire who join the ladies' lunch arranged in a pavilion on the grass. Completely contrasting with Altman's picnic, Fellowes takes every opportunity to allude to Watteau and Brillat-Savarin. The

day is perfect, the heath green, a lake very blue, and the sky wonderfully studded. The pavilion is posh; the stylish table settings of porcelain and sterling
goblets set exactly as they might be at lunch in Downton Abbey's dining
room. There is swank, but everyone wears tweeds of some sort—the ladies
wear high-fashion suits decorated with feathers, the men are dressed in some-
what gruffer tweeds suitable for deer stalking on the moors.

CHILDREN'S PICNICS

> O Oysters," said the Carpenter,
> "You've had a pleasant run!
> Shall we be trotting home again?"
> But answer came there none—
> And this was scarcely odd, because
> They'd eaten every one.
>
> —Lewis Carroll, *Through the Looking-Glass* (1871)
>
> Morning came, eventually, and by ten or eleven o'clock
> a giddy and rollicking company were gathered at Judge
> Thatcher's and everything was ready for a start. It was not the
> custom for elderly people to mar picnics with their presence.
> The children were considered safe enough under the wings
> of a few young ladies of eighteen and a few young gentlemen
> of twenty-three or thereabouts. The old steam ferryboat was
> charted for the occasion; presently the gay throng filed up the
> main street laden with provision baskets.
>
> —Mark Twain, *Tom Sawyer* (1876)

Children's picnic stories are a durable genre that seems to grow exponen-
tially. They coincide with the rise of adult picnicking and are surprisingly
important for encouraging the picnic as a subject for literature and the arts. The
first two literary efforts to include picnics for children are toy books (in verse):
John Harris's *The Courtship, Merry Marriage, and Pic-Nic Dinner of Cock
Robin and Jenny Wren* (1806) and Mary Belson Elliot's *The Mice, and Their Pic
Nic: A Good Moral Tale* (1809). Importantly, Harris is the first author to name
an outdoor meal a *picnic*, a "pic nic dinner" or wedding feast.[96] Elliot, realizing
that the picnic was still new to most people, included a definition:

What was meant by a Pic Nic, they could but wonder,
Yet ventur'd no question for fear of a blunder;
When they did understand, how they open'd their eyes.
For the guests to bring food was indeed a surprise,
"Well, surely," thought some, "oar [our] old country ways
Are more gen'rous by far, for with us the host pays
While here, those invited, subscribe to the treat,
And visit their neighbour to eat their own meat!"[97]

Narratives aside, Harris and Elliot offered some peculiar food choices, partly because their characters are anthropomorphic animals and partly because of other pedagogical motives: Harris to teach social arrangements and Elliot to teach moral rectitude. Being more careless about food choices, Harris's animals bring some unlikely, if not strange, food contributions to the table: Robin brings cherry pie, Owl brings wheat, Raven brings walnuts, Magpie brings cheese, Pigeon brings tares [vetch], Dog brings a bone, but Lamb brings wool! More startling, Robin also brings currant wine, certainly unusual for a children's story, but not for the adults. To this day, no one notices the wine, and in 1965, Barbara Cooney's version of the story, aimed at children, carries on the tradition.[98] However, Cooney also carries on the long-standing tradition of omitting the only human guest at the dinner—Little Mary. She makes her only appearance in Harris's text, accompanied by her mother, who has provided such foods as cheese, apples, bacon, and plums. This is a nice mixture of foods that is short on sweets, cakes, pies, and other sugary stuff that eventually dominates children's picnic baskets. Ironically, it is Robin who brings the sweet cherry pie and currant wine that he uses to induce Jenny Wren, who obviously has a sweet "beak," to marry him (pardon the pun).

The second important story to the birth of children's picnics is Elliot's *The Mice, and Their Pic Nic*. It takes a different tack that reacts to food scarcity and social indulgences among the affluent. Rebelling against perceived excess, Elliot rails against the mice that live in the city, calling them sometimes "epicures," "pic nic mice," or "London mice." Unlike good, traditional, country mice from Devonshire who eat simple grains, "pic nic mice" dine on cold bacon, cold soups, sweetmeats, fricassee chicken, and gorge themselves on pickles, whipped cream, plumb-cake, cheese cake, custards, and Cheshire cheese. Astute readers of her time would recognize that Elliot was satirizing the extravagance of the English prince regent (later George IV) and the Pic Nic Society, already defunct. Though she was only sixteen years old at the time, Elliot's righteous indignation is aimed at teaching her readers (young and adult) that a "pic nic dinner" is hedonistic, gluttonous, and doomed to disaster. In a Christian moral world, such excess will be punished. So when the country Devonshire mice sit down to dine with their London mice cousins in a London townhouse, they are attacked and eaten by the pantry tabby.[99] Elliot's moral is explicit: know your place, stay away from the evil city, and eat simply. She borrowed this moral from Aesop's fable "The Country Mouse and the City Mouse," but she sharply changed the narrative in which the country mice go home safely. Her moral message for children is embedded in a morbid picnic without joy.[100]

Ironically, Elliot, now obscure, would never know her mice would become anthropomorphic models for future juvenile literature and film. In a sense, Walt Disney is in Elliot's debt, as she was to Aesop and Horace, and among his earliest mouse cartoons is *The Picnic* (1930)—the story of Mickey and Minnie who spend their time courting, kissing, dancing, and laughing while their basket is robbed by squirrels, birds, and ants.[101] By the time Mickey and Minnie realize what has happened, their sandwiches, Swiss cheese, mustard, pickles, olives, honey, cookies, cake with icing, and sugar cubes are all gone. Still they laugh it off, and so we do, too. Unlike Elliot's fancy ragouts or fricassees, Disney prefers mounds of comfort food.

By 1930, a children's picnic pleasure principle was fixed on sweets and mounds of food. Kenneth Grahame institutionalized the children's pleasure principle of excess in the form of the largest picnic for one person—ever. In *The Wind in the Willows* (1908), Water Rat's picnic not only begins the story but also associates it with all good things, like the warmth and lightness of spring, messing around in a boat, and spending a leisurely day on the grassy bank of a river. The staggering weight of Ratty's picnic hamper magnifies these elements of the pleasure principle. His "fat wicker luncheon basket" is stuffed with "cold chicken . . . coldtonguecoldhamcoldbeefpickledgherkinssaladfrenchrollscres-sandwidge-spottedmeatgingerbeerlemonsodawater." There is never a hint that this abundance of food might signify hedonism, and in fact, Ratty is generous and invites Mole and later all of his friends to share—though by then, the food has all been eaten. Grahame makes the case that more is better.[102]

Conversely, Graham also included a second picnic that is so glum that it is often overlooked. It takes place in the fall, the dying time of the year, which finds Ratty depressed, moody, and unable to focus. By chance, he meets Sea Rat, an ancient fellow, "lean and keen-featured," who enthralls him with tales of adventure in foreign parts of the world. This time there is no abundance of food. Ratty packs his "luncheon-basket" with simply "a yard of long French bread, a sausage out of which the garlic sang, some cheese which lay down and cried, and a long-necked straw-covered flask wherein lay bottled sunshine shed

Figure 5.10.   E. H. Shepard, *The River Bank* (1931). Illustration for Kenneth Grahame's *The Wind in the Willows* (1908). Hulton Fine Art Collection, British Library/Robana/Getty Images.

and garnered on far Southern slopes."[103] The simple meal signifies the change in Ratty's temperament; the boisterous joy of spring is now the somber anxiety of fall. The shift mirrors his depressed state of mind and the dullness of his soul. It feels to Ratty that he is in a waking dream, and he repacks the basket mechanically, walks home mechanically, and when he is about to head out to find the ancient Sea Rat, Mole happens by and distracts him and holds him until the fit subsides. How much the sausage and the wine have to do with Ratty's behavior is uncertain, but his food choices are strikingly adult and really not the stuff children might pack for a picnic. Even the happy picnic of cold tongue, pickled gherkin salad, and cress wedges are foods unlikely to be touted in cookbooks for children, and in fact, they seldom, if ever, appear, replaced instead with sweet, fatty stuff, lemon soda water, and ginger beer.

Ratty's picnic menus are singularly unappealing to children because they want the stuff that will make them happy, and that is really a combination of butter, jelly, breads, buns, sweets, cakes, pies, jams, and potatoes. Though Arabella Boxer might have attempted recreating Ratty's menu, she retreats. Her *The Wind in the Willows Country Cookbook* (1983) suggests that for a "River-Banker's Lunch," children will want a wedge of French bread with butter, cheddar cheese, and tomato chutney.[104] Boxer also suggests sandwiches of sausages or steak, sausage rolls, potted shrimps, stuffed eggs, hard-boiled eggs, meat loaf, hot meat pastries, and more. Flapjacks cooked at home can be wrapped in aluminum foil for a picnic. The recipe is butter, soft brown sugar, syrup (doesn't specify what kind), and, of course, oats. She pitches for "leafy summer lettuce snacks," but the basket is full of sugar and fat.

Adults and children know that Winnie-the-Pooh loves sweets. These are the foods that Christopher Robin uses to lure Pooh to a party to thank him for saving his friend Roo. Pooh is characteristically reticent and has to be coaxed to attend with the promise of honey and the little cake things with pink icing. The event is an outdoor party in the final chapter of *Winnie-the-Pooh* (1926). It is a pleasant ending to the story, and no one usually notices what is served. But when adapted to Virginia Ellison's *The Pooh Cookbook* (1969), later *Winnie-the-Pooh's Picnic Cookbook, Inspired by A. A. Milne* (1997), the picnic foods are surprisingly unsweet (and very adult)—sandwiches of watercress, radishes with butter, turkey and cheese with honey mustard, peanut butter and banana, and deviled eggs. The cucumber sandwiches are served with nasturtiums, which Pooh calls "mastersalums."[105] This joke only calls attention to the adult food sensibility working here: what youngster knows about nasturtiums, let alone that the flowers are edible? The rest of Ellison's suggestions seem to begin with the word *honey*.

Overall, the foods of successful children picnic stories are sweets. At the Mad Tea-Party, Alice serves herself tea, bread, and butter. Lewis Carroll's humor in *Alice's Adventures in Wonderland* (1865) is carefully aimed at the oddball behavior of the March Hare, Hatter, and Dormouse.[106] But tea parties are not exactly picnics. There is a picnic lunch of oysters that Walrus and the Carpenter dine upon in *Alice through the Looking-Glass* (1871).[107]

In the later novel *Sylvie and Bruno Concluded* (1893), Carroll packs Bruno's picnic backpack with apples, bread, and milk.[108] But this strangely dark novel is one that Lewis's readers have ignored, and Bruno's picnic is obscured by Alice's tea party. The problem for picnic menus, however, is that Carroll has set a pattern for subsequent menus, and the race to include more sweets and carbohydrates was on. Not helping out much, John Fisher's *The Alice In Wonderland Cookbook, A Culinary Diversion* (1976) offers a recipe for donuts. August Imholtz and Alison Tannenbaum's *Alice Eats Wonderland* (2009) makes the culinary adventure an irreverent joke when serving up recipes for iguana tamales, stuffed dormouse, roast hedgehog, and hare. It is stuff you do not want to try on a youngster—and inadvertently proves the point that kids really prefer sweets.[109] Adults with a taste for iguana tamales love it.

The roasted potatoes play an important role in Frances Hodgson Burnett's *The Secret Garden* (1911) for the restoration of spirit and body, but so does Burnett's faith in Christian Science, a belief in the separation of social classes, and joy in experiencing nature.[110] Burnett suggests that if you combine all these, life is a picnic. So each time that Colin Craven and Mary Lennox picnic in the secret garden, they are transformed by a diet of roasted eggs, potatoes, richly frothed new milk, oatcakes, buns, heather honey, and clotted cream, all provided by a helpful, well-meaning housekeeper. When at last Colin walks and Mary smiles, the picnics have done their work through the children's dependency on potatoes, buns, and butter. It is a wonder their arteries have not clogged. It is no surprise that Amy Colter's *The Secret Garden Cookbook* is true to the story or that the section "Garden Picnic" reproduces the Burnett menu of roasted potatoes and eggs; currant buns (called mell cakes, a reference to the last of the harvest called *mell*); crumpets (eaten warm or toasted over a fire); Cornish pastries (cold meat pie via Cornwall); potato pastries (called *tiddy oggies* by the Cornish—*tiddy* is potato); Yorkshire pastries (filed with sweet spices, raisins, and apples); and chocolate picnic biscuits (sugar cookies).[111]

Martinis and foie gras may have been favorites for Ian Fleming's Commander James Bond, but in the juvenile novel, *Chitty Chitty Bang Bang* (1964), Fleming's last book, Commander Caractacus Potts and family like hard-boiled eggs, cold sausages, bread-and-butter sandwiches, jam puffs, and bottles of the best fizzy lemonade and orange soda. The jam puffs are a family joke, for the children are pleased when the Commander tells them they are more jam than puff.[112] When all of this sweet stuff is packed into Chitty Chitty's boot, there is sure to be a glorious picnic, which in fact happens on a sandbar in the English Channel. However, the picnic is a prelude to adventure, and when the family sleeps off the sweet meal, Chitty Chitty Bang Bang flies them to France, where they begin a series of seriocomic escapades.

There is some diversity among picnic foods for kids that are jokey and serious because they attempt to match foods to character, though this practice does not necessarily make good dietary sense. Jean and Laurent de Brunhoff's *Babar the Elephant* stories offer a more contemporary slant on the menu. In *Babar's Picnic* (1949), the youngsters, Celeste, Arthur, Flora, Pom, Alexander, and Zephyr picnic alone in the jungle but have their foods supervised by Babar and Celeste. After shopping in the open market, they set off with a rucksack packed with a baguette, a green bottle of soda or water, some red lettuces, and cookies. The food choices change, however, for the revised *Babar's Picnic* (1965).[113] Now the whole family, Babar, Celeste, their children, cousin Arthur and their friend the Old Lady dine on bananas, pears, apples, grapes, and sandwiches (contents unknown). The amount of food is moderate; gone are the mounds and piles. These elephants are dainty eaters and suggest a restrained alternative to the moundy and elaborate picnics of Ratty and Wilberforce. Unless the sandwiches have meat, Babar's is a vegetarian picnic. The same is true for *Babar Visits Another Planet* (1972), which begins at a picnic meal comprised of water, bananas, peaches or tomatoes, and sandwiches.[114]

The best picnic food joke is in Mark Twain's *The Adventures of Tom Sawyer* (1876), and it is about a single piece of cake that feeds Tom Sawyer and Becky Thatcher when they are lost in McDougal's Cave. It is possible that Twain's story is a satire of Stella Austin's *Stumps* (1873), then a very popular English Victorian story about a girl of four. Austin's picnic is nearly all sweets—apple tarts, plum cake, shortbread, mulberry tart, sponge cake, bread and butter, hard-boiled eggs, plums, pears, greengage plums, and macaroons. But when these diabetes-inducing foods are inspected, Stumps is disappointed because there is no "'trawberry' jam."[115] Twain turns Austin's basket of sweets inside out. At his picnic, Tom and Becky keep from starving by nibbling a single piece of cake for three days.

Tom and Becky's "pic-nic" begins as "a giddy rollicking company" that inadvertently turns topsy-turvy when the two children get lost. But Tom assumes the role of the gallant knight, and Becky plays damsel in distress. Their playacting helps them to overcome adversity and, of course, because Twain intends to make us laugh, the dialog is melodramatic:

"Tom, I'm so hungry!"

Tom took something out of his pocket.

"Do you remember this," said he.

Becky almost smiled.

"It's our wedding cake, Tom."

"Yes—I wish it was as big as a barrel, for it's all we've got."

"I saved it from the pic-nic for us to dream on Tom, the way grown up people do with wedding cake—but it'll be our–"[116]

She dropped the sentence where it was. Tom divided the cake, and Becky ate with good appetite, while Tom nibbled at his moiety. There was abundance of cold water to finish the feast with. *Moiety* is an unusual word to be used by Tom. Perhaps "portion" or "snack" would be more appropriate. Twain's joke suggests that the sweetness of cake is a symbol of romantic love ripe for satire.

Also, a picnic food joke is the exchange between the cartoon duo of Olive Oyl and Popeye when they picnic on the wharf. Olive tries to liven up the menu and provide variety. Perversely, she prepared two picnic baskets packed with salami, fresh rye bread, pickles, root beer, and lemonade, but these are graciously declined by Popeye, an unlikely gourmet, who demurs, "No, thanks, Olive, I'd rather have spinach." Thinking it over, and to placate Olive, Popeye says, "I yam what I yam what I yam. And now that I've had me spinach, how about some of that salami?"[117]

An episode on *Sesame Street*, "The King's Picnic" (1978), makes picnic food a joke when everyone brings watermelon to his picnic. Dismayed at the lack of variety, the king suggests that he likes potato salad. Sure enough, everyone brings potato salad. In desperation, the king realizes his error and suggests that every-one ought to bring something different.[118] At the Simpson's picnic, "There's No Disgrace Like Home" (1990), everyone brings gelatin dessert molds to Mr. Burns's company picnic because they think he loves it.[119] In fact, Mr. Burns hates the stuff, and as each guest arrives the mold is tossed in the trash.

The eating orgy is compounded in Margaret Gordon's popular *Wilberforce Goes on a Picnic* (1982). Perhaps she is alluding to Grahame's riverbank picnic in *The Wind in the Willows*, but Gordon's picnic is only about overeating.[120] The story is about a family of obese bears that pack the picnic basket with hamburgers on rolls, a stack of sandwiches, a jar of catsup, a bowl heaped with mashed potatoes, bananas, oranges, a pound cake, a rolled chocolate cake with vanilla cream, cake (contents unknown), tarts with pink filling, soda, and a thermos of hot drinks. After eating it all, they are so full they immediately fall into a food-induced coma that is supposed to be thought of as contented. But the roly-poly bears look more like beached whales. What the family does not eat, a friendly goat does, ha-ha! Even more, when a rain shower wakes them, the family rushes to pack up so they can be on time to eat a supper of fried eggs, sausages, and tea.

A similar story emphasizing a pattern of overeating is Ronda and David Armitage's story *The Lighthouse Keeper's Picnic* (1993).[121] Now to be fair, the Armitages' intend to illustrate that obesity is not healthy, but if the deeper aim of the narrative is to discourage overeating, anyone who reads this book or looks at the illustrations remembers the mounds of food lovingly illustrated in a two-page centerfold and including hamburgers, hot dogs, beef or lamb kebabs, pizza, scallop sausages, crab salad, sandwiches, melon, layer cake, cream whorls, green jelly, grapes, bananas, pears, apples, peaches, cupcakes, Danish pastry, cherry tart, chocolate éclair, and ice cream with whipped cream. It is all prepared by Mrs. Grinling—and eaten mouthful by mouthful by Mr. Grinling, who utters "delicious and delectable," when he can take a breath without choking.

Gordon's or the Armitages' menus are lockstep with most cookbooks for children. Currently, the trend to revise dietary standards has not made deep changes in what children are expected to like and will eat. The rise of juvenile obesity has not yet produced picnic menus without sweets. Even *Sesame Street* is not immune. Pat Tornborg's *The Sesame Street Cookbook* (1979) includes stuff for comfort, but the recipes are abashedly on the sweet side.[122] The new *Sesame Street "C" Is for Cooking* (2009) basically provides chapters such as "Sweet Sips" "Sweets & Treats," and "Snacks" that account for 20 percent of the text. Special are Alton Brown's "Crispy Sweet and Sticky Rice Bars" and Martha Stewart's "Yummy Oatmeal Raisin Cookies."[123] No one is counting calories. Linda White's *Cooking on a Stick: Campfire Recipes for Kids* (1996) favors sweets.[124] White's menu has a variety of cutesy names for foods, like Snail on a Limb (biscuit dough coiled around a stick), Veggie Herd (vegetables in a pouch), Bird's Nest Breakfast (ham, potatoes, and eggs in an orange shell), and Moose Lips (apple, peanut butter, and marshmallows). Sunset Books' *Best Kids Cook Book* (1992) includes a recipe for a "Rainy Day Picnic" that provides instructions for making a tent at home (take two chairs and cover with a blanket; use another blanket for the floor; eat by flashlight). The menu suggests a variety of foods, provides nutritional analysis, and is as balanced a meal as one finds for a children's picnic: ready-made soup, tuna on pita bread, peanut butter cookies, and strawberry shake.[125]

The *Winnie-the-Pooh's Teatime Cookbook, Inspired by A. A. Milne* (1993) is another book oriented toward comfort foods: sections are titled Breads and Toasts; Scones, Muffins, and Crumpets; Jams and Butters; Sandwiches; Cookies and Biscuits; and Cakes and Pastries.[126] The text's editors suggest that teatime is snack time, but the old refrain is constant. Mostly, this is a tongue-in-cheek adult cookbook masquerading in kid's clothing. The rest is a valiant attempt to entice children with such kiddie foods as pineapple-kiwi cooler, grilled shrimp with garlic, spicy corn and tomato salad, green beans with ginger-honey dressing, and bittersweet chocolate chunk brownies. When Milne's *Pooh* stories became part of Disney Enterprises in 1977, Pooh was rebranded in an animated feature film, and by 1999, the English bear was so Americanized that he invites his friends to a picnic in *Thanksgiving in the Hundred-Acre Wood*. Even in this new incarnation, the food is "everything sweet and tasty," and the cloth is mounded with several honey pots, a cake with pink icing, cookies, muffins, bread, beets, carrots, grapes, and a pumpkin. Christopher Robin, the only human invited, shows up late after everything is eaten; unperturbed, he invites the group to his American Thanksgiving dinner, a strange dinner for a British lad and his pals.

Jane Werner's *Walt Disney's Mickey Mouse's Picnic* (1950) features a picnic basket with mixed foods, some more nutritious than others: peanut butter and jelly sandwiches, cold meat sandwiches, deviled eggs, potato salad, radishes, onions, pink lemonade, and chocolate cake. The radishes and onions are a nice touch, but the rest of the salad is missing.[127] Walt Disney's *Mickey Mouse Cookbook* (1975, 1995) is notable for its useful discussion of kitchen rules, measuring guideline, and kitchen utensils. This is immediately followed by such favorites as Cakes, Frostings, and Cookies. So as not to miss out on the heavy taste of carbs, there is also a chapter on desserts.[128] Subsequently, *Walt Disney's Mickey Mouse Book* (1965) provides us with a humorous depiction of Mickey Mouse as the hard-working movie star who picnics at the beach in order to relax.[129] Minnie unpacks a huge picnic basket filled with triple-decker sandwiches (with lettuce visible at the edges, but other contents are unknown), hard-boiled eggs, cookies, a large chocolate cake with pink icing and a cherry on top, a plate of green veggies, and lots of lemonade. Clearly "movie stars" like Mickey are not immune to the lure of sweets, and cartoon characters, at least, never have to worry about their figures.

There is some food variety in the beach picnic in Laurence Yep's *Dragonwings* (1975) because he mixes typical American and Chinese food selections at a San Francisco beach.[130] It is Yep's way of bringing together disparate cultural groups through food. Among American books, it is the best for understanding Chinese–American relationships. The picnic is a socializing activity bringing together Windrider and Moon Shadow, the Chinese father and son, and Miss Whitlaw, their landlord. The foods suit the characters: Moon Shadow buys Chinese foods at the Tang food shops in Chinatown: meat-filled dumplings and "pastries filled with various kinds of ground meat and shrimp"; Miss Whitlaw packs thick sandwiches of turkey with cranberry sauce and bread stuffing, gingersnap cookies, and lemonade.

Faith Ringgold got slammed for bringing watermelon to the table of the African American's picnic on the roof in *Tar Beach* (1988).[131] Critics claimed that Ringgold, an African American herself, was racist, something disproved when *Tar Beach* was awarded the 1992 Coretta Scott King Illustrator Award for its portrayal of minorities. The rest of the meal is ordinary and includes roasted peanuts, fried chicken, soda, iced tea, and beer. From a dietary point of view, it is hopeful, because Ringgold omits cakes and pies. The story was first painted on a canvas quilt, *Tar Beach 1* (1988), and then a juvenile storybook appeared (1991). The expression *tar beach* is a New York City euphemism for rooftop sun bathing or entertainment on summer evenings. In the storybook, Cassie Lightfoot spends an evening picnicking with family and friends on tar beach. While the food is set out, Cassie flies, like Peter Pan, above the rooftops, leaving the others below. Her magical flight symbolizes the freedom of youth and the ability to overcome the nagging harshness of racism and the confines of big-city living. When she encourages her brother Be Be to join her, he does. Cassie says, "I have told him it's very easy, anyone can fly. All you need is somewhere to go that you can't get to any other way. The next thing you know, you're flying among the stars." Sometimes picnic foods can make you do that.

MYTHS

Pan!" cried Mr. Sandbach, his mellow voice filling the valley as if it had been a great green church. "Pan is dead. That is why the woods do not shelter him." And he began to tell the striking story of the mariners who were sailing near the coast at the time of the birth of Christ, and three times heard a loud voice saying: "The great God Pan is dead."

"Yes. The great God Pan is dead," said Leyland. And he abandoned himself to that mock misery in which artistic people are so fond of indulging. His cigar went out, and he had to ask me for a match.

—E. M. Forster. "The Story of a Panic" (1904)

When artists and writers combine myth and picnicking, the mixture works because picnicking is so simple and myths are complex. It works because it provides interest and vitality but does not detract from the essential narrative of the myth. The problem is that most of the myths are unhappy, and when a picnic is added, it tends to be unhappy. Occasionally when there is humor in the myth, there is humor at the picnic. The combination of myth and picnic begins with Albrecht Dürer's engraving *Hercules at the Crossroad* (ca. 1498) and continues into our contemporary world. It is used humorously by film director Jean Renoir in *Luncheon on the Grass* (1959) and horrifically by novelist Günter Grass in *The Flounder* (1977).

It is an anachronism to call Albrecht Dürer's engraving *Hercules at the Crossroad* a picnic scene, but it is.[132] If the word *picnic* was unknown to him, the concept was not. By the evidence, Dürer was adding visual interest to the myth originally in Xenophon's *Memorabilia of Socrates* (370 BCE) that does not include such information. As Xenophon tells it, the story is an allegory about Hercules's dilemma when asked to decide if he wanted a life of pleasure or of virtue. However, as Dürer illustrates, the moment of choice occurs just as Virtue is about to hit Pleasure with a cudgel, who has been sitting on a blanket in the embrace of Pan. As Hercules heroically stands to ward off the blow, the blanket is upset, and the fruits resembling apples spill. Pleasure raises her hand to ward off the blow. Pan looks on lasciviously. Why Dürer added the picnic aspects is unknown, but from a Christian point of view, the apples suggest sexuality, and the tree behind Virtue is an allusion to the Tree of the Knowledge of Good and Evil. Hercules's choice is never given, but his dilemma is still potent. Among contemporary artists, the theme is still potent. David Legare's painting *Hercules Protecting the Balance between Pleasure and Virtue* (1993) follows not only Dürer's picnic but also accentuates the food—cherries, grapes, and apples that spill out of a bowl onto a blue picnic cloth.[133] This is a double allusion because Legare is referencing Édouard Manet's *The Luncheon on the Grass* (1863), and the blue cloth and fruits are important sexual food details.

Clearly a picnic on the grass, though not identified as such, is Lorenzo Lotto's *The Allegory of Virtue and Vice* (1505), which contrasts a lascivious god Pan with a naked baby.[134] The scene is a grassy lawn that is divided into two and separated by a deformed tree, one side of which is in bloom and the other blighted. On the blooming side, there is the baby, symbolizing innocence and joy, playing in front of a shield with the coat of arms of the bishop of Treviso, perhaps Lotto's patron. On the blighted side, Pan sits, obviously drunk and desperately examining an empty wine jar. Beside Pan is a white rabbit, a sign of promiscuity. The allegory suggests that the innocent can expect a future in heaven, and the profane will have to endure a hell of roiling thunderstorms. The ulterior motive for Lotto to settle on a picnic scene is to suggest familiarity.

Ovid's works include anachronistic picnics, some of which have served artists and writers as themes to exploit. The *Metamorphosis* (8 CE) is the source for Piero di Cosimo's *The Fight between the Lapiths and Centaurs* (1500–1510). It is a version of Ovid's story of the Lapiths and the Centaurs. This is discussed in chapter 5, "Death," because it turns a wedding feast topsy-turvy and contrasts civility with barbarity. Especially picnicky is a New Year celebration, Anna Perenna, that Ovid writes about in *Fasti* (17–19 CE), a calendar of Roman holy days. It is celebrated on the Ides of March, the day given to excessive eating and to excess drinking in a sacred grove outside the city of Rome.[135]

Also from *Fasti*, Giovanni Bellini's painting, *The Feast of the Gods* (1514), is a picnic of the gods who sit on the grass as if posing for a group photo at a high school graduation.[136] Bellini selected his details from two of Ovid's ribald stories, *Fasti* 1 (January) and *Fasti* 6 (June), both of which make a joke about how Priapus failed to rape Vesta, or Lotis, when Silenus's donkey brayed inopportunely. Ovid does not describe the scene more than calling it a feast in a forest or some pastoral setting, but Bellini embellishes the setting and makes it a picnic. Ovid calls the gathering of gods either a feast or a banquet; Bellini suggests they are at a picnic on the grass. There is no demonstrative sign of feasting, but there is of drinking. The moment Bellini chooses for his narrative is near the end of a long day when the gods are tired and drunk. Priapus is waiting to pounce on the sleeping nymph, and the ass emits its "ill-timed bray." It is a picture about timing, and a joke that is about to happen. Obviously, Bellini admired the story, and it is all explained in Carolin Young, *Apples of Gold in Settings of Silver: Stories of Dinner as a Work of Art* (2003).[137] Norman Lindsay's drawing *The Gods' Picnic* (1907) has nothing to do with Ovid, but it is a satire of Bellini's *The Feast of the Gods*.[138] It is meant as a joke at the expense of what Lindsay saw as Australia's tightly wound sense of etiquette. It was his self-appointed task to liberate Victorian prudery, but here he selects the usual gang of gods, led by Pan and Dionysus and naked nymphs charging out from the woods to frighten an unsuspecting family picnicking. It is a perfect example of Lindsay's wicked sense of humor, and obviously a picnic was something familiar to him. Usually, Lindsay is lascivious and paints fully nude women, and partially clothed men, as in *Picnic—Bacchanalia*, a drinking luncheon on the grass.

Among contemporary writers, mythology is a constant resource, but a few standouts in which a picnic is added to the original story are Thomas Hart Benton's painting *Persephone* (1938) and Eudora Welty's story "Asphodel" (1942), both of which take Hesiod's *Theogony* (700 BCE) for a source. The

Figure 5.11. Giovanni Bellini and Titian, *The Feast of the Gods* (1505–1529), oil on canvas. The Widener Collection. Courtesy National Gallery of Art, Washington, D.C.

essential story is that Hades, god of the underworld, has abducted Persephone, and she rules as the Iron Queen in Hades until she is allowed to return to the upper world for the spring and summer in order to restore joy and happiness by ensuring successful harvests. Because the story also suggests a battle of the sexes, Benton and Welty find substitutes for Hades and Persephone. Benton paints an image of himself in the guise of a farmer gazing at the recumbent nude and very sensuous Persephone. It is unclear whether he is thinking of abduction or something else. Persephone, however, is oblivious to the Peeping Tom [Benton, meant as a pun], and she is sleeping next to her wicker picnic basket filled with a collection of daylilies, a rose, and a carnation, modern substitutions for the asphodels that Persephone was picking when she was abducted. Because Benton's Persephone is lasciviously posed and he is ogling her, you sense that he is expressing some deep motive that probably has little to with the myth and picnic, and more to do with Benton's sexuality.[139]

A darker sexual aspect of the myth is also the basis for Eudora Welty's retelling of Persephone's story in "Asphodel" (1942). It is uncertain if she knew of Benton's painting, but Welty makes the picnic a central incident in her narrative of the unhappy marriage of Miss Sabina to Don McInnis, whose adultery forces her to leave Asphodel, her ancestral home. When at last Sabina dies, three of her old friends, Phoebe, Cora, and Irene, decide to picnic on the lawn in front of the ruined, cheerless mansion. To get there they must cross a shallow river that is an allusion to the Styx, the river that separated the world of the living from the dead. Once across and not venturing too near the mansion, they set out a picnic of aromatic ham and chicken, spices and jellies, fresh breads and a cake, peaches, bananas, figs, pomegranates, grapes, and a thin, dark bottle of blackberry cordial. It is all happy, but just as they finish, a naked, bearded man appears on the porch; presumably it is McInnis, Sabina's nemesis, but to the old maids, he might as well be Hades. At the sight of him, the women panic, "the white picnic cloth seemed to have stirred of itself and spilled out the half-eaten fruit and shattered the bottle of wine," and the women run panic-stricken across the river and back to town, chased by a herd of goats. Cora is thankful to escape. Irene says nothing, and Phoebe laughs, "as though the picnic were not already set rudely in the past, but were the enduring and intoxicating present, still the phenomenon, the golden day."[140] It is a comical ending that shows three gossiping old maids turned topsy-turvy.

There is no evidence of a picnic in the myth of Prometheus, the Titan who defied Kronos and gave fire to humans. The story is most famously told in Hesiod's *Theogony* (700 BCE), Aeschylus' three plays *Prometheus Bound*, *Prometheus Unbound*, and *Prometheus Fire-Bringer* (ca. 415 BCE). Afterward it took off, and the story of his heroism has been retold many times in variation. One thing is always sure—Prometheus is punished, but how is sometimes reinterpreted. Originally, Prometheus was chained to a mountain where each day an eagle eats his liver, until very belatedly Zeus pardons him. James G. Davis's painting *Prometheus Bound, Prometheus Unbound* (2006) retells the updated narrative as a picnic on the beach.[141] Davis's Prometheus is dressed in a green bathing suit and is reclining on a white picnic blanket. A black bird that eats his liver is half concealed behind a red barbecue smoker, an allusion to the ritual sacrifice at which he tricked Zeus. The blanket has the usual picnic paraphernalia: a paperback book, a tray with red wine, a partly eaten sandwich, and a portable radio. There is a blue cooler and a red grill and steaks, still wrapped in plastic. Behind Prometheus is a woman, maybe Pandora, the bringer of woe and evil. Below him is a man and woman, who may be an allusion to Prometheus's secret concerning Zeus and Thetis, whose child, if they had one, would overthrow

Zeus. In the background are two cars, and Prometheus looks in their direction as if expecting visitors, though none are in sight. All in all, this is a densely somber picnic that brings an ancient story into a contemporary milieu that is quirky. Prometheus's daring disobedience to Zeus was meant to be cautionary; Davis makes it appear that he is on vacation, having a fine, leisurely day at the beach. It is not clear what Davis is suggesting; perhaps it is a wry innuendo that life *is* or *is not* a picnic, especially when it is not evident that Prometheus is restrained.

The god, Pan, is sometimes linked with picnics because he is associated with woodlands or mountainous terrain. He is variously characterized, sometimes as a bawdy sexual predator and other times as a benign, pipe-playing creature. These two contexts of Pan appealed to E. M. Forster, who used them in connection with stories about picnics, especially "The Story of a Panic" (1904) and "The Curate's Friend" (1904), and then the novel *A Room with a View* (1914). Because these all deal with homosexual and heterosexual love, they are discussed in the section in this chapter, "Lovers." Forster's friend, Leonard Woolf, Virginia's husband, complained that Forster's early stories were "Pan-ridden," but he refrains from speculating on Forster's affinity for Pan.

Another story with a picnic is Forster's "The Other Kingdom" (1909), which is about an unhappy wife who flees her overbearing husband whom she no longer loves. Miraculously, she is transformed into a tree. The story is an allusion to Ovid's *Metamorphosis* in which Daphne is transformed into a laurel tree before Apollo can rape her. It also references Virgil's *Eclogues* (II, 68) and the story of how Corydon was transformed into a beech tree when a boy named Alexis rebuffed him. Forster unlinks the story from its homosexual roots and shows how the only way that the lighthearted Evelyn Worters can escape her dour, unimaginative husband, Harcourt, is to be amalgamated into a grove of beech trees, a beloved wedding present that she calls her "picnic grove." At her happiest, she presides in the grove while unpacking a basket of oranges and biscuits and serving tea (that is terrible tasting). But this cannot last, and she is last seen dancing among the trees, crying, "Oh Harcourt! I never was so happy. I have all that there is in the world." With this exclamation, the picnic in this world ends. Worters is sure that it is a game and looks for her: "Evelyn must be dodging round one of the trunks. You go this way, I that. We'll soon find her."[142] But, fortunately, they never do.

The appearance of the mellow Pan at a picnic is central to George Warner Allen's painting *Picnic at Wittenham* (1947–1948), in which Pan plays his pipes for a sleeping man.[143] At first glance, this is a pastoral scene in Oxfordshire, alluding to Jean-Antoine Watteau's picnicky landscape paintings such as *Champs Elyssée* (1720–1721). But Warner's scene is a picnic among friends who sit dining in an open, sunlit, grassy lawn. The bright colors of the picnickers lead the eye to them first, and only after absorbing these prominent figures does the viewer's eye refocus on the sleeping artist in the foreground and then the figure of Pan standing above him. Refocusing again, it is apparent that a woman in a blue dress, sitting apart, may be looking at the sleeping figure of the artist. It is unclear if she looks with some feeling of love or friendship. Whatever the intention, with Pan involved, the artist is not likely to be interested.

Allen's gentle mythological allusion is contrasted with passionate love, violent rivalry, and death that are at the core of the story of Sir Tristan, Princess Isolde, and King Mark, probably the best-remembered Celtic myth. The story is not picnicky, but Frederick Ashton found the paradox of pleasant entertainment and grief irresistible. Though the myth is skimpy on locale, Ashton adds a picnic on the rocks and ruined stones of Tintagel Castle in Cornwall reputed to be King Arthur's birthplace. The ballet, *Picnic at Tintagel* (1952), modernizes the Celtic mythology and keeps the action in the ruins of the castle.[144] Ashton uses two time frames to tell the story: one 1916, and the second, in mythological time. Ashton begins as a maid and chauffeur set a picnic for a man, his wife, and her lover, who are modern stand-ins for Tristan, Isolde, and Mark. Trying to be alone, the wife and the lover explore ways of avoiding the husband, but they return to the picnic blanket unsatisfied. In scene two, the action shifts to King Arthur's time when Mark, who has returned early from a hunt, finds the lovers, Tristan and Isolde, romantically engaged. Needing to avenge his honor, Mark duels with Tristan, and in the mêlée both Tristan and Isolde are slain. Shifting to 1916, the modern lovers raise a toast to each other but are prevented when the husband intervenes. As the third scene ends, Merlin, the mythical magician, appears holding the swords belonging to Tristan and Mark, a signal that history will repeat itself. Ashton's picnic is an allusion to Mary Elizabeth Braddon's novel *Mount Royal*, discussed in the section of this chapter, "Fiction and Art."

There is nothing gentle about Günter Grass's fiction and his mythological allusions, usually suggesting ugliness, depravity, and violence. Ostensibly, *The Flounder* (1977) is a retelling of the Grimm Brothers' fairy tale "The Fisherman and His Wife."[145] But the chapter "Father's Day" is a provocative retelling of how the Cumaean Sibyl got her wish for death. The story in Ovid's *The Metamorphosis* tells that when Apollo desired Sibyl, he promised her long life, but when Sibyl wanted youth as well, Apollo cursed her with a life of decrepitude in which her only desire was to die at last. This is Grass's gift to Sibyl, here called Sybille, or Billie, at a picnic that coalesces on Ascension Day with the German's celebration of Father's Day. It is a bizarre and barbaric afternoon on the grass that ends in rape and murder that leaves you aghast and stunned.

On this day, Sybille, Maxie, Frankie, and Siggie, four women who prefer to be lesbians, cross-dress as men to attend the Father's Day picnic. Garbed as masculine Hell's Angels, they motorcycle to the Grunewaldsee in Berlin, where they plan to situate themselves in the midst of ten thousand men. Though they mean to be provocative, they ignore the potential consequences of being noticed. Looking for a perfect place to picnic, they explore the parkland until ending their "mythogenic wandering" and settle on the lakeshore "where the forest has been thinned under a clump of mottled pines, on a floor of sand, pine needles [and] quaking grass." Their provisions, almost entirely meat, suggests a ritual meal served at a temple or Homeric feast: inch-thick steaks, lamb kidneys (seasoned with oil, thyme, pepper, and other spices), black bread, sheep's milk cheese, cases of cold beer, and schnapps cooling in an ice bucket. Besides plates, etc., they have the necessary gear for cooking out—an iron grill, poker, and spade (to dig a trench around the fire to avoid a forest fire). At first the women agree that the place is fabulous and that cooking over an open fire is almost magical. But immediately, they bicker about how women and men cook differently in the open. Sybille says it does not matter, but no one is convinced. When the meal is done, they lie about dreaming, until "The Hour of Pan" arrives and then they are aroused by an unbridled sexuality: Maxie climbs a pine tree; Siggie sews a button into her cheek; and Frankie slugs Maxie. They make a friendship pyramid, but it attracts some evil-looking men, black-leather boys with knives, who soon invade their picnic. There is taunting, but the men withdraw while Sybille pulls down her pants and moons them. The women swagger and argue for female dominance, which ends in a free-for-all in which they beat each other bloody. Exhausted, they sleep, and when Maxie, Siggie, and Frankie awaken, they brutally take turns raping Sybille, who is still sleeping. When they are finished with this astonishing display of misogyny, Sybille tries to escape the company of her friends, but she is stalked by the men in black leather, who ferociously and masochistically rape her. When Maxie, Frankie, and Siggie find Sybille, she is "no longer human." What is left is a mass of flesh that has been run over many times by the murderous men in black on black motorcycles until she was dead. If this is a battle of the sexes, the "boring men" have overpowered the women—Sybille is dead, and women who want to be men are found out and intimidated. Grass is cruelly misogynistic. They abandon the picnic and leave the remains of Sybille on the grass, and "after that life went on."

The volatile combination of Sibyl, Pan, Ascension Day, and Father's Day explodes chaotically. The picnic, suggestive of pleasantness and conviviality, segues into vitriol and rape and murder. The "Hour of Pan" brings chaos that upends any picnicky values: compassion, friendship, social discourse, and sympathy are discarded willy-nilly. On another scale, the choice of a picnic on Father's Day intends the desecration of God, "the Father on high, the Father who exceeded all norms," and it ridicules the ascendancy of Christ into Heaven. Grass's picnic is a showcase for insatiability—material, lustful, intellectual, and spiritual—that cannot be fulfilled without dire consequences. Grass's narrator, a dispirited man, comes closest to self-revelation when he says, "Fairy tales only stop for a time, or they start up again after the end. The truth is told, in a different way each time."[146] The same might be said for Grass's picnics. The final episode of *The Flounder* is another picnic on the beach at which the narrator and Maria, another of his women, share perfunctory sex and a pail of lukewarm pork and cabbage they eat out of a dinner pail. It is a glum prelude to the recycling of the whole narrative, a pleasure many readers might want to forgo.

Grass's deadly satire and morbid observations are a perfect foil for Jean Renoir's Pan, recast as an old shepherd who maliciously upsets a stogy picnic and throws everyone into a panic. Contrary to Grass's *The Flounder*, Jean Renoir's film *Picnic on the Grass* (1959) is a frivolous, topsy-turvy satire laced with humor.[147] It's a mélange of Renoir's satiric humor, blending allusions to Edouard Manet's painting *Luncheon on the Grass* (1863) and Aldous Huxley's dystopian sci-fi novel *Brave New World* (1932). The picnickers are Professor Etienne Alexis, who believes that a society based on sex is unnecessary and that procreation should be done by artificial insemination. His fiancé, Marie-Charlotte, an aristocratic German, is disinterested in love, marriage, or sex. By chance, the picnic for their engagement party is situated adjacent to a ruined temple of Diana the virgin goddess. It's a stiff affair, but when Gaspard, a Pan-like shepherd, appears in the temple and begins to play his flute, a great wind arises, causing disorder, panic, and the release of primal passions. The orderly world is turned topsy-turvy. Alexis's rigidly controlled entourage goes wild, and a bacchanal erupts among them. Alexis escapes, but in the mess he finds Nénette, a young, buxom peasant woman, naked and swimming in a river. He's about to turn away, but when Gaspard plays his flute, Alexis responds and makes love to her. Afterward, they picnic with other young couples who simply accept the informality of picnicking—sitting on the grass—as a natural fact of life. When Alexis realizes that Nénette is pregnant and that he is the father, he chucks Marie-Charlotte and marries Nénette. Such is the power of Pan, the matchmaker, to incite love and chaos and still keep the essential charm of picnicking. Renoir's film *Luncheon on the Grass* is all humor, particularly because the old shepherd as the stand-in for Pan intentionally excites passion for the fun of it.

DEATH

> Now a cold wind blows,
> And the grass is gray,
> But the spot still shows
> As a burnt circle—aye,
> And stick-ends, charred,
> Still strew the sward
> Whereon I stand,
> Last relic of the band
> Who came that day!

—Thomas Hardy, "Where the Picnic Was" (1913)

> The coachmen were walking the horses slowly around to
> freshen them up before watering, the lackeys laying table-
> cloths out on the straw left over from the threshing in the ob-
> long shade of the building. Luncheon began near the accom-
> modating well. All around quivered the funereal countryside,
> yellow with stumble, black with burned patches; the lament
> of cicadas filled the sky. It was like a death rattle of parched
> Sicily at the end of August vainly awaiting rain.

—Giuseppe Lampedusa, *The Leopard* (1958)

Surprisingly, death is a constant at real and fictional picnics. The paradox runs deep because in real life social holidays make honoring the dead joyful, but in fiction, death at a picnic is unhappy and anxiety ridden—anything but celebratory.

Honoring the dead is respectful when the Chinese sweep the graves on Qinming and celebratory on El Día de los Muertos, when Latin Americans decorate graves and altars with orange and yellow flowers. Barbara Kingsolver's novel *Animal Dreams* (1990) makes a link between life and death when the Grace family climb a hill in Arizona to the cemetery where they clean and decorate family graves before they picnic. Codi Noline, the narrator, tries to explain that they did this out of a sense of obligation lightened by flowers. "We were a harvester-ant clan ourselves," she writes, "burdened not only with flowers but with food and beer and soft drinks and sundry paraphernalia."[148]

The aspects of death and the picnic have lured other writers and artists, but not always successfully. Composer Charles Ives tried to make music about the devastating fire on the steamer *General Slocomb* (1904) that claimed the lives of one thousand picnickers on New York City's East River.[149] It was an unimaginable picnic, and Ives left only a sketch because the subject was too claustrophobic and disturbing. Not so for William March, whose novel, *The Bad Seed* (1954), asks you to imagine a murder at a school picnic at which Rhoda Penrose brutally smashes and drowns a classmate who bested her at penmanship.[150] Imagine a girl of eight with cute blond braids and a cutesy pink dress beginning her career as a serial killer at a school picnic!

The unhappy fact is that fictional death picnicking already had a four-hundred-and-fifty-year history that can be traced to Piero di Cosimo's *The Fight between the Lapiths and the Centaurs* (ca. 1500–1515), at which a festive picnic turns deadly.[151] Piero's inspiration was the episode in Ovid's *Metamorphoses* (8 CE) in which the Centaurs, invited guests to the king of the Lapiths' wedding feast, get drunk and then begin to kill and rape. The breach of decorum and violation of etiquette are meant to expose the Centaurs' essential barbarity. But Piero added the picnic to Ovid's story knowing, presumably, that such awful violence would be amplified. Happiness is expected at a picnic, and the opposite may be depressing or horrifying. Of course, Piero refrained from calling the feast a picnic because he did not have the word. On the other hand, he did not call the feast a *merenda*; perhaps he considered it too informal to do so.

It did not matter much because after Piero, the picnic death theme lay dormant. Then at the start of the nineteenth century, it inscrutably reemerged in a children's "toy book" published by John Harris in 1806, titled *The Courtship, Merry Marriage, and Pic-Nic Dinner of Cock Robin and Jenny Wren, To Which Is Added, Alas! The Doleful Death of the Bridegroom* (1806). Why Harris linked picnics and death is uncertain. He certainly meant the story to be a cautionary tale about how happiness may be ruined by a rash act. Until it is pointed out, everyone forgets the "pic nic dinner." But everyone remembers that Sparrow killed Cock Robin. Sparrow was aiming for Cuckoo, who was accosting Jenny Wren, but his aim was poor or he was frightened "For the Cuckoo he missed; / But Cock Robin he kill'd." When he added the "pic nic," Harris was probably totally unaware of Piero's painting. His source was a centuries-old ballad *The Death and Burial of Poor Cock Robin*, most recently published (1783), but remembering the scandal of the London theatrical club, the Pic Nic Society, Harris picked up on the picnic to add zest to an old story.

After Harris, there was another hiatus, until 1850 when Sir Edwin Henry Landseer painted *A Dialogue at Waterloo*, in which there is a picnic on a battlefield. This theme has its own history and will be discussed in a section of this chapter, "Battlefields and War." Elsewhere Émile Zola recognized the contradiction of picnic and death, and in the novel *Thérèse Raquin* (1867), he devised a picnic to carry out a murder of a dimwitted husband by two adulterous lovers.[152] Those familiar with the Impressionist paintings of happy Parisians on the banks of the Seine just west of Paris will easily imagine where Thérèse Raquin and her lover Laurent drown the hapless Camille. But if you expected a pleasant *partie carrée* of lovers in the country, you will be disappointed, because Zola's afternoon is filled with anxiety and suspense. Thérèse and Laurent are not ordinary but "human brutes," whose lust is tinctured with morbidity. Contrary to Édouard Manet's pleasantly engaged picnickers in *Luncheon on the Grass*, Zola's picnickers sit in a dark forest grove on crackling red leaves. While Manet's pale picnickers engage in animated conversation, Zola's are so silent and morose it is easy to hear the murmur of the Seine. Though you never know how Manet's picnic ends (it doesn't matter), Zola's ends when Camille, who cannot swim, bites a chunk of Laurent's neck as he is pushed into the Seine. It is so disturbing that you forget that this is a picnic. Moreover, the emotional effects of this deathly picnic never abate, and over the next four years, there is an unrelenting decline in Thérèse and Laurent's relationship until they commit mutual suicide. She falls on Laurent and brushes her lips against the scar on his neck, the ineradicable symbol of the picnic on the Seine and Camille's murder.

Zola's picnic and death episode is repeated in Theodore Dreiser's novel *An American Tragedy* (1925). Like Zola's, this picnic involves a murder in a relationship as a means of resolving the emotional tangles in a love affair gone sour. Dreiser's protagonist is a young man who wants out of a relationship with his pregnant girlfriend. Like Zola, Dreiser is suggesting that his characters illustrate the relative stupidity and brutality that makes lust deadly. On a large scale, Zola indicted the French civilization of the Second Empire, while Dreiser meant his tale as an indictment of rising American materialism after World War I. Dreiser's trio of lovers are Clyde Griffiths, a callow young man with no sure prospects; his pregnant fiancé, Roberta Alden, a factory worker; and his summer love, Sondra Finchley, who is rich and socially prominent. Clyde's character is put to the test when he decides to picnic at Big Bittern Lake and drown Roberta. Wracked by conscience he strives to ignore, what ought to be a perfect summer picnic becomes uneasy, then a nightmare: "At the point of land favored by Roberta, into a minute protected bay with a small, curved, honey-colored beach, and safe from all prying eyes north or east. And then he and she stepping out normally enough. And Roberta, after Clyde had extracted the lunch most cautiously from his bag, spreading it on a newspaper on the shore, while he walked here and there."[153]

When Roberta happily sings snatches from Foster's "My Old Kentucky Home," Clyde thinks of "Fate! Death! Destruction! and Murder!" Despite his apprehensions, nothing stops him. At a "cataclysmic moment" when Roberta reaches out to Clyde, he reflexively knocks her out of the boat. Hearing "her sharp scream," he lets her drown. Predictably, what follows parallels Zola's narrative of disaster: Clyde loses his socialite sweetheart, and he is apprehended, tried, convicted, and executed. Dreiser suggests Clyde is a victim of fate and is only dimly aware of social forces he cannot control and must obey, all of which are exacerbated during the picnic, where imagery combines anxiety and pleasure that results in chaos.

Picnicking in a ruined landscape signifying death is the unhappy lot of Don Fabrizio Corbèra, the prince, the protagonist of Giuseppe Lampedusa's *The Leopard* (1958). The picnic is a relief from the heat and dust traveling from Palermo to the mountain town of Donnafugata, but neither Don Fabrizio nor his family notice the morbid beauty of their surroundings: "the funereal coun-

Figure 5.12. Luchino Visconti, director, *The Leopard [Il Gattopardo]* (1963). Twentieth Century-Fox Film Corporation/Photofest. ©Twentieth Century-Fox Film Corporation/G. B. Poletto.

tryside, yellow with stubble, black with burned patches; the lament of cicadas filled the sky. It was like a death rattle of parched Sicily at the end of August vainly waiting rain."[154]

The old farm where they settle for lunch is virtually a ruin, but most telling is the great, sagging door below a statue of a prancing leopard whose legs have been broken off. If Don Fabrizio had read the symbols, he might have seen them as portentous omens of his unhappiness and malaise. The broken leopard, really a wild cat nearing extinction, parallels the prince's broken line of power and relevance.

Contrary to the text, Luchino Visconti's film adaptation *The Leopard* (1963) ignores the symbolism. Instead, he shifts Lampedusa's meaning and transfigures the scene into an idyllic picnic.[155] In the heat of the day, the Don Fabrizio family lunches on the grass under the shade of a large centuries-old oak. Visconti's memorable picnic scene displays a brilliantly white cloth on the dusty grass with large wicker baskets laden with food, and Don Fabrizio sits regally and contentedly on a chair placed against the oak. Because this is contrary to the picnic in the novel, it allows us to have a false view of what Lampedusa really intended—a picnic symbolizing the tension between the Fabrizio family's decline as they sit in the shade of their former glory. Lampedusa meant it as a death picnic, but Visconti disguises it as being just another picnic. Of course, readers get the symbolism, but not the moviegoers.

Sylvia Plath's demons are manifest. They surface often, especially at a picnic in a hate-filled poem "The Colossus" (1960).[156] Ostensibly, Plath aimed her displeasure at her father, Otto, whose suicide left her with inerasable hatred because she felt abandoned by him when he killed himself when she was eight years old. At the time the poem was written, Plath was also in the process of ending a destructive marriage with the poet Ted Hughes. This probably increased her need for venting, and in order to increase the power of her rant, Plath upends the expectation of an ordinary picnic by contrasting it with a landscape of chaos and pain. The resulting metaphor mixes urges of hate and death, as she opens her "luncheon on a hill of black cypress" amid the ruins of a place like the Roman Forum. Even the air smells bad with the scent of Lysol, the disinfectant, which, of course, will never cleanse her pain. It is a picnic at which nothing is right and whole: her life, the unquiet memories of her father, a distaste for Hughes, and a deep anxiety over her two children consumed her. Instead of leisure and happiness, the picnic sapped her life. This glimpse into the world of Plath's demons contrasts with her pleasant memories when she was twenty. She had bouts of happiness, and she remembered happily picnicking on a sunny beach: laughing, racing over the dunes and switch grass, the blue of the Atlantic, towels on sand, cheese and ham sandwiches with mustard and coleslaw and tomatoes and peaches and ginger ale.[157]

Years after Plath snapped and committed suicide, Ted Hughes described their marriage in the poem "Minotaur 2" (1998) as the "surreal mystery of our picnic quarrel."[158] It is unclear if Hughes is alluding to the death imagery in "The Colossus," but it is more likely he is using the expression of his view of a hellish marriage. He alludes to this in *The Iron Man* (1968), a children's book that he wrote for his children (and himself) about Plath's death.[159] The story opens with the appearance of Iron Man, who terrorizes a town before he is trapped and buried deep underground and covered with a mound of earth. He lies there until the day a family unknowingly picnics on the grass above him. As if responding to their happy presence, the Iron Man begins to stir. Then as the kettle boils, Iron Man is awakened, the grassy mound splits open, and it so frightens the family that they run off without looking back. Eventually Iron Man is placated, and peace is restored. But the whole idea of the story, the demon buried under a picnic, is puzzling. Perhaps it was meant to heal deep pain and sadness. Yet the disrupted picnic has the unintended effect of resurrecting the dead and revivifying the unhappy memory of his life with Plath.

Whatever Hughes's intention, the image of the buried demon beneath the picnic is similar to W. H. Auden's imagery in the long, meditative poem "New Year Letter" (1941). At the time, Auden was working out his personal dilemma of having left England at the start of World War II for the relative safety of the United States. For Auden, however, this peace was as illusory as "a jolly picnic" on the grass over an abyss hidden below. Decades later, feeling the sense of mortality, Auden wrote a death picnic haiku, "Thoughts of His Own Death" (1965–1968), that suggests some vague sense of fragile mortality:

> Thoughts of his own death,
> like the distant roll
> of thunder at a picnic.[160]

Auden's distant "thunder" is just a gentle reminder of mortality, but Vladimir Nabokov provides a staccato image of "picnic, lightning," in his novel, *Lolita* (1955). Instead of vague premonition, Humbert Humbert acutely remembers his mother's death when she was struck by lightning at a picnic. "Picnic lightning" is how he succinctly writes it as if reinforcing the quickness of the bolt of lightning, that "freak accident" of nature, that robbed him of a mother's love. At that moment Humbert explains, "the sun of my infancy had set."[161] Of course, this is Humbert's crafty explanation for suggesting that his mother's accidental death at a picnic made him bad—a murderer, pederast, and rapist. No one is taken in by this mea culpa, but Humbert is a man without shame or principle. As a matter of course, picnics do not encourage bad or good behavior—bad people do bad things; good people do good things; and unhappy people remain unhappy.

It is the unhappy that Anton Chekhov writes about in "The Party" (1888), a story that moves from happiness to unhappiness and then anxiety and death. Perhaps more than anything that happens at Pyotr Dmitritch's nameday party, it is the picnic on the Island of Good Hope that contributes most to the stillborn death of Pyotr and Olga's child. Though outwardly the party and the picnic are happy, guests never notice their hosts' concerns, especially Olga's. Now seven months pregnant, she is anxious and tired. No one cares that Pyotr is distracted by concerns with money, business, and a lawsuit. If the party ended sooner things might have worked out, but when Olga must be rowed across a lake to the late afternoon picnic she nearly snaps, thinking that the boat is a "death-trap." She thinks of leaping out and yelling at everyone "I am sick of you."[162] At great cost, she maintains her pleasant exterior. At last alone, Olga abruptly goes into labor, but the baby is dead. Instead of consoling her, Pyotr callously says, "Why didn't we take care of our child?" With hindsight, they penetrate the surface reality and understand that the day's activities were a contributing cause of the baby's death. As is often Chekhov's pattern, life goes on, but less happy. The day that began happily ends glumly; the tea and desserts served in the afternoon are replaced by the reek of chloroform and Olga's tears of despair.

Allusions to Chekhov's story permeate Katherine Mansfield's story "The Garden Party" (1922). But here the garden party is a metaphor contrasting sixteen-year-old Laura Sheridan's first experience with death and her expectations of a happy day. When a worker is accidentally killed as the party is being set up, Laura is rebuked for wanting to stop the party: "Stop the garden-party? My dear Laura, don't be so absurd. Of course we can't do anything of the kind. Nobody expects us to. Don't be so extravagant."[163] The story is based on Mansfield's memories of her adolescence and is especially tender because she was facing her own imminent death from tuberculosis. As with many writers and artists facing trauma and life-threatening illness, Mansfield attempts to remediate the ravages of tuberculosis in her fiction. If her personal life is not a picnic garden party, there are memories of earlier times, though not without the tinge of death. Around the time she finished "The Garden Party," she wrote to a friend, Dorothy Brett:

> It's misty to-day, and the sun shines and the mist is silver. It's still. And some-where the bell rings over and over that little chime, so forgetful, so easy and so gay. It's like a gay little pattern, gold and butterflies and cherubs with trumpets in the very middle of the page—so that one pauses before one begins the afternoon chapter. We are going on a picnic. We take the jaeger rug and the bastick [chair]. And then we lie under a tree. Stir our tea with a twig, and look up, look down, wonder why.[164]

"The Water-Party" becomes a metaphor of love and death. It is a key episode in D. H. Lawrence's novel *Women in Love* (1920) that takes place when an ostentatious company picnic switches from happiness to despair.[165] Gerald Crich's sister Diana falls from the deck of a steamer and disappears into a lake. When a young doctor attempts a rescue, he, too, is lost. In the ensuing panic, Gerald, responsible for water safety, repeatedly dives into the black, cold water, to no avail. When the bodies are at last found, they are locked in a grotesque embrace, with Diana's arms wrapped around the doctor's neck. Gerald's desperate search for his sister in the black water suggests his obsessive love for the predatory Gudrun Brangwen, who plays with Gerald's psyche and thwarts his desire for sexual pleasure. Metaphorically, he drowns in a pool of unrequited love. Though he does not yet know it, the water-party is his undoing.

The "black water" in "The Water-Party," inspired Joyce Carol Oates to write her novel *Black Water* (1992). Like Lawrence's picnic, hers is a death picnic, though it begins as Kelley Kelleher, a young woman who is trapped in a car, watches it fill with black water as she waits in vain to be rescued. For those who know, the episode is a fictionalized account of an accident in which Senator Edward Kennedy crashed his motorcar and left Mary Jo Kopechne to drown in a tidal creek on Chappaquiddick Island, Massachusetts. Oates's Kelley and her senator share a desire that ends in death. What begins at a Fourth of July party is a cautionary tale of the deadly consequences of sexual predation and impetuous behavior. It is a picnic that celebrates predatory appetites: "slabs of marinated tuna, chicken pieces swabbed with Tex-Mex sauce, raw red patties of ground sirloin the size of pancakes. Corn on the cob, buckets of potato salad and coleslaw and bean salad and curried rice, quarts of Häagen-Dazs passed around with spoons."[166] The picnic turns sexual when the senator, a man in his early fifties, seduces Kelley, a woman half his age. Everyone there sees what is happening, but no one objects. It is a crowd of the "well-to-do" deeply involved in politics, who live by the rule of carpe diem. Hastening to get away, Kelley and the senator ignore his drunken state. When the car skids off a bridge and into a creek, the senator gets out, panics, and leaves Kelley to her fate. He says that it was all an accident and is contrite. But that is the external part of the story. In her flashback, Kelley clings to life as she awaits rescue while being enveloped and drowned in the black water. Oates points to the lust, crass foods, and false values of American elites. The drowning woman, Oates trenchantly suggests, is a symbol of moral decay and that America is drowning its best and brightest.

Death by drowning is also central to John Banville's novel, *The Sea* (2005).[167] At sixty-two, Max Morden, the narrator whose names means "death" in German, is drowning in memories of his wife's death from cancer and trying to get over the persistent memory of his complicity in the death of two friends fifty years earlier. In order to save himself, Morden returns to a town on the Irish coast and relives his summer when he was twelve years old and enamored with the Grace family and devastated by their loss. Purposely, he rents a room in a house where the Graces had lived, but now the house is a pension run by Rose Vavasour, the former nanny of the Grace children, Chloe and Myles. As Morden's memory clicks, he remembers that what began as a summer of picnics on the beach—striped canvas awning, folding chairs and table, a large, straw hamper filled with tins of sandwiches, biscuits, vacuum flasks, and real tea cups and saucers—ends with death when he watched Chloe and Myles Grace commit suicide by drowning. Morden believes he had a hand in leading the twins to their death since he conspiratorially told Chloe that her father was having an affair with the nanny, Rose Vavasour. In fact, when Vavasour reveals that her affair was, in fact, with the mother, Max is stunned. Still the mystery of death is so deep that Morden neither accepts that the drowning was accidental nor that he was a cause of it. Tired, sadder, and wiser, Morden senses that the picnic is finally over, and when he looks back now it is "as if nothing had happened."

A picnic might end as happily as it begins, but the reversal of fortune makes a familiar theme unforgettable. So powerful is the death-ridden story of the novel *Picnic at Hanging Rock* that people believe it is real, and Hanging Rock, Victoria, has become a literary tourist mecca.[168] The outcome of the picnic in Joan Lindsay's novel leaves readers mystified and enthralled because it is so malleable to interpretation. Why do two schoolgirls and a teacher climb the rock and disappear? What really happened? Lindsay admits that when she climbed the rock as a schoolgirl, it was pleasant. But in her late sixties, when she found herself admiring William Ford's painting *At the Hanging Rock, Near Mount Macedon* (1875), something clicked and instead of happy memories, Lindsay's reimagined the St. Valentine's Day picnic as a death picnic. The effect was so charged with displeasure that she might have sardonically titled the novel *No Picnic at Hanging Rock*, but she played it safe and only suggested that when a picnic goes very wrong, it would end in death. This topsy-turvy picnic appealed to Peter Weir, whose film adaptation *Picnic at Hanging Rock* (1975) makes every aspect of the story surreal and foreshadowing death.[169] Impending disaster is tuned up with the eerie, mournful music of panpipes. Lighting is gauzy, and the soft focus provides a sense of apparent threat. Weir also tarts up the picnic with strong hints of suppressed lesbian sexuality among the girls, teenagers dressed in white.

An accident of weather sets in motion a series of tragic and sinister events: a happy picnic and its picnickers' lives are shattered, almost irrevocably, until a second picnic sets things right again. The pair of picnics bookend Ian McEwan's novel *Enduring Love* (1997) by balancing death and life, fate and strength of character.[170] The narrative begins at a romantic picnic Joe Rose and his wife, Clarissa, have to celebrate her birthday on the grass in a park in the Chiltern Hills. Just as Joe is about to open a pricey bottle of wine, he notices an escaped hot air balloon with a child in the basket and a man dangling from a guy rope. Joe and two other bystanders, Jed Parry and John Logan, run to help, but as the balloon rises and falls, the men panic. Each man lets go of the guy rope, except John Logan, who is carried aloft and falls to his death. The irony is that if they had done nothing, the balloon would have landed safely. This freak accident, however, unhinges Jed Parry. It triggers a psychological condition that makes Jed feel obsessive, homoerotic love for Joe, so obsessive that it nearly ruins Joe and his relationship with Clarissa. When Jed stabs Clarissa, he is detained and hospitalized. Clarissa recovers, and relationships are repaired. The second picnic is a reconciliation. Joe, Clarissa, and Jean Logan, the dead man's wife, meet for a picnic on the Thames, just outside of Oxford. As fate would have it, this is the vicinity that Lewis Carroll picnicked with Alice Liddell and her sisters, the pleasant idylls on the river that gave him the impetus to write *Alice in Wonderland*.

Fate also plays a central role in Jim Crace's novel, *Being Dead* (1999), which is among the most macabre death picnics. It is the story of Joseph and Celice. After being murdered while picnicking at Baritone Bay, Joseph and Cecile become beach food for the sea critters and birds. There is an ironic sense of justice here because they are biologists who teach evolution and the ineluctable power of nature. While this proves a valuable science lesson, they are not capable of knowing it. The picnic is meant to be celebratory because this is the beach where Joseph and Celice met thirty years before and courted as biology students. Settling into the grass to avoid the wind, they prepare a blanket, eat sandwiches, and make love. What they cannot know is that a psychopath will shortly smash their skulls for a bag of clothes and a few biscuits. Crace's narrator writes that they paid "a heavy price for their nostalgia." The murderer thinks, "They'd brought this bad luck on themselves." For six days before their bodies are recovered, Joseph and Celice meld into the ecological niche of the beach. Joseph and Cecile were ordinary people unlucky enough to picnic at the wrong place. In the end, when the picnic is over and evidence of the murder is gone, "The natural world had flooded back. The brightness of the universe returned."[171] Then Crace seems to suggest, it is time to picnic again, if not here on earth, then in the "everending days of being dead."

Linking lynching to the Fourth of July undermines the essential American belief in freedom and equal civil rights. This is the point of James Baldwin's story "Going to Meet the Man" (1957), which was published about the time that Martin Luther King Jr. was emerging as a leader of the Southern Christian Leadership Conference. Baldwin's story is an excoriating character study of Deputy Sheriff Jesse, whose life as a man pivots on his memory of attending a lynching when he was about eight years old. Whether Jesse's hatred of African Americans is a bias of American southern culture or something acquired because he is masochistic is unknown, but hatred rules his life, especially with regard to racial equality, which he abhors. His key memory is of his father taking him to watch an African American man being lynched and matter-of-factly telling him, "We're going on a picnic. You won't ever forget this picnic—!"[172] In Jesse's mind, the lynching is a Fourth of July picnic because everyone looked "excited and shining." The unintended effect of the memory is that over time it has unmanned his masculinity and made him fearful of the African American male's sexuality.

When an adult picnics with his or her teddy bear it is either just an instance of delayed maturity, or worse. In William Trevor's story "The Teddy Bears' Picnic" (1982), the images of well-educated and well-off "twenty-somethings" picnicking with bears and sharing banana sandwiches, biscuits with icing, chocolate and coffee cakes, squash, and milk is a sardonic portrait of a rising generation's immaturity and lack of virtue in 1980. It characterizes an exchange between Edwin Chalm, who complains to his wife, Deborah, "You call sitting down with teddy-bears a bit of fun? Grown-up people?" Undeterred, Deborah snaps back, "I wish you wouldn't keep on about grown-ups. I know we're grown-ups. That's the whole point."[173] Of course, Edwin does not get it, and he becomes petulant and gets very drunk and very mean. His behavior comes to a crisis when he acts impetuously and deliberately and knocks down his host, an old man of ninety-two, who cracks his skull and dies. Since no one has seen him do it, Edwin nonchalantly walks away, but when the body is discovered, he is the first on the scene. Since this is all done while a phonograph is playing "The

Teddy Bears' Picnic" with adults playing children's games, the cold-blooded homicide rings mordantly in contrast to the lyrics. This is Taylor's salvo at the rising generation he sees being either juvenile or vicious. It is a grim picnic—one, alas, that is not the only one of its kind.

BATTLEFIELDS AND WAR

> Good heavens, woman, this is a war, not a garden party! You've got to stay. Melanie needs you.
>
> —Dr. Meade, character in *Gone with the Wind* (1939).
> Ben Hecht, screenplay

> All except Lankes climb on the pillbox. Roswitha spreads out a bright flowery tablecloth. From the bottomless basket she produces little cushions with tassels and fringes. A pink and bright green parasol is opened, a tiny gramophone with loudspeaker is set up. Little plates, little spoons, little knives, egg cups, and napkins are distributed.
>
> —Günter Grass, *The Tin Drum* (1961), translated by Ralph
> Manheim

The Illustrated London News cover for June 14, 1919, ran a headline "Picnics on the Old Front: Motor Tours on the Battlefields." With an illustration by staff artist L. Sabattier, the copy encouraged readers to take a new look at the battlefield. "With an old ammunition-box," the caption continues, "a party of sightseers lunching in a camouflaged shelter on a former battle front in France" sit in wreckage on a cold day. Presumably, the editors were attempting to direct attention from the war to the peace then being negotiated in Versailles. "The countryside has been all pounded and devastated," the *News* reports, "and there are only patches of green and stumps of trees. But the land of desolation is not wholly without resources to aid the tired traveller."[174] It's cold comfort to picnic on a battlefield, a reminder of happier times in the past and better times for the future.

Incredibly, the *Illustrated London News* was participating in a centuries-old association of making an odd couple of picnics and battlefields. The mismatch grabs your attention and then dashes your typical expectation for a picnic.

Figure 5.13.   L. Sabattier, "Picnics on the Old Front: Motor Tours on the Battlefields," *Illustrated London News*, June 14, 1919.

Around 1500, Piero di Cosimo seems to have initiated the theme in a painting *The Fight between the Lapiths and the Centaurs*. It is an illustration of a story from Ovid's *Metamorphoses* (completed 8 CE) about how drunken centaurs, invited guests, disrupt the wedding feast of the king of the Lapiths. Piero's warlike picnic seems like a one-shot moment because the theme did not stick, and it did not resurface until the nineteenth century. It then became common and normalized as a metaphor contrasting war and peace in literature, drama, and film.

The picnic war/peace metaphor is depicted in Sir Edwin Henry Landseer's painting *A Dialogue at Waterloo* (1850), which contrasts the peaceful aspects of a battlefield near Waterloo with still-vivid memories of the terrible battle there thirty-five years earlier in 1815. The chief figure is the Duke of Wellington, who is in dialog with a young girl selling mementos on the former field of battle while her family prepares a hunters' lunch behind her. Most likely she has no knowledge of whom she is pitching her wares to, and it is just as likely that the duke is amused by her ignorance. But if the picnic, so entirely associated with pleasantries and happiness, is meant to signify peace, the metaphor fell flat because an annoyed reviewer sneered, "We are not clear as to what it all means. Some of the objects seeming rather to have been dragged in than naturally to have come thither; the tablecloth spread in the ploughed field appearing rather out of character."[175] The rebuke chagrined Landseer, and he refrained from historical narrative painting and anything picniclike after that. The fallout, however, is that other artist and writers recognized Landseer's *Dialogue* as a powerful theme for contrasting the folly of war with the picnic's happy expectations.

If Landseer was too timid to explore the caustic possibilities, others have been more aggressive. J. G. Farrell's picnic in his historical novel *The Siege of Krishnapur* (1973) suggests that for an audience watching a military battle, it is just another day for an outing in the country. "During the daytime," Farrell writes, "it had become the custom of a vast crowd of onlookers to assemble on the hill-slope above the melon beds to witness the destruction of the Residency. They came from all over the district, as to a fair or festival; there was music and dancing; beyond the noise of the guns the garrison could hear the incessant sighing of native instruments, of flutes and sitars, accompanied by finger-drums; there were merchants and vendors of food and drink, nuts, sherbets and sugarcane."[176] Farrell makes the picnic on the battlefield an entertainment and a metaphor for the brutality and stupidity of war; people are getting killed while onlookers dance and eat sherbets and sugar cane.

War and a garden party make an indelible metaphor in *Gone with the Wind* by Margaret Mitchell. In David Selznick's film, Sidney Howard's screenplay (1936) exchanges dialog that explicitly associates the siege of Atlanta with a garden party picnic at Twelve Oaks. In the film, the garden party at the Wilkeses' plantation occurs days after hostilities began in Charleston, South Carolina. Rhett Butler informs of impending war, but Scarlett does not care, since it is her love life that matters, and it is not progressing with Ashley Wilkes. The party is just a venue for Scarlett to flirt with her beaux. At southern picnics you flirt, court, and romance, and it is this southern joie de vivre that is captured in Selznick's adaptation of *Gone with the Wind* (1939), directed by Victor Fleming. Before the devastating siege of Atlanta, Dr. Meade, Scarlett, and Aunt Pittypat have an exchange that reminds you that the life of the Old South is already gone with the wind. Meade's tone to Scarlett's request to evacuate Atlanta is incredulous, and his use of the picnic-on-the-battlefield metaphor makes the response indelible. Instead of merely berating her, Meade reminds her of the recent past, picnics at plantation homes, and the former glory of southern civilization:

Dr. Meade: [to Scarlett] Now you've got to listen to me! You must stay here!

Aunt Pittypat: Without a chaperon, Dr. Meade? It simply isn't done!

Dr. Meade: Good heavens, woman! This is a war—not a garden party![177]

Meade's exasperation expresses the brutality of the siege and the probability of the Confederacy's defeat.

The trend toward a picnic on the battlefield began with the first battle of Bull Run, aka Manassas. There are hazy stories about U.S. congressmen and Washington socialites anticipating a Union victory picnicking with fine china and crystal above the battlefield. Southerner Mary Chesnut gloats over the Unionists' false sense of victory, and her diary entry for July 27, 1861, scoffs at U.S. congressmen who were "making a picnic" of the war.[178] The picnic metaphor is in the lead story "Bull Run and Its Consequences" (August 17, 1861) for the *Illustrated London News*. However, whether or not these members of Congress and company packed picnics is moot, though for sure the war correspondent William Howard Russell reported that he also picnicked on the third day of the battle when he left Washington, D.C., packing a lunch: a flask of Bordeaux, a bottle of water, a paper of sandwiches, and a flask of brandy.[179]

Also watching battle events closely, author Herman Melville picked up the metaphor in "The March into Virginia Ending in the First Manassas (July, 1861)." Though it was composed contemporaneously with the Union army defeat, it was not published until 1866. Melville's distress centered on a war that he could not take lightly with his patriotic fervor, and his metaphor is that war is not a picnic:

The banners play, the bugles call,
The air is blue and prodigal.
No berrying party, pleasure-wooed,
No picnic party in the May.[180]

A year after Bull Run, Alexander Gardner staged a photograph of a picnic beside a bridge in Antietam, Maryland, the bloodiest battle of the Civil War. Many of Gardner's photographs of this battle (and the war) have become iconic. He took two photographs of Antietam Bridge: the former is a snapshot published with a caption, "The stone wall extending from the bridge still bears evidences of the battle, and it is the only monument of many gallant men who sleep in the meadow at its side."[181] The latter is *A Pic-Nic Party at Antietam Bridge, Virginia, 22 September 1862*, which he meant as an antiwar metaphor and for which he never wrote a caption. This photograph is remarkable because at a glance the picnic is ordinary—two women sitting by the Antietam Creek are being served food while sitting in a shallow bottom skiff moored on the bank of the creek. They are looking placidly at the camera, though not quite smiling.

Figure 5.14. Alexander Gardner, *A Pic-Nic Party at Antietam Bridge, Virginia, 22 September, 1862*. Courtesy of the Library of Congress.

But closer examination reveals some odd details: a Union soldier, leaning forward, stirs the contents of a tin cup with his bayonet. Just off to the side, another soldier tends a horse and shay, unaffected by the tumult of the preceding days. A most important incongruity is that while the title is remembered as *A Pic-Nic Party*, the scene is situated just below the main battlefield on Antietam Creek, four days after the battle during which twenty-three thousand soldiers died. "22 September 1862" was an infamous date, and Antietam was a source of sorrow. Consequently, making the situation a picnic is intended to startle and disorient the viewer.

Ironically, Gardner's scene was repeated during World War II when Winston Churchill picnicked on the Rhine River almost in view of the German troops. A vintage 1944 photograph from London's Imperial War Museum shows Winston Churchill, Britain's prime minister, having a picnic lunch in Holland on the west bank of the Rhine River with General Bernard Montgomery and Field Marshall Alan Brooke. It is an arresting image of three men at a folding card table near a river. It is only when you know that the river is the Rhine and that the Allies had only days earlier invaded Germany that you realize these are not just any three men at a table but the men who are leaders of the Allied invasion of Germany. Though the area was secure, Germany artillery and snipers were a threat. It is unclear what was served, but Cita Stelzer's survey of Churchill's food preferences, *Dinner with Churchill* (2013), suggests that the lunch was probably ham or beef sandwiches with mustard on very thinly sliced bread.[182]

Sometimes the metaphor is used to honor, heal, or recoup the sense of loss. After the Union victory at Gettysburg (July 1863), Thomas Prichard Rossiter reimagined the metaphor in a painting *Pic-Nic on the Hudson* [*Constitution Island*] (1863).[183] The painting honored General Gouverneur Kemble Warren, a hero at Gettysburg. Warren, the central figure, reclines at ease away from the war and now, momentarily, he is at peace. Like Gardner's *Antietam*, this is staged propaganda and meant as an idyllic picnic moment promoting the Union's impending victory. Despite Warren's picnic bravado on the shore of Lake Mahopac, New York, when he returned to the war, General Grant chastised him for being timid. Looking at the picnic without context, no one would know the backstory. At the turn of the century, Arthur Conan Doyle used the picnic metaphor in his history *The Great Boer War* (1900). Sadly, he explains that at Vaalkrantz (then a memorable disaster for the Brits, now a forgotten skirmish) the massacre was no picnic: "It was a horrible ordeal for raw troops. The men were miners and agricultural labourers, who had never seen more bloodshed than a cut finger in their lives. They had been four months in the country, but their life had been a picnic, as the luxury of their baggage shows. Now in an instant the picnic was ended, and in the grey cold dawn war was upon them—grim war with the whine of bullets, the screams of pain, the crash of shell, the horrible rending and riving of body and limb."[184] The incident was indelible in Doyle's memory of a war in the service of which he was knighted.

Eric Newby's *merenda* in Italy took place after he escaped from a German prisoner-of-war camp in Italy during World War II. In gauzy hindsight, he retells the episode in his memoir *Love and War in the Apennines* (1971). When local partisans helped him to escape, he remembers a local farmer who treated him to a typical Italian *merenda* meal—polenta, white bread made of pasta dura, culatello and spall (both ham), cheese, and lambrusco wine. "Afterwards," he says, "we lay on our stomachs on the grass on the slope of the embankment, looking out over the top of it across the river." The picnic was one of the best days of his life, and he "hated the thought that it was almost at an end."[185] Shortly after, the idyllic picnic ended, and he was recaptured.

Richard Attenborough's film *Oh! What a Lovely War* (1969) is an antiwar story that makes World War I a symbol for all wars.[186] As women and children, dressed in white, serve a picnic on the grass, they cannot know that wraiths of their dead families are wandering among them looking for a place on the grass. It begins innocently as a family spreads a blanket, and while they sit on the cloth, a boy asks his mother what his dead father did during the war. The tranquility of the sunny picnic and the misery of war join for a moment as the dead father comes out of a fog, looking at his family picnicking, and he lies down on the grassy hillside covered with red poppies. Then the camera pulls back, revealing that the picnickers on the grass are in a military cemetery filled with endless rows of white crosses for the war dead. *Oh! What a Lovely War* makes no pretense of the stupidity of war and the poignancy of picnicking among the dead to honor them. Attenborough's picnic is aimed directly at exposing the myth that national pride is no substitute for the appalling suffering and disruption caused by war.

Alberto Moravia's bitter story "Back to the Sea" is a metaphor of the new Italy recovering from the effects of World War II. It is set as a picnic on the beach at Ostia outside of Rome in 1945. Though the shooting war is over, social and political hostilities still roil, so that life is a waking nightmare realized by the picnickers, Lorenzo, a fascist, and his estranged wife, who no longer loves him. The picnic is doomed even before it begins, and the beach landscape is symbolically littered with war detritus and unexploded mines. Ostensibly, Lorenzo wants to renew his relationship with his wife, but he crudely attempts to rape her. She escapes, leaving him without a car. The picnic over, Lorenzo decides to walk on the beach. "He removed his shoes and socks, folded his trousers up to below the knee, and picked his way through the barbed wire to the water's edge. He set out walking in the ebbing and flowing water, with his shoes in hand, his head bowed and eyes lowered."[187] As if searching for something, he casually jumps across a thatch of "black shining seaweed," steps on an unexploded mine, and is blown to bits. It is a chance happening, but in Moravia's world, nothing happens by chance. The walk on the beach is symptomatic of illusions of peace even after the hostilities of war have ceased. As the picnic is timed to coincide with the end of the Second World War, Moravia is suggesting the brutal necessity of ridding Italy of its past, and that its future will not be a picnic. Moravia's picnic is without a shred of joy—*la vita non è uno scherzo*.

The metaphor is turned from grim realism to surrealistic in Fernando Arrabal's one-act drama *Picnic on the Battlefield* (1959) and Günter Grass's novel *The Tin Drum* (1969). Both revile war by upending the common expectations of picnicking. Some obvious similarities suggest Grass's indebtedness to Arrabal, but both picnics stand independently as unique interpretations. While Arrabal's picnic is an antiwar argument, Grass's picnic is a deeper satiric analysis of the German mind and its midcentury civilization.

Arrabal's ploy is that a picnic on the battlefield defies logic and exposes universal stupidity. His scene is simple: Monsieur and Madame Tépan, the parents of Private Zapo, arrive on the battlefield with a basket of food, an umbrella, and a phonograph. When they find Zapo crawling on his stomach, he tells mom and dad that they cannot come to the war unless they are soldiers. The parents proceed to unpack the picnic basket, spreading sausage, hard-boiled eggs, ham sandwiches, salad, cakes, and red wine on a cloth. Zapo reminds his parents "discipline and hand-grenades are what's wanted in a war, not visits." But they do not listen. "I don't give a damn," retorts M. Tépan, "we came here to have a picnic with you in the country and to enjoy our Sunday."[188] Compounding their folly, they invite an enemy soldier to share their picnic, and he accepts. For a moment everything is picnicky, as they share their picnic basket. After an insipid conversation and some wine, they all get enthusiastic, and dance a *pasadoble* to the music on their phonograph until machine-gun fire kills them all dead. The shocked audience sits watching stretcher bearers remove the bodies, listening to a stuck phonograph needle repeat the *pasadoble* tune—an obvious reminder that if war never ends, a Sunday picnic does.

Grass's *Tin Drum* picnic begins with a "real" picnic on the beach and then morphs into a kind of magic realism, a blend of realism and fantasy. The day is historically accurate because it is June 5, 1944, the day before the Allied invasion of Europe in Normandy. But Oskar Matzerath, the tin drummer and the entertainment troupe he is a member of, take a day off from work for a leisurely picnic on the beach. Oskar works hard, and he is pleased with the war, because it is good for the entertainment business and his sex life, since he tours with his mistress Roswitha Raguna, an Italian somnambulist. The picnic immediately turns topsy-turvy when the group settles on the cement roof of a pillbox, a German defensive military fortification facing the English Channel:

Kitty: Oh, yes, a picnic in the open.

Felix: Nature has whetted our appetites.

Roswitha: Oh, sacred act of belly-filling that will unite the nations as long as men eat breakfast!

Bebra: Let us feast on the concrete. Let us have human rituals built on solid foundations!

All except for Lankes climb up on the pillbox. Roswitha spreads out a bright, flowery tablecloth. From the bottomless basket she produces little cushions with tassels and fringes.[189] Though in wartime food is scarce, here it is abundant, and the picnic basket is decorated with artificial flowers. Perhaps supposing that if you eat your enemies, it will make you strong, the basket contains French pâté de foie gras, Soviet caviar, Danish butter cookies, Dutch hot chocolate in a thermos bottle, South African ginger and plum preserves, Danish boiled eggs, English corned beef, American cookies, and French bread with plum jam and honey.

As with Arrabal's *Picnic on the Battlefield*, Grass provides his picnickers with a phonograph for entertainment and a bright green umbrella for shade. As the picnickers finish their meal, they see a party of nuns from Lisieux who are picnicking and looking for shellfish to eat. For amusement, Roswitha plays "Sleigh Bells in St. Petersburg" (an imaginary song and reference to the Siege of Leningrad that ended in January 1944) on the phonograph, to which the the nuns react by dancing on the beach. Because their happiness is a disturbance, Corporal Lankes, the commander of the pillbox, gets a call from his superior officer demanding that the beach be cleared, he immediately shoots the nuns. Knowing that this noise will be bothersome, Oskar asks Roswitha to stop up her ears, and Felix masks the gunshots by playing a recording of "The Great Pretender," sung by The Platters, an American rock and roll group in 1955. Given the circumstances, this time warp seems logical. When the record sticks, it is time to go, and the picnic ends. The picnic's coda is that the next morning, June 6, the Allies storm the beach, and in the bombardment, Roswitha is killed while getting a cup of coffee. By distorting the picnic, Grass suggests that happiness is impossible in wartime, something that is lost on Oskar, who is meant to symbolize the German mind-set of world domination. Years after the war ended, Oskar and Lankes meet on the beach and share a picnic. This time it is a fresh-caught codfish that they grill over a fire made with beach debris, and they eat as if nothing ever happened before: "We made a table by laying a big piece of tarboard over some empty buckets. We had our own forks and knives and tin plates."[190]

The American mind-set gone off kilter is Francis Ford Coppola's film *Apocalypse Now*, a loose adaptation of Joseph Conrad's *Heart of Darkness* (1979).[191] This is an indictment of the United States' war in Vietnam, and Coppola's picnic comes after a day of strafing and killing. To reward his troops, Captain Bill Kilgore, the leader of an Air Cavalry unit, treats them with an evening barbeque picnic on the beach. Beer and T-bone steaks are cooked on the beach. Kilgore likes his steak rare, but not cold. Coppola's symbolism is intended to undermine the expectations of picnicking, especially the college beach picnic at which twenty-somethings get drunk and go wild. Shortly before the picnic, Kilgore orders one of the soldiers, a surfer named Lance Johnson, to show his prowess even though the battle is still in progress. Lance is disbelieving but Kilgore is insistent, and a bit insane. Kilgore's split personality allows him to kill and surf simultaneously, and his picnic is a metaphor of the irrationality of war.

A picnic in a barn during World War II in E. L. Doctorow's novel *City of God* (2000) presents a deceptive moment of leisure during a war that was as yet to be won. In fact, it is a grim reality during a war that was yet to be won. The picnickers are Ronald, a U.S. Air Force sergeant on leave in the Cotswolds, and Miss Manderleigh, an English war widow. This is not innocent, as Ronald learns, because the predetermined purpose of his visit will be to father a child with this woman in order to carry on an aristocratic line. On the surface this seems crass, but in a ravaged world, procreation and carrying on the family is important and primal. Under such circumstances, Ronald might be expected to be angry or decline the invitation, but he is so war weary and touched by death that the idea of making life is a mission to him. And Miss Manderleigh is very attractive—a young woman with widespread eyes, full red lips, and dark hair, cut pageboy style. For their mating, she has arranged a picnic, and she greets him carrying a heavy portable radio and a picnic basket filled with wine, cucumber sandwiches, and deviled eggs. When it rains, they enter an old barn, where they eat on the straw. The mix upends picnic expectations. And just as they forget the war, the radio clicks on Hitler making a speech, "rudely denying/any pastoral exception."[192] As it happens at many picnics, Ronald and Manderleigh get aroused and make love. The next morning Ronald feels no intimacy, and Manderleigh is stoic. The picnic idyll is over, and Ronald is back to the war.

Upon parting, the picnic in the barn is a pleasant memory of two people acting out their sense of duty and determination to defeat the forces of evil. It is reason enough for conceiving a child—and perhaps saving a world at war. Both share the knowledge that the picnic "had to be done," and as such it runs against the grain of picnic pleasure, exposing instead the incongruities of war. Doctorow, not an author to get romantic, abandons his usual prose style and tells the picnic story in free verse. Poetry always helps. The name Miss Manderleigh is a sly allusion to Daphne du Maurier's novel *Rebecca* (1939) that takes place in Cornwall and begins, "Last night I dreamt I went to Manderley again."

LOVERS

> And so it came about, in the end, that Mr. Spenlow told me this day week was Dora's birthday, and he would be glad if I would come down and join a little picnic on the occasion. I went out of my senses immediately.
>
> —Charles Dickens, *David Copperfield* (1850)

> Yes; Fate, impatient perhaps of any wavering of the balance in so insignificant a matter as George Gilbert's destiny, threw this penny-post letter into the scale, and, lo! it was turned. The young man read the letter over and over again, till it was crumpled and soiled with much unfolding and refolding, and taking out of, and putting back into, his waistcoat-pocket. A picnic! a picnic in the Hurstonleigh grounds, with Isabel Sleaford!
>
> —Mary Elizabeth Braddon, *The Doctor's Wife* (1864)

Love, food, and picnics are inextricably linked throughout picnic history and repeated across all genres of literature, art, and other media. Mostly, the attraction is being outdoors, supplied with food and drink; the possibility of romance enhances the excitement. When picnics satisfy these expectations, there is happiness. But because expectations are malleable, picnics may be awful, nasty, and dispiriting. Sometimes they are peculiar, like for Michel Leiris, surrealist writer and ethnographer, whose first blush with sexuality happened at a picnic when he was six or seven and realized that he had an erection. Leiris was really at a loss to explain the connection between his manhood and being at a picnic because there was no love object there.[193] Typically, happy picnics are scenes of courtship, romance, and love, but they may also be scenes of lust, disaffection, adultery, and even death. The range is broad but follows established trajectories already known in literature and the arts.

Courtship and Romance

Fictive picnics may be a carryover from the author's personal experiences, though creative imaginations have license to reimagine tender or erotic assignations. *The Confessions* (1781), Jean-Jacques Rousseau's memoirs (partly true, partly fiction) are often charged with sexual innuendo. Among these episodes involves a picnic with two young women, Misses Graffenried and Galley, who he found sexually attractive. Though there is no overt sexual contact, dessert is fresh cherries, which are suggestive:

> After dinner, we were economical; instead of drinking the coffee we had reserved at breakfast, we kept it for an afternoon collation, with cream, and some cake they had brought with them. To keep our appetites in play, we went into the orchard, meaning to finish our dessert with cherries. I got into a tree, throwing them down bunches, from which they returned the stones through the branches. One time, Mademoiselle Galley, holding out her apron, and drawing back her head, stood so fair, and I took such good aim, that I dropped a bunch into her bosom. On her laughing, I said to myself, "Why are not my lips cherries? How gladly would I throw them there likewise."[194]

To his credit, Rousseau remained respectful. There is no wine, but even without it, he is emotionally intoxicated.

Charles Dickens was emotionally intoxicated while writing *David Copperfield*, his most autobiographical novel. But it was probably not his pregnant thirty-four-year-old wife, Catherine, who charged his imagination but a dream of a younger woman. Outwardly, it was a happy time of picnics and rustic games at a villa on the Isle of Wight. But when he translated family fun into fiction, he used a picnic for the chapter "Blissful" for discreetly masking his disaffection for Catherine by recalling memories of young, romantic love, as he was later to find with Ellen Ternan, a woman eighteen-years-old when he first met her. "Blissful" is how David Copperfield feels about his love for Dora Spenlow. But it is also about Dora's birthday picnic and how giddy David feels about his courtship of her and how jealous he is of anyone coming between them.[195] Because Dickens was a man who kept secrets, family life carried on "happily," with the family socializing at picnics, games, and parties. His friend John Leech satirized this good life in the cartoon *Awful Appearance of Wopps at a Picnic*, a mock tragedy about what can go wrong at a picnic outdoors when a gigantic wasp attacks and the picnickers panic. Everything is turned topsy-turvy, and as people scattered, a heroic figure of Charles Dickens stands with his left arm around his wife, Catherine, and his right hand brandishing a dinner knife. The secret of Dickens's romantic life was closely guarded, and as much as Leech knew, Dickens dearly loved his wife.[196]

More innocent and romantic is the picnic at Settignano above Florence in E. M. Forster's *A Room with a View* (1908). It is the start of a long courtship that earnestly begins when George Emerson rushes to save Lucy Honeychurch before she falls off the hillside. It is a pivotal scene that takes place while a group of English tourists gather at a picnic to enjoy the view of Florence. Near the edge of a promontory, Lucy steps out on a small terrace, and she suddenly finds she standing in a place of great beauty filled with blue violets. George sees her and is enthralled; however, thinking that she is in danger, he rushes forward, shouting, "Courage and Love!"[197] His momentary sense of panic is self-imposed. What George doesn't know is that Lucy is merely impressed with the view. But George is on a mission, and so rushing to save her, he impulsively kisses her. It is the apex of the picnic and an emotional high that neither George nor Lucy ever fully understand. George has broken a code of social decorum; Lucy is embarrassed because she feels a whiff of an unknown sensation. The spell is broken immediately when others call and join them. Though neither Lucy nor George can understand, love has happened, which Forster suggests is brought on by the presence of Pan, "not the great god Pan, who has been buried these two thousand years, but the little god Pan, who presides over social contretemps and unsuccessful picnics."[198] From Forster's point of view, this picnic is a comedy of errors—no one dies, trouble is ameliorated, and all seems to end well, eventually.

Young lovers bring foods that sometimes give a sense of their newness to love and their uncertainty of it. Colette's novel *The Ripening Seed* (1923) follows Phil Adebert, sixteen, and Vinca Ferret, fifteen, as they walk down the rocky cliffs of Brittany like "explorers, to eat out of doors in one of the deep clefts in the cliffs: a time-honoured pleasure."[199] Phil leads the way to the surf, carrying nets and gear, and he looks back consciously to ask if Vinca needs help with the picnic baskets. She flashes her blue eyes and says, "Don't bother!" They settle on a small, open space of clean, smooth sand, spread a blanket, and eat lunch just before noon: liters of sparking cider and mineral water, a baguette for sandwiches of buttered lettuce and cubes of gruyere, salt, ripe pears, and sardines. The picnic is very grown-up; Vinca and Phil emulate their parents, and, like them, use flatware and drink from glasses. Vinca serves and cleans up, while Phil relaxes. It is a contrast to Dickens "Blissful" because Phil is involved in a love affair with an older woman (in her thirties) whose house he visits regularly. It is so very French of Colette, whose own love affairs included her estranged husband's adolescent son. Life with either Colette or Dickens was no picnic.

Of course, Dickens and Colette were reworking a long-standing narrative theme that recalls Omar Khayyam's often-quoted verse from *The Rubáiyát of Omar Khayyám*. Everyone knows his about the lovers at a picnic and the lines that combine such strong feelings of desire and food:

> Here with a Loaf of Bread beneath the Bough,
> A flask of Wine, a Book of Verse—and Thou
> Beside me singing in the Wilderness—
> And Wilderness is Paradise enow.[200]

A similar scene is alluded to in Margaret Atwood's novel *The Blind Assassin* (2000), where lovers picnic on the summer grass of a park beneath an apple tree while eating hard-boiled eggs. The woman says, "Here's the salt for it." "Thanks." the man says. "You remembered everything."[201] Sitting under an apple tree confirms, symbolically, that the affair is sexual.

The combination of wine, bread, and romance is so prevalent at picnics that it suggests it is a kind of sacrament devoutly to be offered and accepted. The theme is potent, and from a picnic point of view, there is a substantial body of fictional picnics spanning from the early twelfth century to the present, where it is still resilient and popular. It is taught in the seventeenth century to young courtiers. *New Mirror for Youth* (1617), Crispijn van de Passe's pedagogical handbook, is aimed at elucidating the ways of the world, especially in socializing and courting women with music, song, dance, and food. The setting is a garden, and the season and the mood are playful and lusty. The legend accompanying van de Passe's pictorial visualization of the scene advocates seizing the day:

> How fertile are these sights! In springtime: nourishing
> As Earth brings forth flowers of all kinds.
> These incite frolic and youthful celebration
> Freeing you for all desires and delights.[202]

Desires and delights suggest more than a whiff of sensuality. Many of the couples are engaging in physical courting; they touch, hold hands, embrace, dance, and recline.

The couples at lunch may or may not be courting in Jean-Antoine Watteau's painting *La Collation* or *Lunch in the Open* (ca. 1721).[203] This is Watteau's most explicit picnic scene and is obviously a tryst, though the moment Watteau has chosen to show is while they are dining on wine, bread, and a roast chicken. Paradoxically, there are no plates or cutlery, so the emphasis is on the wine, which is being liberally poured for two women holding crystal wine glasses. The scene may hold some narrative secrets, but because no one touches this may be just a lunch on the grass after all. Other picnic scenes may be more circumspect and symbolic. Bernard Fleetwood-Walker's painting *Amity* (ca. 1933) is misleading.[204] Though the young man and young woman appear physically separate, they are intensely in thought. He stares at a daisy, a symbol of love, and she, facing away from him, seems disengaged, in deep thought or pouting. Her body holds a suggestive pose, breasts thrust out. The white daisy suggests youth and innocence, but her red shoes do not. The picnic basket is filled with apples, an allusion to sexuality that the couple's relationship may or may not progress beyond friendship. Other artists have been more succinctly amorous and approach sexuality more directly.

Singularly, E. M. Forster is extraordinarily adept at ingratiating picnics and sightseeing in his stories and novels. The most revealing, especially because it is autobiographical, is "The Story of a Panic" (1904), which his coming-out story.[205] The picnic takes place while sightseeing in the hills above Ravello, Italy, on a grand day in May. The panic is a reference to the god Pan, the sexual predator, whose presence causes pandemonium that so unnerves the picnickers that they run heedlessly. Only Eustace, an effeminate fourteen-year-old boy, remains, and when the others reassemble, they find Eustace awakening from a trance. Judging from the goat hoof prints surrounding the boy, it suggests that he has been "raped" by Pan. He is so changed that he scrambles and cavorts as if he were a goat. The change is noted but not fully understood, except by a waiter at the hotel, who recognizes Eustace as a kindred spirit and gives his life so the boy may go free. It is a bizarre ending and turns the idea of a picnic topsy-turvy. It makes sense if Forster's need to express his homosexuality in fiction but hide in life is understood. He does the same in the story "The Curate's Friend" (1907), in which Harry, the curate, discovers a faun while enjoying the view of the Wiltshire Hills, which he thinks is "the most beautiful in England." After spreading a rug, making tea, and getting out the food for his other companions, a young woman named Emily and her mother, a faun accosts Harry. Surprised but not frightened, Harry strikes up a relationship with the faun, who gently seduces him, "Dear priest, be placid: why are you frightened?"[206]

There is quasi-homoerotic picnic in the novel *Brideshead Revisited* (1945). Evelyn Waugh passes this off with an allusion to Omar Khayyam's wine and bread metaphor as Sebastian Flyte and Charles Ryder spend an afternoon picnicking instead of attending classes at Oxford. "I've got a motor-car and a basket of strawberries and a bottle of Chateau Peyraguey," says Sebastian, "—which isn't a wine you've ever tasted, so don't pretend. It's heaven with strawberries." Alone in a farmer's field, they eat the strawberries, drink the very expensive sauterne, and smoke Turkish cigarettes on the grass under some elms. Sebastian is melancholy: "Just the place to bury a crock of gold," he says. "I should like to bury something precious in every place where I've been happy and then, when I was old and ugly and miserable, I could come back and dig it up and remember."[207] Charles is quiet and intense in his feelings for Sebastian, but he keeps his innocence and does not act. The scene is memorable because it captures the young men's friendship and aloofness. Sebastian is a gay man, but at this time in his life, as far as Charles knows, he has not come out.

Nothing is left to chance for the liaison of Randolph Henry Ash and Christabel LaMotte when they have their tryst. Ash has even been thoughtful enough to supply wedding bands for the two of them, a symbolic but mock marriage. Ash and LaMotte, one of two pairs of central characters in A. S. Byatt's novel *Possession, A Romance* (1990), are the adulterers. And it is this secret Roland Mitchell and Maud Bailey seek to uncover. The Ashe/LaMotte tryst takes place in North Yorkshire, on the North Sea, and the picnic takes place at Boggle Hole, where Ash collects sea creatures for study. Ironically, Mitchell and Bailey picnic on the same rocky shore at Boggle Hole where they, too, begin a love affair. They take a simple lunch: brown bread; white Wensleydale cheese; crimson radishes; yellow butter; scarlet tomatoes; round, bright green Granny Smiths; and mineral water. But the experience is complex, for they are abandoning a friendship for a relationship. They are not quite sure what it is, but they experience something new on a perfect day. It is only when Roland unbraids Maud's golden hair and lets it free that he senses the new relationship and is roused: "Roland felt as though something had been loosened in himself, that had been gripping him. . . . Maud pushed aside her hair and looked out at him, a little flushed."[208] She agrees that it feels better. Letting her hair down is a cliché, but it works here because Byatt is so sly about it all.

The contrasting patterns of innocence and sexuality is common enough so that in 1608, lovers' picnics were a relevant theme for Thomas Trevelyon's *Miscellany*, in which there are two picnics that contrast innocent and sexual lovers at a picnic in a garden. The first picnic for lovers is romantic. It is set in a May garden where a woman anticipates the arrival of her lover as he approaches carrying a bouquet of flowers in one hand and the horse's reigns in the other. Alongside of the woman is a wicker bower in which a table is set with fruit and wine. The legend suggests the carpe diem theme—seize the day—but the allusion is innocent: "Rise early now this month of May. And walk the fields that be so gay. From surfeiting see thou refrain. Forfend it will procure thy pains." The second picnic is explicitly sensual and alludes to the belief that love intensifies in the spring, which is also the birthday of Venus.[209] Here, beside a table of fruits, bread, nuts, and wine, a woman named Strumpet is doing her best to seduce a young scholar, who would otherwise be tending his university studies and not his sexual education. Strumpet appeals to the young man's physical senses, and she admonishes him to play, a euphemism for sexual lovemaking:

"Come my wanton let us play,
In this fair Arbor, fresh and gay."
And as the man is attracted to her beauty and needs little goading, he responds,
"All sweet content contained in thought
May here be found in her, be sought
Then here I seek and here I find
The pleasure most contents my mind."[210]

Food does not end lovers' problems in Somerset Maugham's novel *The Razor's Edge* (1944). The discussion is never resolved about what foods are appropriate to stir a young man's heart and satisfy a young woman's desire to get a husband. Mrs. Louisa Bradley wants a practical picnic lunch for her daughter, Isabel, to confront her fiancé, Larry Darrell, about his future. She suggests stuffed eggs and a chicken sandwich. But Elliott Templeton, Isabel's effete uncle, suggests, "You can't have a picnic without pâté de foie gras. You must give him curried shrimps to start with, breast of chicken in aspic, with a heart-of-lettuce salad for which I'll make the dressing myself, and after the pâté if you like, as a concession to your American habits, an apple pie."[211] Mrs. Bradley prevails, but the picnic fails its objective, suggesting that Templeton might have been right. But nothing really can move Larry's heart unless it is spiritual food, which neither Mrs. Bradley nor Templeton can conceive. Larry Darrell lives by some romantic notion about finding himself and happiness, neither of which is helped by devilled eggs or pâté.

Happy love is at the heart of Jean Renoir's satire *Luncheon on the Grass (Déjeuner sur l'herbe* (1959), a film that mines allusions from the picnics of his father Pierre-Auguste Renoir, Édouard Manet, Claude Manet, and Aldous Huxley's dystopian novel *Brave New World* (19932). Renoir's preposterous story begins during the election for president of the United States of Europe, and the leading candidate Professor Alexis, a rational atheistic technocrat, who believes sex is no longer necessary for breeding when it can be done more efficiently in a laboratory. The comedy begins when Nénette, a buxom young woman, asks to make love to him because she wants his child. At first, Alexis is repulsed. He is also committed to Marie-Charlotte, a chaste German, who is leader of a militarist, sexless league of girl scouts. To prove that despite his efforts, the world is not perfect (yet) and at the press conference, staged as a picnic, announcing their engagement, all hell breaks loose. The cause is Gaspard, an old shepherd, who looks suspiciously like an old Pan, whose panpipes play an irresistible melody that causes pandemonium, the result of which is a release of passion. Amidst the tumult, Alexis is separated from Marie-Charlotte and wanders until he stumbles on Nénette, naked and swimming in a creek. Irresistibly, they make love. Now changed irrevocably (though he does not know it), Alexis joyously picnics with Nénette and her friends on the grass. Forced back to "real" world, Alexis is on the verge of marrying Marie-Charlotte when he reconnects with Nénette (now very pregnant) and walks her down the aisle. Like his father's painting *Luxury, Calm, and Pleasure*, Renoir suggests the picnicky qualities of life are physical, sexual, and happy.

Love and Lust

Auguste Barthélemy Glaize's painting *Souvenir of the Pyrenees* or *The Picnic* (1851) is a portrait of Alfred Bruyas, the highlighted central figure, who is surrounded by young and comely women.[212] He offers a toast to two women seated next to him, but they do not touch. No one seems to touch, and they exist in separate spheres that rob the picnic of its conviviality. Around Bruyas other men are also being attended to, and there is only a whiff of courtship. The men are respectful; the women seem intent on serving and are engaged in preparing a profusion of food and wine. The picnic suggests homage to Bruyas's self-restraint and makes this is a perfectly civil and honorable gathering. Perhaps it is tame so that it reflects Bruyas's personal sense of his own saintliness. Judging from their docility, Glaize seems to suggest that for Bruyas women are meant for nurturing and serving.

Glaize's picnic is starkly contrasted by the purposeful sexual innuendos and food metaphors of Édouard Manet's masterful painting *Luncheon on the Grass*, aka *Le déjeuner sur l'herbe* (1863).[213] Manet's narrative suggests that wine, cherries, peaches, figs, bread, cheese, and oysters are love foods with a history of symbolic sexual associations. Oysters, especially, are regarded as aphrodisiacs; cherries and peaches have suggestive contours resembling the female torso; and the overturned basket may suggest loss of innocence. Manet is said to have privately referred to the painting as that *partie carrée*, a meeting or tryst for sexual liaison. So it can be presumed that if there are no outward signs of lust and debauchery the food is as suggestive as the nude woman staring insouciantly, daring the viewer to think otherwise. Critics and viewers searching for meaning in *Luncheon on the Grass* are continually engaged in debate about what a painting that was originally called *The Bath* means. More than a century later, details of the painting are much discussed, especially in Paul Hayes Tucker's *Manet's Le dejeuner sur l'herbe* (1998), and they are as yet unsettled.[214]

Lovers at a picnic motivated Paul Cezanne, and his first *Dejeuner sur l'herbe*, aka *The Luncheon on the Grass* (1870–1871), is a glum allusion to Manet's *Luncheon*.[215] Where Manet is sure, Cezanne is uncertain. And his picnickers provide a peek at his (then) conflicted attitude toward sexual relationships with women, whom he considered distractions to his dedication to his art. The clarity and brightness of Manet's painting contrasts with Cezanne's somber palette of blues, blacks, and whites. There are solid clouds and a blue sky, but half of the white picnic blanket is in shadow. Manet's chief female figure is nude and brazen, but Cezanne's is a fully clothed femme fatale dressed in white offering a man an apple, a sure symbol of sexuality and disobedience. Manet's men chat among themselves, but Cezanne's male figure, recognizable as the artist, sits looking intently at the woman and her offering as if in deep thought, without any hint of action. Beside him is an overturned wine bottle and a golden mongrel dog; behind a top hat and umbrella. But what these objects represent is moot. Subsequent picnic scenes in his early paintings show how Cezanne attempted to work out his sense of self and sexual relationships with women. How he changed paintings such as *Idyll*, aka *Pastoral* (1870) and *Le Festin*, aka *The Banquet* (ca. 1870) is discussed in Mary Tompkins Lewis's *Cezanne's Early Imagery*.[216] In 1874, *Picnic on a River* shows a brighter palette with picnickers at ease; however, it was not until decades later that Cezanne formulated his own *Le dejeuner sur l'herbe* (1898), in which the picnickers are convivial, if not cheerful, and on the white cloth filling the central portion are displayed red apples and oranges. Obviously as Cezanne matured and aged, his idea of a picnic mellowed.

Picnics are always sad, somber, and sexually charged for Émile Zola. In his critical review of the Manet's *Luncheon* and other paintings, "Édouard Manet" (1867), Zola acted as Manet's defender, castigated reviewers and viewers who thought the painting lewd.[217] However, Zola is disingenuous. If Manet's *Luncheon on the Grass* is just a picnic on the grass, as he suggests in his art criticism, Zola's picnic on the grass is clearly a sexual tryst. Influenced by Manet's *Luncheon on the Grass*, Zola wrote the novel *Madeleine Férat* (1868) that begins with a picnic of intense, high-spirited, sexual romance that remorselessly disintegrates and ends in murder and suicide. Madeleine Férat's food choices reflect her physical desire, which Zola describes metaphorically using fruits—"giving her lover a bite of her peaches and pears."[218] William, the lover, "was enraptured to see her by him; each day, her beauty seemed more dazzling; he watched, with admiring surprise, the development of health and strength which the fresh air was imparting to her." Fresh air, fruits, and an active sex life make Madeleine "become a powerful woman, with a broad chest and a clear laugh. Her skin, though slightly tanned, had not lost its transparency. Her gold-red hair, carelessly tied up, fell on her neck in a thick glowing coil. Her whole body gave evidence of superb vigour." The enhancement of Madeleine's vigor and beauty is an allusion to Manet's model Victorine Meurent, whose insouciant stare enthralls viewers.

Compare Zola's picnic with the lovers' picnic in Carson McCullers's novel, *The Heart Is a Lonely Hunter* (1940), and a very emotionally flat picnic is discovered.[219] Some might find it touching, but the romance is mirrored by what is in the picnic basket—cold liver pudding, jelly sandwiches, Nehi—about as unromantic as you can get. It may be that this is exactly what Carson McCullers intends for Mick Kelly (a thirteen-year-old girl) and Harry Minowitz (about fifteen years old), two awkward adolescents who have a causal friendship. It is a remarkably awkward episode in the novel during a first-time sexual encounter without love, after which Mick and Harry go on as if nothing happened. Both say they don't ever want to marry. However, adolescents often change their minds. McCullers seems to be projecting herself through Mick. The picnic, however, is such an emotional and sexual dud that you hope it had no basis in her real life, though in fact her life was turmoil and while writing this novel her marriage was disintegrating.

The birthday picnic in Vladimir Nabokov's novel *Ada* (1969) is the beginning of a life-long affair.[220] No matter that Ada, twelve years old, and Van Veen, fifteen years old, are brother and sister. Nabokov seems to suggest (wink, wink) that a picnic is as good a time to begin an affair as any. The event is a circus of chatter and expensive foods and wines—crustless sandwiches, roasted turkey, Russian black bread, Gray Bead beluga caviar (the most expensive), candied violets, raspberry tarts served on china, and white and ruby port, watered claret for the children, and cold, sweet tea served in crystal. For entertainment Ada dances to a tune on a music box, and Van Veen walks on his hands. On the ride home, Ada sits on Van Veen's hard lap, and he can scarcely keep from having an orgasm. Four years, later, after these youthful preliminaries, they meet for Ada's birthday. As quickly as they can, Ada and Van Veen rush off into the woods to make love. No blissful romanticism for Nabokov's Ada and Van Veen, just erotic sexuality. Afterwards, they return for the conventional social part of the picnic.

D. H. Lawrence's *Sons and Lovers* (1913) includes a tryst meant only for love. For hero Paul Morel, it is the pretense of a picnic with Clara Dawes that makes the moment memorable. The anticipation makes him ache with desire that takes his breath away. In the Grove, a park along the River Trent, they walk "up the slippery, steep red path" looking for a place to settle. They carry no food, no blanket, only a bouquet of red carnations Clara grasps in her hand. Finally, they climb down to the rushing river. "Stop a minute," he said, and, "digging his heels sideways into the steep bank of red clay, he began nimbly to mount (the embankment). He looked across at every tree-foot. At last he found what he wanted. Two beech-trees side by side on the hill held a little level on the upper face between their roots. It was littered with damp leaves, but it would do."[221] He threw down his rainproof jacket and waved to her to come. "When they had finished, they are pleased but the many scarlet carnation petals, like splashed drops of blood; and red, small splashes fell from her bosom, streaming down her dress to her feet." The flower symbolism suggests passion; the loose petals staining her dress foreshadows that the relationship will not last. It does not.

Raw lust and sexual energy is what drives Bess into Crown's arms in DuBose Heyward's novel *Porgy and Bess*. In fact, this ruins another happy picnic for the residents of Catfish Row and proves to be heartache for Porgy, despair and drug addiction for Bess, and death for Crown. The essential problem is that Bess cannot manage her lust for Crown, or he for her, and when given the chance to reject passion for stability, Bess unhesitatingly takes passion. When Bess's restraint is tested during a picnic at Kittiwah Island, a palmetto-forested island in Charleston harbor, she cannot resist the excitement of her lust for Crown's body. The original scene in Dubose Heyward's novel *Porgy* (1927) ends as Crown tells Bess that she is doomed to love him, and when he snatches her body, Bess inhales and emits "a wild laugh out against the walls of the clearing."[222] Because the episode is crucial, it is repeated in all versions of it, *especially* the Broadway opera/musical *Porgy and Bess* (1935) with music by George Gershwin. The picnic's contradictory elements suggest a conflict between love and lust, even good and evil, because if nothing else Porgy is good and Crown is evil. The day's outing is a church picnic, and congregants of Catfish Row strut and festively march to the wharf carrying the banner "The Sons and Daughters of Repent Ye Saith the Lord." But none repent, and after eating and drinking and dancing and singing they rally to the drug dealer, Sportin' Life, who sings, "It Ain't Necessarily So," an irreverent song that paradoxically suggests that Bess's attachment to Porgy is anything more than friendship. The picnic ends disastrously for Porgy. The episode is the climax and leads directly to catastrophe, not the least of which sexual. This turnaround undercuts the usual expectations that a picnic must be happy and that a romantic love affair ought not to end in tragedy.

George Orwell's lovers' picnic purposely undermines expectation. Though it is held in a typical English spring landscape, with leaves from trees and a forest floor carpeted with bluebells, it is dystopian and the beginning of the deconstruction of Winston Smith, the hero of the novel *1984* (1948). At first Smith thinks he's in Eden because it is so contrary to life in grimy London. He's about to engage in a sexual liaison with Julia, a clerk and member of the Junior Anti-Sex League, who invites him to leave London for a day in the country where she intends to seduce him. The paradox is overwhelming for Smith because he is unused to seeing. The lovers, however, have brought no provisions, not even a blanket. Smith is so unnerved he complains, "I'm thirty-nine years old. I've got a wife that I can't get rid of. I've got varicose veins. I've got five false teeth."[223] But the beautiful, dark-haired Julia doesn't care; she has some dark, shiny chocolate, and breaking it in half, she gives one of the pieces to Smith. The "first whiff of its scent" stirs "up some memory which he could not pin down, but which was powerful and troubling." Delighted with the taste, Winston is aroused, and their lovemaking is lustful. Sparked by the picnic, the chocolate, and the beauty of nature, Smith's frame of mind and health improves, but there is a heavy cost. Big Brother knows about the picnic and is watching them and waiting to pounce. Retribution is sure and inexorable. Julia betrays Smith; Smith betrays Julia. Their moment of love evaporated, the picnic in the field of bluebells is a blip in the routine of glum reality.

Seduction and lust is the central theme of William Inge's *Picnic* (1953). Slowly, and inexorably, Madge Owens, a nubile woman of eighteen, is seduced by Hal Carter, about twenty-eight, of dubious character and great sexual power. Beautiful Madge is aware of her beauty, but not of her sexuality. Her sensual awakening coincides with the community picnic on Labor Day in early September. Though you expect to get to the picnic, Inge does not include it. There is no picnic in *Picnic*. Instead, on the morning of the picnic, everything is in a state of incipient, seething sexuality. Madge dailies with Hal, and when they dance, it becomes increasingly impossible for either of them to resist their animal magnetism. Madge ineffectually says that the others are waiting and the baskets are in the car. But neither is inclined to meet the other:

Hal: Baby!

Madge: I . . . I get so tired of being told I'm pretty.

Hal: (Folding her in his arms caressingly) Baby, baby, baby.

Madge: (Resisting him, jumping to her feet) Don't. We have to go. We have all the baskets in our car and they'll be waiting. (Hal gets up and walks slowly to her, their eyes fastened and Madge feeling a little thrill of excitement as he draws nearer) Really—we have to be going. (Hal takes her in his arms and kisses her passionately. Then Madge utters his name in a voice of resignation) Hal!

Figure 5.15. *Picnic* (1955). Directed by Joshua Logan. Columbia Pictures/Photofest. ©Columbia Pictures.

Hal: Just be quiet, baby.

Madge: Really. . . . We have to go. They'll be waiting.

Hal: (Picking her up in his arms and starting off. His voice is deep and firm.) We're not goin' on no goddamn picnic.[224]

So the curtain falls ending Act Two, and no one is ever likely to remember that left behind in the car are deviled eggs, potato salad, and three dozen bread and butter sandwiches.

Because the picnic ought to be an obligatory scene, Joshua Logan's film adaptation of *Picnic* (1955) was extensively revised by screenwriter Daniel Taradash. For what seems an eternity, the film meanders through a Labor Day Community Picnic and features an a capella quartet.[225] The film is iconic because the actors are Kim Novak and William Holden, who are now cult figures in Hollywood lore. The picnic is remembered because of a steamy dance scene between Madge and Hal. American prudery on stage and film in the 1950s left much to the imagination. What a contemporary see-all-tell-all revision of *Picnic* might include now can only be anticipated.

Neither depressing nor sensual, John O'Hara's story "A Few Trips and Some Poetry" (1968) is about a picnic-sex episode that provides a memory that lasts a lifetime. Jim, the narrator, and Isabel Barley, his sporadic lover, are long-time friends who share passion without compassion, pleasure but not love. Isabel turns off the main road and drives along a dirt road to a picnic ground furnished with rough tables, benches, and a small bandstand. Without discussion, Isabel prepares for love: "I don't want to lose you entirely," she says matter of factly. "When we're really ready I'll lie on a picnic table." Jim asks if this is wise, but Isabel has it figured out. "She got out of the car and lay on the table, with her shirtwaist open and her skirt rolled up . . ." Isabel's cheerful tagline, "back to nature," seems to be spit out through clenched teeth.[226] But Jim, the ever-unreliable narrator, says that their lovemaking is quick but "immensely pleasurable." For the reader, this is a comically sordid, picnic-sex fantasy at which no food is required and none is served.

Jealousy

Strong feelings are displayed when two men compete for a picnic basket donated by a woman they desire. In *Oklahoma!*, ostensibly the auction is a typical fund-raiser/social event. But the bidding is a duel of wills, for whoever wins the basket wins the woman who donated it, Laurey Williams. Never has a basket of meat pies, gooseberry tarts, and apple jelly been the subject of such contentious rivalry overlaying seething sexual hostility and masculine animosity. At last, the goodhearted Curly McLain outbids the black-hearted Jud Fry. The final moments are very tense as Curly gives up what is most dear to him, a saddle, horse, and gun. Laurey is pleased because she loves Curly and fears Jud's sexuality. But Jud leaves disgruntled and angry while the lovers plan for their future happiness. Though the happy ending follows the usual trajectory, Laurey and Curly have not seen the last of Jud, who returns to fights with Curly and is killed. The cost is dear, and Jud's life ends unhappily because he could not beat a bid of $53. The sale is such a downer that the auctioneer, Aunt Eller, says with surprise, "Whut's the matter with you folks? Ain't nobody gonna cheer er nuthin'?"[227]

Unhappiness

Picnic fare in Martin Amis's novel *Dead Babies* (1975) is meant to be licentious and disgusting, like the people eating and drinking. His picnic on the grass is bucolic and rustic but situated in a cow pasture with manure. Though it is intended as an ordinary picnic or *partie de plaisir*, Amis's is a metaphor for an abusive group of twenty-somethings reveling in a cow pasture in their dependency on alcohol, drugs, and destructive conversation. The picnickers' eat "gingerly," but the "pieces of meat were picked up between finger and thumb and held aloft like live worms before being quickly dispatched; offending portions of salad and cheese were disgustedly spat out on the grass; water biscuits, apples, celery, and radishes enjoyed fair popularity, but little truck was had with such greasy and malodorous dishes as sardines, liver sausage, and anchovies. The company snorted when bananas were mentioned and actually gagged in unison when boiled eggs were produced."[228] Their picnic ends abruptly when a heifer crashes the party and they all scamper for safety, all getting scratched, especially the breasts of the naked women. Talking about sex, dining on disgusting food, and drinking excessive quantities of wine and spirits suggest that this is a *partie de plaisir* turned topsy-turvy.

Another picnic in Émile Zola's novel *L'Assommoir* (1877) is depressing. It is without food or drinks and set in a wasteland just beyond Montmartre, then an outskirt of Paris. Gervaise Macquart, a laundress, and Goujet, a locksmith who loves her, finally sit in "a vacant lot between a sawmill and a button factory."[229] Their bench is a dead tree near which a tethered goat munches the sparse grass. Their situation seems hopeless, and when Goujet asks her to run away with him, she cannot. Impulsively, Goujet kisses her, but she does not respond. Neither of them can really arouse passion. Not knowing what else to do, Goujet picks dandelions and throws them into Gervaise's basket, so that when they leave it is filled with the yellow flowers that uncharacteristically signify sadness and defeat.

John Galsworthy's adaption of Zola's sad picnic is genteel, and though a chauffeur drives his characters to the country, the excursion is no less dispiriting. Like Zola's, Galsworthy's picnic takes place by a tree, this time an apple tree in bloom from which the story takes it name, "The Apple Tree," and it is a symbolic sexual allusion to the second sin.[230] Zola's putative lovers never embrace, but Galsworthy's have a romantic, passionate love affair. This ends badly when Frank Ashurst leaves Megan David, a farm girl, to return to his own social class. Now twenty-six years later, Ashurst and his wife, Stella, inadvertently picnic in a meadow near the apple tree beside which is a grave, Megan David's grave. The youthful memories of his old love resurface, and when he relives the whole episode Ashurst is left achy, guilty, and forlorn over his lost youth and passion. Though the picnic rug is carefully placed and the luncheon basket open, he cannot picnic. By heightening expectations and then depressing them, Zola and Galsworthy have depicted that if you expect a picnic for lovers to be joyous, you might well be disappointed and saddened. Undermining the picnic by omitting food, which everyone knows makes people happy, only serves to intensify sentimentality and joylessness.

When it comes to adultery, Guy de Maupassant's tale "A Day in the Country" (1881) is a surprising example.[231] As the story goes, a bourgeois Parisian family takes its long-awaited outing in the country, where they will dine at a restaurant along the Seine. At the time, this was a popular pastime for Parisians because the destination was a short ride by train or carriage. Because it is a warm day, after eating, the men sleep, but the mother and her eighteen-year-old daughter are alert. So when two handsome boaters approach the women, they agree to a boating adventure on the river. For the mother, the adventure leads to lust, and she and her young boatman shore up in the brush to make love. The daughter is reticent and resists her boatman's advances. When they return to the men, the mother is happy, but the daughter has mixed feelings about the lost opportunity. Later, the boatman tries to find the young woman, but she has married her bourgeois suitor, and he ruefully realizes that a moment has been lost. This is typical Maupassant irony, and may have been drawn from life since he was an expert rower and frequented restaurants on the Seine west of Paris. The story with its kindly wink at adultery may be an allusion to Émile Zola's picnic murder in *Thérèse Raquin* (1876). Jean Renoir's film, *A Day in the Country*, aka *Partie de campagne* (1936), is a faithful adaptation of Maupassant's story.[232] Renoir is more forthcoming about the menu: friture [fried fish], rabbit fricassee, bread, and white wine. He is more emphatic about developing the relationship between the lovers and its sad dénouement when they meet by chance at another picnic. Sadly, however, the lovers realize they have missed the opportunity for a sustained relationship, and they irrevocably separate. Sentiment rules, and the lovers are irrevocably parted.[233]

Deep sadness and remorse permeate Thomas Hardy's picnic memory of his wife, Emma, who had long ceased to love ardently. The poem "Where the Picnic Was" (1913) suggests a deep sadness at her passing. Yet he was already engaged in a passionate relationship with Florence Dugdale (his secretary) and would soon marry her. The mixture of old grief and new ardor left Hardy in a kind of limbo, as if living parallel lives—one in which he felt the strong presence of Emma and the physical presence of Florence. The actual picnic in the poem was happy and attended by Emma and poets William Butler Yeats and Henry Newbolt, who give him the Royal Society of Literature's gold medal. You might expect that because the picnic was happy that it would be reimagined with at least some sense of its original feelings. But Hardy refuses to provide anything you might expect. The grassy lawn on the picnic is empty, and Emma is dead—not mourned or remembered fondly. If there was a picnic basket, it is not mentioned. Its absence suggests loss, among the dreariest adjectives you would expect for a picnic:

> But two have wandered far
> From this grassy rise
> Into urban roar
> Where no picnics are,
> And one—has shut her eyes
> For evermore.[234]

How Florence put up with Hardy's torment is a wonder, and she never complained that he did not picnic with her.

Suicide

Bo Widerberg's film, *Elvira Madigan* (1967), with its double suicide, shadows the highs and lows of romantic love and romantic death in the great tradition of Romeo and Juliet.[235] Like Shakespeare, Widerberg frames the story between lovers meeting, but instead of a balcony and tomb there are two picnics on a grassy lawn beneath a great oak. The first picnic is pure romance. Having abandoned their obligations, Elvira Madigan and Sixten Sparre make love, drink wine, and eat cheese. For the second picnic, the lovers bring a picnic basket, wine, and a service revolver. Having run out of money, the lovers face a self-imposed choice of separating or suicide. So twisted by romantic feelings of gloom, the final picnic ends with two clear pistol shots. The moment is perhaps the least dried-eyed picnic imagined, especially because you never want this picnic to end, particularly in this manner. Widerberg's aching romanticism suggests that when life is not a picnic, it's not worth living. As the Danish say, *Livet err ikke skovtur*, "life is not a picnic." Madigan and Sparre are beautiful people blinded by a passion they refuse to let go of, even when they know the dire consequences. Their final picnic makes their tragedy potent. You expect, you want, the couple to be as happy as they are at the picnic at the start of their love affair when loving had no end in sight. You know that it never is, but wouldn't it be a pleasure, if it were.

SELECTED
BIBLIOGRAPHY

GENERAL

Albala, Ken. *The Banquet: Dining in the Great Courts of Late Renaissance Europe.* Urbana: University of Illinois Press, 2007.

Angelo, Henry. *Reminiscences of Henry Angelo.* London: H. Colburn and R. Bentley, 1830.

Battiscombe, Georgina. *English Picnics.* London: Harvill Press Limited, 1949.

Bellioli, Andrea P. A., ed. *A Day in the Country: Impressionism and the French Landscape.* Los Angeles, CA: Los Angeles Museum of Art.

Bendiner, Kenneth. *Food in Painting from the Renaissance to the Present.* London: Reaktion Books, 2004.

Boreth, Craig. *The Hemingway Cookbook.* Chicago: Chicago Review Press, 1998, 2012.

Borrel, Anne, Alain Senderens, and Jean-Bernard Naudin. *Dining with Proust.* New York: Random House, 1992.

Brumley, Albert E. *All-Day Singin' and Dinner on the Ground: A Collection of Favorite Old Time Songs and Hymns and Choice Recipes from Days of Yesteryear.* Camdenton, MI: Albert E. Brumley, 1972.

Burckhardt, Jacob. *The Greeks and Civilization,* translated by Sheila Stern, edited by Oswyn Murray. New York: St. Martin's Press, 1872; 1999.

Burns, John and Elisabeth Caton. *The Urban Picnic: Being an Idiosyncratic and Lyrically Recollected Account of Menus, Recipes, History, Trivia, and Admonitions on the Subject of Alfresco Dining in Cities Both Large and Small,* edited by Jennifer Lyon Illus. Vancouver, BC: Arsenal Pulp Press, 2004.

Combe, William. *The Pic Nic.* London: R. Exton for J. F. Hughes, 1803.

Craigie, Carter W. "A Movable Feast: The Picnic as Folklife Custom in Chester County, Pennsylvania, 1870-1925." PhD dissertation, University of Pennsylvania, 1976.

Davidson, Alan and Tom Jaine. *The Oxford Companion to Food*. 2nd edition 2006, New York: Oxford University Press, 1999.

Dunbabin, Katherine M. D. *The Roman Banquet: Images of Conviviality*. Cambridge: Cambridge University Press, 2003.

Eyre, Karen and Mireille Galinou. *Picnic*. London: Museum of London, 1988.

Fitzgerald, Gerard J. and Gabriella M. Petrick. "Good Taste: Rethinking American History with Our Palates." *Journal of American History* 95, no. 2 (September 2008): 392–404.

Fussell, Betty. *My Kitchen Wars*. New York: North Point Press, 1999, 120–46.

Gowing, Lawrence. *Cezanne: The Early Years 1859–1872*. New York: Harry N. Abrams, 1988.

Grigson, Jane. *English Food: An Anthology*. London: Penguin Books, 1974.

Gurney, Jackie. *The National Trust Book of Picnics*. Newton Abbot: David and Charles, 1982.

Harris, John. *The Courtship, Merry Marriage, and Pic-Nic Dinner of Cock Robin and Jenny Wren. To Which Is Added, Alas! The Doleful Death of the Bridegroom*. Volume 2. London: J. Harris, 1806.

Isaacson, Joel. *Monet: Le Déjeuner sur l'herbe*. London: Allen Lane, The Penguin Press, 1972.

Johnston, Susanna and Anne Tennant, eds. *The Picnic Papers: A Few Literary Thoughts on the Ultimate Outdoor Spread*. London: Hutchinson, 1983.

Jones, Evan. *A Food Lover's Companion*, illustrated by Lauren Jarret. New York: Harper and Row, 1979.

Joyes, Claire. *Monet's Table: The Cooking Journals of Claude Monet*, photographs by Bernard Naudin. New York: Simon & Schuster, 1989.

Kay, Pamela and Susie Ward. *The Art of the Picnic: An Anthology of Theme Picnic*. London: Cassell, 1988.

King, Shirley. *Dining with Marcel Proust: A Practical Guide to French Cuisine of the Belle Époque*. Lincoln, NE: Bison Books, 1979; 2006.

Kraig, Bruce. *Hot Dog: A Global History*. London: Reaktion Books, 2009.

Lane, Maggie. *Jane Austen and Food*. London: Hambledon Press, 1995.

Le Faye, Deirdre. *Jane Austen: The World of Her Novels*. London: Francis Lincoln, 2002.

Levy, Walter. "Picnic History." In *Scribner's Encyclopedia of Food and Culture*, edited by Solomon H. Katz. New York: Charles Scribner's and Sons, 2003.

——. "Picnics and Fairy Tales, or Let Them Eat Cake." In *Nurture: Proceedings of the Oxford Symposium on Food and Cookery 2003*, edited by Richard Hosking. Bristol, UK: Footwork, 2004, 167–79.

——. "The Morality of Anti-Picnics." In *Food and Morality: Proceedings of the Oxford Symposium on Food and Cookery 2007*, edited by Susan R. Friedland. Totnes, UK: Prospect Books, 2008, 165–72.

———. "American Picnics." In *The Oxford Encyclopedia of Food and Drink in America*, edited by Andrew F. Smith and Bruce Craig, 2nd ed. New York: Oxford University Press, 2012.

Lewis, Mary Tompkins. *Cezanne's Early Imagery*. Los Angeles, CA: University of California Press, 1989.

Leyda, Jay. *The Melville Log: A Documentary Life of Herman Melville, 1819–1891*. Volume 2. New York: Harcourt, Brace and Company, 1951.

Madeline, Laurence. *Picasso / Manet: Le déjeuner sur l'herbe*. Paris: Musée D'Orsay, 2009.

Malaguzzi, Silvia. *Food and Feasting in Art*, translated by Brian Phillips. Los Angeles: The J. Paul Getty Museum, 2006.

McGee, Diane. *Writing the Meal: Dinner in the Fiction of Early Twentieth-Century Woman Writers*. Toronto: University of Toronto Press, 2001.

Mennell, Stephen. *All Manners of Food: Eating and Taste in England and France from the Middle Ages to the Present*. Oxford: Basil Blackwell, 1985.

Miller, Angela. *The Empire of the Eye: Landscape Representation and American Cultural Politics, 1825–1875*. Ithaca, NY: Cornell University Press, 1993.

Opie, Peter and Iona Opie. *The Oxford Dictionary of Nursery Rhymes*. New York: Oxford University Press, 1997.

Pettifer, Julian and Nigel Turner. *Automania: Man and the Motor Car*. London: Collins, 1984.

Phébus, Gaston III, Count de Foix. *The Hunting Book of Gaston Phébus* [1389], translated by Wilhelm Schlag. London: Harvey Miller Publishers, 1998.

Pleji, Herman. *Dreaming of Cockaigne: Medieval Fantasies of the Perfect Life*, translated by Diane Webb. New York: Columbia University Press, 2001.

Post, Emily. *Etiquette: In Society, in Business, in Politics, and at Home*. New York: Funk & Wagnalls Co., 1922.

Rothkopf, Katherine, Richard R. Brettell, and Charles S. Moffet. *Impressionists on the Seine: A Celebration of Renoir's* Luncheon of the Boating Party, ed. Eliza E. Rathbone. Washington, DC: The Phillips Collection, 1996.

Rothschild, Deborah, ed. *Making It New: The Art and Style of Sara & Gerald Murphy*. Berkeley, CA: University of California Press, 2007.

Rousseau, Jean-Jacques. *The Confessions* [1781], translated by J. M. Cohen. Baltimore, MD: Penguin Books, 1954.

Schlossman, Norma A. *Pastoral Pleasures: The Picnic in American Art before 1870*. San Jose: San Jose State University, 1997.

Sherrill, Charles H. *French Memories of Eighteenth-Century America*. New York: Scribner's Sons, 1915.

Sitwell, Osbert. *Sing High! Sing Low!* London: Macmillan, 1944. Reprint, 1977. Plainview, NY: Ayer Printing.

Stern, Michael and Jane Stern. *Auto Ads*. New York: Random House, 1978.

Strong, Roy. *Feast: A History of Grand Eating*. Orlando, FL: Jonathan Cape, 2002.

Symons, Michael. *One Continuous Picnic: A History of Eating in Australia*. Adelaide: Duck Press, 1982.

Tandon, Bharat, ed. *Jane Austen,* Emma: *An Annotated Edition*. Cambridge, MA: Belknap Press of Harvard University Press, 2012.

Tomlinson, Janis A. *Francisco Goya: The Tapestry Cartoons and Early Career at the Court of Madrid*. Cambridge: Cambridge University Press, 1989.

Trollope, Frances. *Domestic Manners of the Americans*, edited by Donald Smalley. New York: Alfred A. Knopf, 1949. Originally published in 1832.

Tucker, Paul Hayes, ed. *Manet's* Le déjeuner sur l'herbe. New York: Cambridge University Press, 1998.

Visser, Margaret. *The Rituals of Dinner: The Origins, Evolution, Eccentricities, and Meaning of Table Manners*. New York: Grove Weidenfeld, 1991.

Wolfe, Linda. *The Literary Gourmet: Menus from Masterpieces*. New York: Simon & Schuster, 1989.

Young, Carolin C. *Apples of Gold in Settings of Silver: Stories of Dinner as a Work of Art*. New York: Simon & Schuster, 2003.

Zeldin, Theodore. *An Intimate History of Humanity*. New York: Harper Perennial, 1994.

COOKBOOKS

Batali, Mario. *Mario Tailgates NASCAR Style: The Essential Cookbook for NASCAR Fans*. St. Louis, MO: Sporting News, 2006.

Beard, James. *Cook It Outdoors*. New York: M. Barrows and Company, Inc., 1941.

——. *The Complete Book of Outdoor Cookery*. New York: Harper & Row, 1955.

——. *Delights and Prejudices*. Philadelphia: Running Press Book Publishers, 1964; 2001.

——. *Menus for Entertaining*. Revised edition 1997. New York: Marlowe & Company, 1965.

——. *American Cookery*, illustrated by Earl Thollander. New York: Little, Brown, 1972.

——. *Beard on Bread*. New York: Ballantine Books, 1973.

Beeton, Isabella. "Bill of Fare for a Picnic of 40 Persons." In *Mrs. Beeton's Book of Household Management*. London: S. O. Beeton, 1859–1861. Reprint, New York: Oxford University Press, 2000.

Black, Maggie and Deirdre Le Faye. *The Jane Austen Cookbook*. London: The British Museum Press, 1995.

Boxer, Arabella. The Wind in the Willows *Country Cookbook: Inspired by* The Wind in the Willows *by Kenneth Grahame*, illustrated by Ernest H. Shepard. New York: Charles Scribner's Sons, 1983.

Brennan, Jennifer. *Curries and Bugles: A Memoir and Cookbook of the British Raj*. New York: HarperCollins, 1990.

Brillat-Savarin, Jean Anthelme. *The Physiology of Taste, or Meditations on Transcendental Gastronomy* [1825], translated by Fayette Robinson. http://www.gutenberg.org/cache/epub/5434/pg5434.html.

Claiborne, Craig. The New York Times *Menu Cook Book*, drawings by Bill Goldsmith. New York: Harper & Row Publishers, 1966.

———. *Craig Claiborne's a Feast Made for Laughter*. New York: Holt, Rinehart and Winston, 1982.

Colwin, Laurie. *Home Cooking: A Writer in the Kitchen*. Reprint, Harper Perennial, 1993.

———. *More Home Cooking: A Writer Returns to the Kitchen*. New York: HarperCollins, 1993, 114–22.

Crookenden, Kate, Caroline Worlledge, and Margaret Willes. *The National Trust Book of Picnics*. London: The National Trust, 1993.

David, Elizabeth. *A Book of Mediterreanean Food*. New York: New York Review of Books, 1950; 2002.

———. *Summer Cooking*. London: Penguin, 1955, enlarged 1965.

———. *An Omelette and a Glass of Wine*, edited by John Thorne. New York: The Lyons Press, 1997.

———. *Of Pageants and Picnics*. London: Penguin, 2005.

Day, Alexandra and Abigail Darling. *The Teddy Bears' Picnic Cookbook*. Seattle, WA: Green Tiger Press, 2002.

Edge, John, T. *A Gracious Plenty: Recipes and Recollections from the American South*. New York: Putnam, 1999.

Ellison, Virginia. *The Pooh Cook Book*. New York: Dutton, 1969; 2010.

———. *The Winnie-the-Pooh Cookbook*. New York: Dutton Children's Books, 2010.

Fisher, M. F. K. *The Gastronomical Me*. New York: Macmillan, 1943. New York: North Point Press, 1989.

———. *Here Let Us Feast: A Book of Banquets*. New York: North Point Press, 1946.

———. *An Alphabet for Gourmets*. New York: Macmillan, 1989.

———. *A Stew or a Story: An Assortment of Short Works by M. F. K. Fisher*, edited by Joan Reardon. Emeryville, CA: Shoemaker & Hoard, 2006, 198–207.

Hazelton, Nika. *The Picnic Book*. New York: Atheneum, 1969.

Hemingway, Joan and Connie Maricich. *The Picnic Gourmet: Over 300 Delectable Dishes for Every Kind of Picnic Meal—from Simple Backpacking Hikes to Elegant Basket Lunches*. New York: Random House, 1975.

Jekyll, Agnes. *Kitchen Essays*. London: Persephone Books, 1922; 1969.

Larned, Linda Hull. *One Hundred Picnic Suggestions*. New York: Charles Scribner's & Sons, 1915.

Lewis, Edna. *The Taste of Country Cooking*. New York: Random House, 1976.

Leyel, Mrs. C. F. *Picnics for Motorists*. London: G. Routledge & Sons, 1936.

Leyel, Mrs. C. F. and Miss Olga Hartley. *The Gentle Art of Cookery*. London: Chatto & Windus/The Hogarth Press, 1925; 1983.

Linn, Stephen, ed. *The Ultimate Tailgater's SEC Handbook*. Nashville, TN: Rutledge Hill Press, 2005.

Madden, John and Peter Kaminsky. *John Madden's Ultimate Tailgating*. New York: Viking, 1998.

McNair, James K. *The Complete Book of Picnics: A Portable Feast of Ideas for Preparing & Packing Delicious Snacks, Meals, Elaborate Feasts for Any Time, Any Place*. San Francisco: Ortho Books, 1979.

National Council of Negro Women. *The Black Family Reunion Cookbook: Recipes and Food Memories*, edited by Libby Clark, 1993 edition. New York: Touchstone, 1991.

Naudin, Jean-Bernard, Jean-Michel Charbonnier, and Jacqueline Saulnier. *Renoir's Table*. New York: Simon & Schuster, 1994.

Neustadt, Kathy. *Clambake: A History and Celebration of an American Tradition*. Amherst, MA: University of Massachusetts, 1992.

Olsen, Kirstin. *Cooking with Jane Austen*. Westport, CT: Greenwood Press, 2005.

O'Neill, Molly. *American Food Writing: An Anthology with Classic Recipes*. New York: Library of America, 2007.

Roden, Claudia. *Picnic: The Complete Guide to Outdoor Food*, illustrated by Linda Kitson. London: Jill Norman, 1981.

———. *Everything Tastes Better Outdoors*, illustrated by Alta Ann Parkins. New York: Alfred A. Knopf, 1984.

———. *Picnic: And Other Outdoor Feasts*, illustrated by Linda Kitson. London: Grub Street, 2001.

———. *Arabesque: A Taste of Morocco, Turkey, and Lebanon*. New York: Alfred A. Knopf, 2006.

Rodriguez-Hunter, Suzanne. *Found Meals of the Lost Generation: Recipes and Anecdotes from 1920s Paris*. Boston: Faber and Faber, 1997.

Scholliers, Peter, ed. *The Dining Nobility: From the Burgundian Dukes to the Belgian Royalty*. Brussels: VUB Press, 2008.

Sesame Street *"C" Is for Cooking: Recipes from the Street*. New York: Houghton Mifflin Harcourt, 2009.

Sloan, Robert. *The Tailgating Cookbook: Recipes for the Big Game*. San Francisco: Chronicle Books, 2005.

Smith, Andrew F. and Bruce Craig, eds. *The Oxford Encyclopedia of Food and Drink in America*, 3 vols. New York: Oxford University Press, 2012.

Southworth, May E. *The Motorist's Luncheon Book*. New York: Harper Brothers, 1923.

Spang, Rebecca L. *The Invention of the Restaurant: Paris and Modern Gastronomic Culture*. Cambridge, MA: Harvard University Press, 2002.

Spry, Constance and Rosemary Hume. *The Constance Spry Cookery Book*. London: J. M. Dent & Sons, 1957.

Sunset Best Kids Cookbook, edited by Elizabeth L. Hogan. Menlo Park, CA: Sunset Books, 1992.

Tarr, Yvonne Young. *The Complete Outdoor Cookbook*. New York: Quadrangle Books/ The New York Times, 1973.

Toklas, Alice B. *The Alice B. Toklas Cook Book*. London: Serif, 1954; 2004.

Tornborg, Pat. *The Sesame Street Cookbook*. New York: Platt & Munk, 1978.

Ward, Cynthia Whitney. *Picnics of New England: With Recipes to Inspire and Paintings to Enchant*. Boston: Museum of Fine Arts, 1997.

Waters, Alice. *Chez Panisse Menu Cookbook*, in collaboration with Linda P. Guenzel, recipes edited by Carolyn Dille, and designed and illustrated by David Lance Gaines. New York: Random House, 1982.

Wenger, Shaunda Kennedy and Janet Kay Jensen. *The Book Lover's Cookbook: Recipes Inspired by Celebrated Works of Literature and the Passages That Feature Them*. New York: Ballantine Books, 2003.

White, Linda. *Cooking on a Stick: Campfire Recipes for Kids*. Layton, UT: Gibbs Smith, 1996.

Wyvern [Arthur Kenney-Herbert]. *Culinary Jottings: A Treatise in Thirty Chapters on Reformed Cookery for Anglo-Indian Exiles, Based Upon Modern English and Continental Principles with Thirty Menus for Little Dinners Worked out in Detail, and an Essay on Our Kitchens in India*. Fifth edition. London: Richardson and Co., 1879.

NOTES

INTRODUCTION

1. Georgina Battiscombe, *English Picnics* (London: Harvill Press Limited), 1949.
2. Osbert Sitwell, "Picnics and Pavilions," in *Sing High! Sing Low!* (London: Macmillan, 1944); Carter W. Craigie, "A Movable Feast: The Picnic as Folklife Custom in Chester County, Pennsylvania, 1870–1925," PhD dissertation, University of Pennsylvania, 1976; Carter W. Craigie, "The Vocabulary of the Picnic," *Midwestern Language and Folklore Newsletter*, 1978, 2–6; Roxana Barry, *Land of Plenty: Nineteenth Century American Picnic and Harvest Scenes*, The Katonah Gallery, Katonah, New York, November 14, 1981–January 10, 1982; Karen Eyre and Mireille Galinou, *Picnic* (London: Museum of London, 1988); Angela L. Miller, "Nature's Transformations: The Meaning of the Picnic Theme in Nineteenth-Century American Art," *Winterthur Portfolio* 24 (Summer/Autumn 1989): 113–38; Jeanne-Marie Darblay and Caroline de Beaurepaire, *L'art du Pique-Nique* (Paris: Editions du Chene, 1994); Julia Csergo, "The Picnic in Nineteenth-Century France: A Social Event Involving Food: Both a Necessity and a Form of Entertainment," in *Eating out in Europe: Picnics, Gourmet Dining, and Snacks since the Late Eighteenth Century*, edited by Marc Jacobs and Peter Scholliers, 139–59 (Oxford: Berg, 2003); Francine Barthe-Deloizy, *Le pique-nique: Ou l'éloge d'un bonheur ordinaire*, edited by Frédéric Chappey with contributions by Salomé Berthon and Michel Gillot (Paris: Editions Bréal), 2008; Mary Ellen W. Hern, "Picnicking in the Northeastern United States, 1840–1900," *Winterthur Portfolio* 24, no. 2–3 (Summer/Autumn 1989): 139–52.
3. Robert Louis Stevenson, "An Autumn Effect," in *Essays of Travel* (London: Chatto & Windus, 1905), http://www.gutenberg.org/files/627/627-h/627-h.htm.
4. Gertrude Stein, "Every Afternoon," in *Geography and Plays* (Boston: The Four Seas Company, 1922), 254, http://www.gutenberg.org/files/33403/33403-h/33403-h.htm.

5. Benedikt Koehlen, *Piano Pictures: Satie—Sports et Divertissements and George Antheil—La Femme 100 têtes*, EMG Classical, 1998, remastered 2011; Erik Satie, "Picnic," translated by Virgil Thompson, in *Sports et Divertissements*, illustrated by Charles Martin (New York: Dover 1923).

6. Alice B. Toklas, *The Alice B. Toklas Cook Book* (London: Serif, 1954; 2004).

CHAPTER 1

1. J. K. Rowling, *Harry Potter and the Deathly Hallows* (New York: Scholastic Press, 2007), 581.

2. Allan Pinkerton, *Criminal Reminiscences and Detective Sketches* (New York: G. W. Dillingham Co., 1878), 18.

3. Robertson Davies, "What Every Girl Should Know," in *One Half of Robertson Davies* (New York: Penguin, 1977), 50.

4. Banksy, *Picnic* (2005).

5. *The Charming Effects of Barricades, or Durable Friendship of the Brothers of Bacchic Picnic: Burlesque in Verse* (Paris, 1649), http://books.google.com/books?id=-nt KAAAAcAAJ&printsec=frontcover&source=gbs_ge_summary_r&cad=0#v=onepage &q&f=false.

6. John Harris, *The Courtship, Merry Marriage, and Pic-Nic Dinner of Cock Robin and Jenny Wren, To Which Is Added, Alas! The Doleful Death of the Bridegroom* (London: J. Harris, 1806).

7. Thomas Nash, *Strange News* (1593), first published in 1592, http://www. oxford-shakespeare.com/Nashe/Strange_News.pdf; *A Pleasant Comedy, Called Summer's Last Will and Testament* (1600), http://www.oxford-shakespeare.com/Nashe/ Summers_Last_Will_Testament.pdf. The play was performed in 1592.

8. Miguel de Cervantes, *Don Quixote de la Mancha* [1605–1615], edited and translated by Edith Grossman (New York: Ecco, 2003); Francisco de Quevedo, *The Swindler* [1626], in *Lazarillo de Tormes and the Swindler: Two Spanish Picaresque Novels*, translated by Michael Alpert (London: Penguin, 2003).

9. Editors, *Columbian Cyclopedia* (Buffalo, NY: Garretson, Cox & Company, 1897).

10. Patience Gray, *Honey from a Weed: Fasting and Feasting in Tuscany, Catalonia, the Cyclades and Apulia* (New York: Harper & Row, 1987), 42–51.

11. James Beard, *Menus for Entertaining* (New York: Marlowe & Company, 1965, revised edition 1997). M. F. K. Fisher, "The Pleasures of Picnics [1957]," in *A Stew or a Story: An Assortment of Short Works by M. F. K. Fisher*, edited by Joan Reardon (Emeryville, CA: Shoemaker & Hoard, 2006), 200.

12. Jeremy Black, "The New Year Ceremonies in Ancient Babylon: 'Taking Bel by the Hand' and a Cultic Picnic," *Religion* 11 (1981): 39–59.

13. Menander, *The Bad-Tempered Man*, in *Menander: The Plays and Fragments*, translated by Maurice Balme (New York: Oxford University Press, 2001), ll. 445–48.

14. Katherine M. D. Dunbabin, *The Roman Banquet: Images of Conviviality* (Cambridge: Cambridge University Press, 2003). Also Paul Zanker and Björn C. Wald, *Living with Myths: The Imagery of Roman Sarcophagi* (New York: Oxford University Press, 2013).

15. Ovid, *Fasti*, edited by James George Frazer (Cambridge, MA, and London: Loeb Classical Library, Harvard University Press, and William Heinemann Ltd., 1931), http://www.archive.org/stream/ovidsfasti00oviduoft/ovidsfasti00oviduoft_djvu.txt.

16. John Thurloe, *A Collection of the State Papers of John Thurloe*, edited by Thomas Birch (London: F. Gyles, 1654, 1742, vol. 2, 652). Thomas Carlyle, *Oliver Cromwell's Letters and Speeches: Including the Supplement to the First Edition; with Elucidations*, volume 2 (New York: Harper & Brothers, 1868), 130.

17. Osbert Sitwell, "Picnics and Pavilions." In *Sing High! Sing Low!* (London: Macmillan, 1944), 142.

18. John Anthony, "Pic-Nics," *Notes and Queries* 7, no. 181 (1853): 388, http://archive.org/stream/notesandqueriesn21445gut/pg21445.txt.

19. Jean-Antoine Watteau, *The Collation [Imbiss Im Freien]* (ca. 1721), oil on canvas. Winterthur, Germany: The Oskar Reinhart Collection "Am Römerholz," http://www.roemerholz.ch.

20. Jean-Antoine Watteau, *The Halt during the Chase [Rendezvous De Chasse]*. London: The Wallace Collection, ca. 1717–1720, http://wallacelive.wallacecollection.org/eMuseumPlus?service=ExternalInterface &module=collection&objectId=65350.

21. Robert Darnton, *Poetry and the Police: Communication Networks in Eighteenth-Century Paris* (Cambridge, MA: Harvard University Press, 2010), 180.

22. Jean-Jacques Rousseau, "Livre VII," *Les Confessions* (1789), http://athena.unige.ch/athena/rousseau/confessions/rousseau_confessions_00.html. Gutenberg translation uses the expression *tête-à-tête*, http://www.gutenberg.org/files/3913/3913-h/3913-h.htm; J. M. Cohen uses *Dutch treat*. Jean-Jacques Rousseau, Book 11, *The Confessions*, translated by J. M. Cohen (Baltimore, MD: Penguin Books, 1954), 324.

23. Jean-Jacques Rousseau, Book IV, "Lunch with De Warens at Montagnole," in *The Confessions* (1781). French text is http://athena.unige.ch/athena/rousseau/confessions/rousseau_confessions_00.html.

24. Jean-Jacques Rousseau, Book IV, "Lunch with De Graffenried and Galley," in *The Confessions* (1781), http://www.gutenberg.org/files/3913/3913-h/3913-h.htm.

25. Jean-Jacques Rousseau, Book VI, in *The Confessions*, translated by J. M. Cohen, 535. Date is June 8, 1762.

26. Rousseau, *Confessions*, http://athena.unige.ch/athena/rousseau/confessions/rousseau_confessions.html.

27. Rebecca Spang, "Rousseau in the Restaurant," in *The Invention of the Restaurant: Paris and Modern Gastronomic Culture* (Cambridge, MA: Harvard University Press, 2000), 61.

28. Philip Dormer Stanhope, "Letter, October 29, 1748," in *The Letters of Philip Dormer Stanhope, Earl of Chesterfield with the Characters* [1773–1774], edited by John

Bradshaw (London: George Allen & Unwin Ltd.), http://www.gutenberg.org/cache/epub/3352/pg3352.html.

29. Mary Coke, "Letter to Lady Strafford 23 September 1763," in *Letters and Journals of Lady Mary Coke*, edited by J. A. Home, 7 (Edinburgh, 1763). Reprint Bath, UK: Kingsmead, 1970, 7.

30. Samuel Foote, *The Nabob: A Comedy in Three Acts* (London, 1772), Act I, scene 2.

31. Ellis Cornelia Knight, "February 10, 1777," in *Autobiography of Miss Cornelia Knight, Lady Companion to the Princess Charlotte of Wales with Extracts from Her Journals and Anecdote Books*, volume 2, edited by J. W. Kaye (London, W. H. Allen, 1861), 45.

32. William Combe, *The Pic Nic* 1 (January 8, 1803)–14 (April 9, 1803) (London: R. Exton for J. F. Hughes, 1803).

33. James Gillray, "Blowing Up the Pic-Nics: – or – Harlequin Quixote attacking the Puppets," 1802. See James Gillray, *The Works of James Gillray, the Caricaturist: With the Story of His Life and Times*, edited by Joseph Grego (London: Chatto & Windus, 1873), http://www.npgprints.com/image/32334/james-gillray-hannah-humphrey-blowing-up-the-pic-nics-or-harlequin-quixotte-attacking-the-puppets.

34. John Keats, "Letter to George Keats 18 December 1818, No. 137," in *Letters of John Keats*, edited by Robert Gittings (New York: Oxford University Press, 1970), http://www.gutenberg.org/files/35698/35698-h/35698-h.htm#Page_187.

35. Dorothy Wordsworth, "Excursion Up Scawfell Pike, October 7th, 1818," in *Journals of Dorothy Wordsworth*, edited by Ernest de Selincourt (London: Macmillan & Co. Ltd., Reprint, 1952), 427–28.

36. Charles Dickens, "A Jaunt to the Looking-Glass Prairie and Back," in *American Notes for General Circulation* (London, 1842), edited by John S. Whitley and Arnold Goldman (New York: Penguin, 1972), 220–28, http://www.gutenberg.org/files/675/675-h/675-h.htm.

37. William Wordsworth, Book IX, "Discourse of the Wanderer, and an Evening Visit to the Lake," in *The Excursion* (London, 1814), ll. 416–678. See Andrew Hubbell, "How Wordsworth Invented Picnicking and Saved British Culture," *Romanticism* 1 (2006): 44–51.

38. Bharat Tandon, ed., *Jane Austen*, Emma: *An Annotated Edition* (Cambridge, MA: Belknap Press of Harvard University Press, 2012), volume 3, chapter 6.

39. Jimmy Kennedy and John Walter Bratton, "The Teddy Bears' Picnic," 1907, 1932. Kennedy wrote the lyrics; Bratton composed the music.

40. Washington Irving, *Salmagundi; or, the Whim-Whams and Opinions of Launcelot Langstaff, Esq., and Others* (1808), in *The Complete Works of Washington Irving*, volume 6, edited by Bruce Granger and Martha Hartzog (New York: Twayne, 1977). Date is February 13, 1807.

41. James Fenimore Cooper, *The Pioneers* [1823], edited by James Franklin Beard, Lance Schachterle, and Kenneth M. Andersen (Albany, NY: State University of New York Press, 1980), 178, http://www.gutenberg.org/files/2275/2275-h/2275-h.htm.

42. James Fenimore Cooper, *Home as Found*, in *The Complete Works of James Fenimore Cooper* (New York: G. P. Putnam's Sons, 1838), 293, http://www.gutenberg.org/files/10149/10149-h/10149-h.htm.

43. "Picnic Excursions," *Appleton's Journal of Popular Literature, Science, and Art* 1, no. 20 (August 14, 1869): 625, http://quod.lib.umich.edu/cgi/t/text/text-idx?c=moa jrnl&idno=acw8433.1-01.020.

44. Winslow Homer, *The Picnic Excursion*, *Appleton's Journal of Popular Literature, Science, and Art* (August 14, 1869): 624, http://americanart.si.edu/collections/search/artwork/?id=37081.

45. Sitwell, "Picnics and Pavilions," 143.

46. Georgina Battiscombe, *English Picnics* (London: Harvill Press Limited, 1949), 3.

CHAPTER 2

1. Laurie Colwin, "Picnics," in *More Home Cooking: A Writer Returns to the Kitchen* (New York: HarperCollins, 1993), 114–22.

2. Bruce Kraig, *Hot Dog: A Global History* (London: Reaktion Books, 2009).

3. Felix Belair Jr., "King Tries Hot Dog and Asks for More and He Drinks Beer with Them," *New York Times*, June 12, 1939. Also http://www.fdrlibrary.marist.edu/aboutfdr/royalvisit.html, and Will Swift, *The Roosevelts and the Royals: Franklin and Eleanor, the King and Queen of England, and the Friendship That Changed History* (Hoboken, NJ: John Wiley & Sons, Inc., 2004), 143–44. The day is all but ignored by the White House chef and housekeeper; Nesbitt, Henrietta. *White House Diary*. Garden City, NY: Doubleday & Co., 1948.

4. James Beard, *Cook It Outdoors* (New York: M. Barrows and Company, Inc., 1941), 185–86.

5. Alice Waters, *Chez Panisse Menu Cookbook*, in collaboration with Linda P. Guenzel, recipes edited by Carolyn Dille, and designed and illustrated by David Lance Gaines (New York: Random House, 1982).

6. Isabella Beeton, "Bill of Fare for a Picnic of 40 Persons," In *Mrs. Beeton's Book of Household Management* (London: S. O. Beeton, 1859–1861), 960, items 2149–2152, http://www.gutenberg.org/cache/epub/10136/pg10136.html.

7. Madhur Jaffrey, "Thirteen: Family Picnics in Delhi," in *Climbing the Mango Trees: A Memoir* (New York: Alfred A. Knopf, 2005).

8. Krishnendu Ray, "Memories of a Bengali Picnic," 2008, personal communication.

9. See Shizuo Tsuji, *Japanese Cooking: A Simple Art, 25th Anniversary Edition* (New York: Kodansha USA, 2012).

10. Barbara Banks, "A Tibetan Picnic," in *Travelers' Tales, Tibet: True Stories*, edited by James O'Reilly and Larry Habegger (Berkeley, CA: Publishers Group West, 2003), 3–6.

11. Eric Newby, *Love and War in the Apennines* (London: HarperCollins Publishers Ltd., 1971).

12. Nadine Gordimer, *The Lying Days* (New York: Simon & Schuster, 1953).

13. Peter Mayle, "Passing 50 without Breaking the Speed Limit," in *Toujours Province* (London: Hamish Hamilton, 1991), 37–45.

14. Claudia Roden, *Everything Tastes Better Outdoors*, illustrated by Alta Ann Parkins (New York: Alfred A. Knopf, 1984), 167–68.

15. Norma Jean Darden and Carole Darden, "Fourth-of-July Picnic, Weekend Concoctions, and Old-Time Favorites, Told by "Bud"–Walter T. Darden," in *Spoonbread & Strawberry Wine: Recipes and Reminiscences of a Family* (New York: Doubleday, 1994), 148–68.

16. Robert Lewis Taylor, *W. C. Fields: His Follies and Fortunes* (Garden City: Doubleday, 1949), 282–83.

17. Ford Madox Ford, "Banquet at Calanques," in *Provence: From Minstrels to the Machine* (New York: Ecco Press, 1979), 885–89.

18. James Beard, *Menus for Entertaining* (New York: Marlowe & Company, revised edition 1997), 272.

19. M. F. K. Fisher, "The First Oyster [1924]," in *The Gastronomical Me* (New York: Macmillan, 1943; New York: North Point Press, 1989), 23.

20. M. F. K. Fisher, "The Pleasures of Picnics [1957]," in *A Stew or a Story: An Assortment of Short Works by M. F. K. Fisher*, edited by Joan Reardon (Emeryville, CA: Shoemaker & Hoard 2006, 198–207).

21. Jean Anthelme Brillat-Savarin, *The Physiology of Taste, or Meditations on Transcendental Gastronomy* [1825], translated by Fayette Robinson, http://www.gutenberg.org/cache/epub/5434/pg5434.html.

22. Constance Spry and Rosemary Hume, *The Constance Spry Cookery Book* (London: J. M. Dent & Sons, 1957).

23. Craig Claiborne, *Craig Claiborne's a Feast Made for Laughter* (New York: Holt, Rinehart and Winston, 1982), 174–83. See *Life*, "Magnificent Pique-Nique: Five Celebrated Chefs on a Cookout," August 27, 1965, volume 59, number 9. Photographs by Mark Kauffman.

24. Nika Hazelton, *The Picnic Book* (New York: Atheneum, 1969), vii.

25. Hazelton, *Picnic Book*, 84.

26. Mrs. C. F. Leyel, *Picnics for Motorists* (London: G. Routledge & Sons, 1936). Also, Mrs. C. F. Leyel and Miss Olga Hartley, *The Gentle Art of Cookery* (London: Chatto & Windus/The Hogarth Press, 1925; 1983).

27. Osbert Sitwell, "Picnics and Pavilions," in *Sing High! Sing Low!* (London: Macmillan, 1944), 142–63.

28. William B. Jerrold, "Picnic Reform," in *The Epicure's Year Book for 1869* (London, 1869).

29. Joan Hemingway and Connie Maricich, *The Picnic Gourmet: Over 300 Delectable Dishes for Every Kind of Picnic Meal—from Simple Backpacking Hikes to Elegant Basket Lunches* (New York: Random House, 1975).

30. Elizabeth David, *Summer Cooking*, enlarged 1965 edition (London: Penguin, 1955), 209.

31. Elizabeth David, *A Book of Mediterranean Food* (New York: New York Review of Books, 1950; 2002), 153–54.

32. Edna Lewis, "Sunday Revival Dinner," in *A Taste of Country Cooking* (New York: Random House, 1976), 119.

33. Linda Hull Larned, *One Hundred Picnic Suggestions* (New York: Charles Scribner's & Sons, 1915), http://www.loc.gov/exhibits/treasures/trr118.html.

34. Agnes Jekyll, *Kitchen Essays* (London: Persephone Books, 1922), 2008. See "A Winter-Shooting Party Luncheon," 109–16, "Luncheon for a Motor Excursion in Winter," 117–23, and "Food for Travellers," 177–85.

35. Bee Wilson, *Sandwich: A Global History* (London: Reaktion Books, 2011).

36. Alan Davidson and Tom Jaine, "Sandwich," in *The Oxford Companion to Food* (New York: Oxford University Press, 1999; 2006).

37. Fisher, "The Pleasures of Picnics," 203.

38. Ernest Matthew Mickler, *White Trash Cooking* (Berkeley, CA: Ten Speed Press, 1986).

39. Ernest Hemingway, *Islands in the Stream* (New York: Scribner's, 1971). Also Ernest Hemingway, "Big Two-Hearted River, Part 2," in *In Our Time* (New York: Boni & Liveright, 1925). A. E. Hotchner, *Papa Hemingway: A Personal Memoir* (New York: De Capo Press, 1955).

40. Laurie Colwin, "Picnics," in *More Home Cooking: A Writer Returns to the Kitchen* (New York: HarperCollins, 1993), 114–22.

41. Laura Shaine Cunningham, *A Place in the Country* (New York: Riverside Books, 2001), 20–25.

42. Edward Gibbon, "November 24, 1762," in *Memoirs of My Life and Writings—Miscellaneous Works: The Journals of Edward Gibbon, 1762–1764*, edited by John Baker Holroyd (London, 1796), http://www.gutenberg.org/files/6031/6031-h/6031-h.htm; and Pierre-Jean Grosley, *A Tour to London: Or, New Observations on England and Its Inhabitants* (1770), translated by Thomas Nugent (London: Exshaw, Williams, Moncrieffe, and Jenkin, 1772).

43. Bernard Clermont, *The Professed Cook, or the Modern Art of Cookery, Pastry, & Confectionary Made Plain and Easy*, tenth edition (London, 1812). Based on Menon, *The Professed Cook; or, the Modern Art of Cookery, Pastry, & Confectionary, Made Plain and Easy: Consisting of the Most Approved Methods in the French, as Well as English Cookery . . . With the Addition of the Best Receipts, Which Have Ever Appeared in the French or English Languages*, translated by Bernard Clermont (London: C. Richards, 1769), http://books.google.com/books?id=LpMEAAAAYAAJ&pg=PA37&dq=intitle:art+intitle:of+intitle:confectionary+date:1700-1880&lr=&as_brr=1&output=html_text#PA37.

44. Mary Montagu, *Elizabeth Montagu, the Queen of the Blue-Stockings: Her Correspondence from 1720–1761*, volume 2, edited by Emily J. Climenson (London: J. Murray, 1906), 12.

45. Edward Spencer, *Cakes & Ale: A Memory of Many Meals, the Whole Interspersed with Various Recipes, More or Less Original, and Anecdotes, Mainly Veracious* (London: G. Richards, 1897), 53, http://babel.hathitrust.org/cgi/pt?id=nyp.33433006644474;se q=9;view=1up;num=iii.

46. Judith Martin, *Miss Manners' Guide to Excruciatingly Correct Behavior* (New York: W. W. Norton, 2005), 172.

47. Frances Milton Trollope, *Domestic Manners of the Americans* (1832), edited by Donald Smalley (New York: Alfred A. Knopf, 1949).

48. Alice B. Toklas, *The Alice B. Toklas Cook Book* (London: Serif, 1954; 2004), 77–78.

49. Judith Martin, *Miss Manners'*, 172. Hemingway and Maricich, *The Picnic Gourmet*.

CHAPTER 3

1. Austin Dobson, ed., *Complete Poetical Works of Oliver Goldsmith* (London: Henry Frowde, 1906), 87, http://archive.org/stream/cihm_79307#page/n157/ mode/2up/search/retaliation.

2. *The Letters of Philip Dormer Stanhope, Earl of Chesterfield*, http://babel.hathitrust.org/cgi/pt?id=miun.acr9672.0001.001;seq=1;view=1up.

3. Thomas Wright, *A History of Domestic Manners and Sentiments in England during the Middle Ages* (London: Chapman & Hall, 1862), 493.

4. Wright, *A History of Domestic Manners*, 438.

5. Scott McKendrick, "Reviving the Past: Illustrated Manuscripts of Secular Vernacular Texts, 1476–1500," in *Illuminating the Renaissance: The Triumph of Flemish Manuscript Painting in Europe*, edited by Scot McKendrick and Thomas Kren (Los Angeles: The John Paul Getty Museum, 2003), 74.

6. Rebecca L. Spang, *The Invention of the Restaurant: Paris and Modern Gastronomic Culture* (Cambridge, MA: Harvard University Press, 2002), 61.

7. George Sand, *Histoire De Ma Vie*, volume 4, edited by Calman Levy (Paris: Michel Levy Freres, 1879), 334–35.

8. Émile Zola, chapter 3, *L'Assommoir*, translated by Ernest Alfred Vizetelly (London: 1877), www.gutenberg.org/files/8558/8558-h/8558-h.htm.

9. William Combe, "February 26, 1803," *The Pic Nic*, volume 3, http://books.google.com/books?id=AsIPAAAAQAAJ&printsec=frontcover&dq=william+combe+the+pic+nic&hl=en&sa=X&ei=AL9NUvWZJ5Ly9gSDuoCwAw&ved=0CC8Q6AEw AA#v=onepage&q=william%20combe%20the%20pic%20nic&f=false.

10. "Pic-Nic Suppers," *The Times*, March 26, 1802, 3, http://newspaperarchive.com/flashviewer/seofullviewer?img=7196212&sterms=.

11. Henry Angelo, *Reminiscences of Henry Angelo* (London: H. Colburn and R. Bentley, 1830), 223–29, http://archive.org/stream/reminiscenceshe00angegoog#page/n6/mode/2up.

12. James Gillray, "Blowing up the Pic Nics; – or – Harlequin Quixote attacking the Puppets," 1802, see figure 1.1.

13. Mary Belson Elliot, *The Mice, and Their Pic Nic: A Good Moral Tale* (London: W. and T. Darnton, 1809).

14. Maria Edgeworth, *The Absentee*, 1812, http://www.gutenberg.org/files/1473/1473-h/1473-h.htm.

15. Bharat Tandon, ed., *Jane Austen*, Emma: *An Annotated Edition* (Cambridge, MA: Belknap Press of Harvard University Press, 2012), 402–3.

16. Anna Laetitia Barbauld, *A Legacy for Young Ladies; Consisting of Miscellaneous Pieces, in Prose and Verse*, edited by Anna Aikin (London, 1826), http://textbase.wwp.brown.edu/WWO/php/wAll.php?doc=barbauld.legacy.html.

17. Charles Dickens, *The Mystery of Edwin Drood* (London: Chapman & Hall, 1870), http://www.gutenberg.org/files/564/564-h/564-h.htm.

18. "A Capital Idea for Rainy Weather in Winter—Make Believe That the Drawing Room Is a Shady Spot in the Woods and Give a Picnic in It," *Harper's*, December 1858.

19. G. K. Chesterton, "The Wildness of Domesticity," in *What's Wrong with the World* (New York: Dodd, Mead and Co., 1910), 49; http://www.gutenberg.org/files/1717/1717-h/1717-h.htm.

20. Margaret Mitchell, chapter 1, part 1," *Gone with the Wind* (Macmillan: New York, 1936), 1, http://gutenberg.net.au/ebooks02/0200161h.html.

21. Augustus Leopold Egg, *Travelling Companions* 1862, oil on canvas. Birmingham, England: City Museums and Art Gallery of Birmingham, http://www.bmagic.org.uk/objects/1956P7.

22. D. H. Lawrence, *Aaron's Rod*, 1922, http://www.gutenberg.org/files/4520/4520-h/4520-h.htm.

23. Constance Spry and Rosemary Hume, *The Constance Spry Cookery Book* (London: J. M. Dent & Sons, 1957), 1076.

24. Jacob Lawrence, *Panel no. 45, The Migrants Arrived in Pittsburgh, One of the Great Industrial Centers of the North, The Migration Series*, Washington, DC: The Phillips Collection, 1941, http://www.phillipscollection.org/collection/browse-the-collection/index.aspx?id=1174.

25. Paul Theroux, *O-Zone* (New York: G. P. Putnam's Sons, 1986), 46.

26. NASA, *Composite Air-to-Ground and Onboard Voice Tape Transcription of the GT-3 Mission*, 1965, http://www.jsc.nasa.gov/history/mission_trans/GT03_TEC.PDF.

CHAPTER 4

1. James Beard, *Cook It Outdoors* (New York: M. Barrows and Company, Inc., 1941); Yvonne Young Tarr, *The Complete Outdoor Cookbook* (New York: Quadrangle Books / The New York Times, 1973); Claudia Roden, *Picnic: The Complete Guide to Outdoor Food*, volume illustrated by Linda Kitson (London: Jill Norman, 1981).

2. John Harris, *The Courtship, Merry Marriage, and Pic-Nic Dinner of Cock Robin and Jenny Wren*, volume 2 (London: J. Harris, 1806), see www.library.uiuc.edu/edx/earlyeng.htm for 1806 by Darton==SE.D349FACSIM.

3. John Thurloe, *A Collection of the State Papers of John Thurloe*, volume 2, edited by Thomas Birch (London: F. Gyles, 1654; 1742), 652, http://india.british-history.ac.uk/image-pageScan.aspx?pubid=610&sp=1&pg=652.

4. Samuel Pepys, *Diaries of Samuel Pepys*, 11 volumes, edited by Robert Latham and William Matthews (Oxford: Oxford University Press, 1970–1983). See http://www.pepysdiary.com/diary/1664/06/26/.

5. Dorothy Wordsworth, "Letter to Mrs. Clarkson (Catherine), August 3, 1808," in *Letters of the Wordsworth Family from 1787–1855*, volume 1, edited by William Knight (New York: Ginn and Co., 1907), 369, http://books.google.com/books?id=8AE lAAAAMAAJ&q=picnic#v=snippet&q=picnic&f=false.

6. M. F. K. Fisher, "The Pleasures of Picnics [1957]," in *A Stew or a Story: An Assortment of Short Works by M. F. K. Fisher*, edited by Joan Reardon (Emeryville, CA: Shoemaker & Hoard, 2006), 199.

7. Laurie Colwin, "How to Avoid Grilling," in *Home Cooking: A Writer in the Kitchen* (Harper Perennial, 1988; 1993), 101.

8. Colwin, "How to Avoid Grilling," 101.

9. Laurie Colwin, "Picnics," in *More Home Cooking: A Writer Returns to the Kitchen* (New York: HarperCollins, 1993), 116.

10. Georgina Battiscombe, *English Picnics* (London: The Harvill Press Limited, 1949), 3.

11. Ray Bradbury, "The Million-Year Picnic," in *The Martian Chronicles* (Garden City: Doubleday & Company, Inc., 1958).

12. NASA, *Composite Air-to-Ground and Onboard, Voice Tape Transcription of the GT-3 Mission*, 1965, http://www.jsc.nasa.gov/history/mission_trans/GT03_TEC.PDF.

13. Jean-Baptiste Charcot, *Le Pourquoi-pas? Dans L'Antarctique 1908–1910* (Paris: Ernest Flammarion, 1910), http://books.google.com/books?id=g1ugAAAAMAAJ&p rintsec=frontcover&dq=peary+the+north+pole&hl=en&sa=X&ei=JnFcUanwJMXw0 gHWoIGwCw&ved=0CDcQ6AEwAQ#v=onepage&q=picnicking&f=falseand www.south-pole.com/p0000095.htm.

14. Robert E. Peary, *The North Pole* (New York: Frederick Stokes & Co., 1910), 262.

15. David K. Shipler, *Russia: Broken Idols, Solemn Dreams* (New York: Viking, 1983), 188.

16. Gertrude Bell, "August 21, 1921," *Gertrude Bell Archive* (Newcastle, England: Newcastle University Library, 1921), http://www.gerty.ncl.ac.uk/.

17. Agatha Christie Mallowan, *Come, Tell Me How You Live* [1985] (New York: Bantam Books, 1999), 14. Christie's married name is Mallowan.

18. Charles Dickens, *Letters of Charles Dickens 1847–1849*, volume 5, edited by Graham Storey and Kenneth Fielding (Oxford: Clarendon Press, 1981), 588.

19. Nathaniel Hawthorne, *The American Note-Books*, edited by Claude M. Simpson (Columbus: Ohio State University Press, 1972), 295. The picnic climb was August 5, 1850. http://www.gutenberg.org/files/8089/8089-h/8089-h.htm.

20. Beard, *Cook It Outdoors*, 13, 15.

21. Beard, *Cook It Outdoors*, 183.

22. James Beard, *Menus for Entertaining* [1965] (New York: Marlowe & Company, 1997), 272.

23. Mrs. C. F. Leyel, "Preface," *Picnics for Motorists* (London: G. Routledge & Sons, 1936).

24. Alice B. Toklas, *The Alice B. Toklas Cook Book* [1954] (London: Serif, 2004), 77–78.

25. Elizabeth David, "The Markets of France: Valence," in *An Omelette and a Glass of Wine* [1984], edited by John Thorne (New York: The Lyons Press, 1997), 271.

26. Elizabeth David, *Summer Cooking*, enlarged 1965 edition (London: Penguin, 1955), 208.

27. Alice Waters, *Chez Panisse Menu Cookbook*, in collaboration with Linda P. Guenzel, recipes edited by Carolyn Dille, and designed and illustrated by David Lance Gaines (New York: Random House, 1982).

28. Nika Hazelton, *The Picnic Book* (New York: Atheneum, 1969), vii.

29. Claudia Roden, "A Middle Eastern Affair," in *Everything Tastes Better Outdoors* (New York: Alfred A. Knopf, 1984), 167–70.

30. Roden, *Everything Tastes Better Outdoors*, 3.

31. Logan Pearsall Smith, "The Ideal," in *All Trivia: Trivia, More Trivia, Afterthoughts, Last Words* (New York: Harcourt, Brace and Company, 1920), 142, http://www.gutenberg.ca/ebooks/smithlp-alltrivia/smithlp-alltrivia-00-h.html.

32. Princess Margaret, "Picnic at Hampton Court," in *Picnic Papers*, edited by Susanna Johnston and Anne Tennant (London: Hutchinson, 1983), 132–33.

33. Deborah M. Gordon, *Ants at Work* (New York: Simon & Schuster, 1999), 46.

CHAPTER 5

1. Elizabeth Bowen, "Out of a Book (1946)," in *Collected Impressions* (New York: Alfred A. Knopf, 1950), 265.

2. Pablo Picasso and Carl Nesjar, *Luncheon on the Grass* (1964–1966), sandblasted concrete. Stockholm, Sweden: Museum of Modern Art, Stockholm.

3. Alfred Tennyson, "Audley Court," in *English Idylls and Other Poems*, London, 1842, ll. 1–3. See *The Poems of Tennyson 1830–1865* (London: Cassell & Co., 1907), http://books.google.com/books?id=LG81AAAAMAAJ&dq=poems+of+tennyson&source=gbs_navlinks_s.

4. Gustave Flaubert, *The Letters of Gustave Flaubert: 1830–1857*, translated by Francis Steegmuller (Cambridge, MA: Harvard University Press, 1980), 195.

5. William S. Gilbert and Arthur Sullivan, *Thespis or the Gods Grown Old* [1871], in *Complete Annotated Plays of Gilbert and Sullivan*, edited by Ian Bradley (New York: Oxford University Press, 2005). See http://math.boisestate.edu/gas/thespis/html/index .htm.

6. Anthony Trollope, chapter 9, "Miss Todd's Picnic," *The Bertrams*, volume 1 (London: Chapman & Hall, 1858), http://www.gutenberg.org/files/26001/26001-h/26001-h.htm.

7. Margaret Mitchell, part 1, chapter 1, *Gone with the Wind* (Macmillan: New York, 1936), http://gutenberg.net.au/ebooks02/0200161h.html; the film adaptation of *Gone with the Wind* is directed by Victor Fleming, screenplay by Sidney Howard, and produced by David O. Selznick.

8. Barbara Kingsolver, *The Poisonwood Bible: A Novel* (New York: HarperCollins, 1998), 49.

9. Calvin Trillin, "Fly Frills to Miami," in *Alice, Let's Eat* (New York: Smithmark Publisher's, 1978), 30, 49–58.

10. Philip K. Dick, chapter 12, *Eye in the Sky* (New York: Collier Books, 1957).

11. Marcel Proust, part two, "Place Names: The Place," *Within a Budding Grove* [1919], translated by C. K. Scott Moncrieff, revised by D. J. Enright (New York: Modern Library, 2003), 661, http://gutenberg.net.au/ebooks03/0300401.txt.

12. Stephen Crane, "Shame," in *Whilomville Stories*, illustrated by Peter Newell, 1900, http://www.gutenberg.org/files/39644/39644-h/39644-h.htm.

13. Miguel de Cervantes, chapter L, "The Shrewd Controversy which Don Quixote and the Canon Held, Together with Other Incidents," *Don Quixote de la Mancha* [1605–1610], translated by Edith Grossman (New York: Ecco, 2003), http://www.gutenberg.org/files/2000/2000-h/2000-h.htm.

14. Mary Elizabeth Braddon, chapter 3, "Half in Sea, and Half on Land," *Mount Royal: A Novel*, 1883, http://archive.org/stream/mountroyalnovel01brad#page/n3/mode/2up.

15. Frederick Ashton, *Picnic at Tintagel*, 1952. Music is Arnold Bax's *The Garden of Fand* (1916). First performed by the New York City Ballet, New York. George Platt Lynes, *Picnic at Tintagel* (Cambridge, MA: Houghton Library, Harvard College Library, Harvard University, 1952).

16. Francisco de Goya, *The Picnic at the Edge of the Manzanares River* [*La merienda a orillas del Manzanares*], oil on canvas (Madrid: Museo del Prado), http://www.museo-delprado.es/en/the-collection/online-gallery/on-line-gallery/obra/picnic-on-the-banks-of-the-manzanares/.

17. Charles Dickens, chapter 19, "A Pleasant Day with an Unpleasant Termination," in *The Posthumous Papers of the Pickwick Club* (London: Chapman & Hall, 1837), http://www.gutenberg.org/files/580/580-h/580-h.htm.

18. Thomas Cole, *The Pic-Nic Party* (1846), oil on canvas. New York: Brooklyn Museum of Art, http://www.brooklynmuseum.org/opencollection/objects/1356/The_Pic-Nic; Henri Cartier-Bresson, *Sunday on the Banks of the Marne*, New York: Magnum Photo-

graphs, 1938, http://www.magnumphotos.com/C.aspx?VP3=SearchResult&ALID=2TY
RYD1D518O.

19. Louis Legrand Noble, *The Life and Works of Thomas Cole* [1853], edited by
Elliot S. Vessell (Cambridge, MA: Belknap Press of Harvard University, 1964), 201,
http://archive.org/details/lifeworksofthoma00nobl.

20. Attributed to Antonio Carracci, *Landscape with Bathers* (ca. 1616), oil on canvas. Boston: Museum of Fine Arts, http://www.mfa.org/collections/object/landscape-
with-bathers-32849.

21. Édouard Manet, *Luncheon on the Grass* (1863), oil on canvas. Paris: Musée
de Louvre, http://www.musee-orsay.fr/index.php?id=851&L=1&tx_commentaire_
pi1%5BshowUid%5D=7123.

22. Mary Elizabeth Braddon, chapter VII, "On the Bridge," in *The Doctor's
Wife* (London: John and Robert Maxwell, 1864), http://www.gutenberg.org/
files/35485/35485-h/35485-h.htm.

23. Claude, Luncheon on the Grass [Central Fragment]. 1865. Paris: Musée
d'Orsay..

24. Claire Joyes, *Monet's Table: The Cooking Journals of Claude Monet*, photographs
by Bernard Naudin (New York: Simon & Schuster, 1989), 67–69.

25. Lewis Carroll, "The Walrus and the Carpenter," in *Through the Looking-Glass
and What Alice Found There*, illustrated by John Tenniel (London: Macmillan, 1871),
http://www.gutenberg.org/files/12/12-h/12-h.htm.

26. Carroll, *Through the Looking-Glass.*

27. James Tissot, *Holyday*, oil on canvas. London: Tate Britain, 1876, http://www.
tate.org.uk/art/artworks/tissot-holyday-n04413/text-catalogue-entry.

28. Oscar Wilde, "The Grosvenor Gallery," in *Miscellanies by Oscar Wilde* (London:
Methuen & Co., 1877), http://www.gutenberg.org/files/14062/14062-h/14062-h.htm.

29. John Sloan, *South Beach Bathers* (1907–1908), oil on canvas. Minneapolis, MN:
Walker Art Center, http://www.walkerart.org/collections/artworks/south-beach-bathers.

30. Guy de Maupassant, "Boule de Suif," in *Original Short Stories*, edited by
A. E. Henderson, Albert M. C. McMaster et al., 1880, http://www.gutenberg.org/
files/3077/3077-h/3077-h.htm#link2H_4_0003.

31. William Styron, *Sophie's Choice* (New York: Random House, 1979), 90–91.

32. Maya Angelou, *I Know Why the Caged Bird Sings* (New York: Random House,
1969), 113–16.

33. Roark Bradford, *Ol' Man Adam an' His Chillun, Being the Tales They Tell
About the Time When the Lord Walked the Earth Like a Natural Man*, illustrated by
A. B. Walker (New York: Harper & Brothers Publishers, 1928); Marc Connelly, *The
Green Pastures: A Fable Suggested by Roark Bradford's Southern Sketches "Ol' Man
Adam an' His Chillun"* (New York: Farrar & Rinehart, 1930), www.musee-orsay.
fr/en/collections/index-of-works/resultat-collection.html?no_cache=1&zoom=1&tx_
damzoom_pi1%5Bzoom%5D=0&tx_damzoom_pi1%5BxmlId%5D=025651&tx_

damzoom_pi1%5Bback%5D=en%2Fcollections%2Findex-of-works%2Fresultat-collection.html%3Fno_cache%3D1%26zsz%3D9.

34. Alexander Pope, "Letter 159; To Martha Blount, August 11, 1734," *Alexander Pope: Selected Letters*, edited by Howard Erskine-Hill (New York: Oxford University Press, 2000), 254. Alexander Pope, "Letter to Martha Blount, 11 August 3-d," in G. S. Rousseau, "A New Pope Letter," *Philological Quarterly* 45 (1966): 409–18.

35. Walter Thornberry, *Life of J. M. W. Turner*, volume 1 (London: Hurst and Blacket, 1862), 216.

36. Thomas Rowlandson, *Richmond Bridge* (1808), pen and ink on paper. London: Museum of London, http://www.museumoflondonprints.com/image/139087/thomas-rowlandson-richmond-bridge-19th-century.

37. J. M. W. Turner, *Richmond Hill and Bridge, Surrey* (1828), watercolor on paper. London: Tate Britain, 1828, http://www.tate.org.uk/art/artworks/turner-richmond-hill-and-bridge-tw0426; http://www.tate.org.uk/art/artworks/turner-richmond-hill-and-bridge-surrey-t04582.

38. John Ruskin, *Notes by Mr. Ruskin on His Collection of Drawings by the Late J. M. W. Turner, R.A., Exhibited at the Fine Art Society's Galleries* (London: Fine Art Society, 1878), http://archive.org/stream/notesbymrruskin01socigoog/notesbymrruskin01socigoog_djvu.txt.

39. Thornberry, *Life of J. M. W. Turner*, volume 1, 206. Engravings by J. M. W. Turner, *Plymouth Dock Seen from Mount Edgecumbe, Devonshire* (1816), engraving on paper, engraved by W. B. Cook. London: Tate Britain, http://www.tate.org.uk/art/artworks/turner-plymouth-dock-seen-from-mount-edgecombe-devonshire-engraved-by-wb-cooke-t05972; and J. M. W. Turner, *Plymouth Devonshire [Mount Edgecumbe]*, (1832), engraving on paper, 1816, Engraved by W. J. Cooke. London: Tate Britain, http://www.tate.org.uk/art/artworks/turner-plymouth-devonshire-engraved-by-wj-cooke-t06095.

40. J. M. W. Turner, *England: Richmond Hill, on the Prince Regent's Birthday* (1819), oil on canvas. London: Tate Britain, http://www.tate.org.uk/art/artworks/turner-england-richmond-hill-on-the-prince-regents-birthday-n00502.

41. Claude Lorrain, *Landscape with Dancing*, aka *Landscape with the Marriage of Isaac and Rebecca* (1648), oil on canvas. London: National Gallery; Jean-Baptiste Camille Corot, *View Near Naples* (1841), oil on canvas. Springfield, MA: Museum of Fine Arts, www.nationalgallery.org.uk/paintings/claude-the-mill; www.wikipaintings.org/en/camille-corot/view-near-naples-1841.

42. J. M. W. Turner, *Melrose Abbey* (1833), watercolor on paper. Edinburgh: The National Gallery of Scotland, http://www.tate.org.uk/art/artworks/turner-melrose-tw0176; http://www.tate.org.uk/art/artworks/turner-melrose-t05142.

43. Philip Gilbert Hamerton, *The Life of J. M. W. Turner, R.A.* Boston: Roberts Brothers, 1879, 234, 232, 233.

44. Jane Austen, chapter 12, *Sense and Sensibility* [1811], edited by Claudia L. Johnson (New York: W. W. Norton & Co., 2002), http://www.gutenberg.org/files/161/161-h/161-h.htm.

45. Jane Austen, chapter 6, *Emma* (London: John Murray, 1816). See Bharat Tandon, ed., *Jane Austen, Emma: An Annotated Edition* (Cambridge, MA: Belknap Press of Harvard University Press, 2012), 397–417.

46. George Lambert, *A View of Box Hill, Surrey* (1733), oil on canvas. London: Tate Britain, http://www.tate.org.uk/art/artworks/lambert-a-view-of-box-hill-surrey-n05981.

47. Maggie Black and Deirdre Le Faye, *The Jane Austen Cookbook* (London: The British Museum Press, 1995); Maggie Lane, *Jane Austen and Food* (London: Hambledon Press, 1995).

48. Dorothy Wordsworth, "Excursion Up Scaw Fell Pike, October 7th, 1818," in *Journals of Dorothy Wordsworth*, edited by Ernest de Selincourt (London: Macmillan & Co., Ltd., 1952), 427–28, http://babel.hathitrust.org/cgi/pt?id=mdp.39015008506035;view=1up;seq=477.

49. Thomas Allom, *View from Langdale Pikes, Looking Towards Bowfell, Westmorland* (1832), steel engraving. In *Westmoreland, Cumberland, and Durham*, edited by Thomas Rose (London: Fisher, Son & Company), http://www.google.com/culturalinstitute/asset-viewer/views/fgG-VSPe9-5Ngg?hl=en.

50. Nathaniel P. Willis and William H. Bartlett, *View from Mount Holyoke* [Massachusetts], engraving, in *American Scenery, or Land, Lake, and River: Illustrations of Transatlantic Nature*, volume 1 (London: George Virtue, 1840), http://archive.org/stream/americanscenery01willrich#page/10/mode/2up/search/Holyoke.

51. Mary Shelley, "July 25, 1818," in *The Journals of Mary Shelley: 1814–1844*, volume 1, edited by Paula R. Feldman and Diana Scott-Kilvert (New York: Oxford University Press, 1987), 119.

52. Percy Shelley and Mary Shelley, "Letter IV: St. Martin-Servoz-Montanvert-Chamouni-Mont Blanc," in *History of a Six Weeks' Tour* (London: T. Hookham and C. and J. Ollier, 1817), 165, http://archive.org/details/sixweekhistoryof00shelrich.

53. Shelley, *Six Weeks' Tour*, 167.

54. Mary Shelley, *Frankenstein, or the Modern Prometheus*, volume 2 (London: Lackington, Hughes, Hading, Mavor & Jones, 1818), http://ebooks.adelaide.edu.au/s/shelley/mary/s53f/.

55. Carl Ludwig Hackert, *Vue de la mer de glace et l'hospital de blain du somet due montan vert dans le mois* (1781), hand-colored etching. Geneva: Centre d'Iconograhie, http://www.christies.com/lotFinder/lot_details.aspx?intObjectID=4765476.

56. Charles Dickens, chapter 13, "A Jaunt to the Looking-Glass Prairie and Back," in *American Notes for General Circulation* (London, 1842), 123–40.

57. Isabella Lucy Bird, "Niagara Falls," in *The Englishwoman in America* [1856], edited by Andrew Hill Clark (Toronto: University of Toronto Press, 1959), 218, www.gutenberg.org/cache/epub/7526/pg7526.html.

58. Anton Chekhov, *The Duel*, translated by Constance Garnett, 1891, http://www.gutenberg.org/cache/epub/13505/pg13505.html.

59. Anton Chekhov, "Letter to Alexei Suvorin May 28, 1892," in *Anton Chekhov's Life and Thought: Selected Letters and Commentary*, translated by Simon Karlinsky and Michael Henry Heim (Evanston, IL: Northwestern University Press, 1997), 2226.

60. Elizabeth von Arnim, *Elizabeth and Her German Garden* [1898] (London: Virago, 1985), 185, www.gutenberg.org/files/1327/1327-h/1327-h.htm.

61. E. M. Forster, "Caves," *A Passage to India* (London: Edward Arnold, 1924), see chapters 14–17, http://archive.org/stream/APassageToIndia_109/APassageTo India_djvu.txt.

62. Forster, *A Passage to India*, 161, 281.

63. Virginia Woolf, *The Voyage Out* (London: Duckworth, 1915), http://www.gutenberg.org/files/144/144-h/144-h.htm.

64. See Julian Pettifer and Nigel Turner, *Automania: Man and the Motor Car* (London: Collins, 1984).

65. Walt Disney, *The Picnic* (1930), http://images.google.com/imgres?imgurl=http://www.disneyshorts.org/years/1930/graphics/picnic/picnic1thumb.jpg&imgrefurl=http://www.disneyshorts.org/years/1930/picnic.html&usg=__bnjmwro8FRHXLo9RVN ZaRbd6fl4=&h=267&w=400&sz=48&hl=en&start=5&um=1&tbnid=bzAEVfIG vQYlZM:&tbnh=83&tbnw=124&prev=/images%3Fq%3Dmickey%2Bmouse%2B %2522picnic%2522%26hl%3Den%26client%3Dfirefox-a%26rls%3Dorg.mozilla: en-US:official%26sa%3DG%26um%3D1.

66. Grace Margaret Gould, "The Motor Picnic," *Motor: An Illustrated Monthly Magazine Devoted to Motoring* 5 (1905): 50.

67. James Beard, *Delights and Prejudices* (Philadelphia: Running Press Book Publishers, 1964; 2001), 238.

68. Linda Hull Larned, *One Hundred Picnic Suggestions* (New York: Charles Scribner's & Sons, 1915), http://archive.org/details/onehundredpicnic00larn.

69. Agnes Jekyll, *Kitchen Essays* [1922] (London: Persephone Books, 2008), 185.

70. Jowett Motors, "This Freedom," in Pettifer and Turner, *Automania*, 155.

71. Katherine Mansfield, "Letter to Anne Estelle Rice [Drey], March 1920," *The Collected Letters of Katherine Mansfield: 1919–1920*, volume 3, edited by Margaret Scott and Vincent O'Sullivan (London: Clarendon Press, 1984), 250.

72. Ford Motors, "Everyday without a Ford Means Lost Hours of Healthy Motoring Pleasure," [1925], Benson Ford Research Center, The Henry Ford Research.Center@ thehenryford.org.

73. May E. Southworth, *The Motorist's Luncheon Book* (New York: Harper Brothers, 1923), 1, http://catalog.hathitrust.org/Record/009116064; www.loc.gov/exhibits/treasures/images/vc132.jpg.

74. Mrs. C. F. Leyel, *Picnics for Motorists* (London: G. Routledge & Sons, 1936), 4.

75. Henry James, *English Hours*, illustrated by Joseph Pennell (London: Heinemann, 1905), 176. William Powell Frith, *The Derby Day* (1856), oil on canvas. London: Tate Britain, http://www.tate.org.uk/art/artworks/frith-the-derby-day-n00615.

76. John Madden and Peter Kaminsky, *John Madden's Ultimate Tailgating* (New York: Viking, 1998), 2.

77. Mario Batali, *Mario Tailgates NASCAR Style: The Essential Cookbook for NASCAR Fans* (St. Louis, MO: Sporting News, 2006), 12.

78. Gertrude Stein, "Letter to Carl Van Vechten, June 28, 1928," *The Letters of Gertrude Stein and Carl Van Vechten 1913–1946*, volume 1, edited by Edward Burns (New York: Columbia University Press, 1986), 165.

79. Alice Toklas, "Food to which Aunt Pauline and Lady Godiva Led Us," *The Alice B. Toklas Cook Book* (London: Serif, 1954; 2004), 57–94.

80. Ernest Hemingway, "Scott Fitzgerald," in *A Moveable Feast* (New York: Charles Scribner's Sons, 1964), 157.

81. Marion Post Wolcott, *Guests of Sarasota Trailer Park, Sarasota, Florida, Picnicking at the Beach with Their Family and Neighbor's Children*, January 1941, black/white negative film. Washington, DC: Library of Congress, http://loc.gov/pictures/item/fsa2000037488/.

82. Agatha Christie, "Picnic 1960," in *Poems* (New York: Dodd, Mead & Company, 1973), 124.

83. Paul Bowles and James Schuyler, *A Picnic Cantata: For Four Women's Voices, Two Pianos, and Percussion*, 1954, http://www.lib.udel.edu/ud/spec/findaids/hoyt.htm.

84. Marlia Mundell Mango, "The Sevso Treasure Hunting Plate," *Apollo Magazine* (July 1990): 2–13, 65–67.

85. Katherine M. D. Dunbabin, *The Roman Banquet: Images of Conviviality* (Cambridge: Cambridge University Press, 2003), 144–45.

86. Gaston Phébus III, *The Hunting Book of Gaston Phébus* [1389], edited by Marcel Thomas and Francis Avril, translated and commentary by Wilhelm Schlag (London: Harvey Miller Publishers, 1998); Gaston Phébus III, "Master of the Hunt Morgan Library Exhibition" (2008), www.themorgan.org/collections/swf/exhibOnline.asp?id=823; http://classes.bnf.fr/phebus/grandes/c38_616.htm.

87. Edward, Duke of York. *The Master of Game* [1406–1413], edited by William A. Baillie-Grohman and F. Baillie-Grohman (London: Chatto & Windus, 1909), http://www.archive.org/stream/masterofgameoldexx00edwa/masterofgameoldexx00edwa_djvu.txt; Jacques du Fouilloux, *La Venerie* (Rouen, 1561), http://www.archive.org/stream/laveneriedejacqu00foui#page/6/mode/thumbsee.

88. George Gascoigne, *The Noble Arte of Venerie or Hunting* (London: Imprinted by Henry Bynneman, for Christopher Barker, 1575). See Stephen Hamrick, "'Set in portraiture': George Gascoigne, Queen Elizabeth, and Adapting the Royal Image," *Early Modern Literary Studies* 11.1 (May 2005): 1.1–30, http://purl.oclc.org/emls/11-1/hamrgasc.htm. See George Turberville's issue, which he filched by signing his name to Gascoigne's text: http://archive.org/stream/turbervilesbook00turbgoog#page/n7/mode/2up.

89. Gillian Austen, *George Gascoigne* (Cambridge: D. S. Brewer, 2008), 106–10.

90. Jean-Antoine Watteau, *The Halt during the Chase*, aka *Rendezvous de Chasse* (1717–1720), oil on canvas. London: The Wallace Collection, www.wallacecollection.org/newsite/public/templates/tmpl_artwork.php?artworkid=338&openmenu=1_27_0

http://wallacelive.wallacecollection.org/eMuseumPlus?service=ExternalInterface&mod
ule=collection&objectId=65350&viewType=detailViewNote 95.

91. Francois Le Moyne, *Hunting Picnic*, aka *Déjeuner de chasse* (1723), oil on canvas. Alte Pinakothek, Munich; Nicolas Lancret, *The Picnic After the Hunt* (1735-1740), oil on canvas. Washington, DC: National Gallery of Art, http://www.nga.gov/fcgi-bin/ tinfo_f?object=41605; Jean-Francois de Troy, *A Hunt Breakfast*, aka *Un déjeuner de chasse* (1737), oil on canvas. Paris: Musée de Louvre, http://www.louvre.fr/en/ oeuvre-notices/hunt-breakfast; Charles Andre van Loo, *The Halt during the Hunt*, aka *Halte de chasse* (1735), oil on canvas. Paris: Musée de Louvre, http://commons.wiki-media.org/wiki/File:Charles_Andr%C3%A9_van_Loo_-_Halt_During_the_Hunt_-_WGA13429.jpg.

92. Charles Dickens, chapter XIX, "A Pleasant Day with an Unpleasant Termination," *The Posthumous Papers of the Pickwick Club* (London, 1837), http://www.gutenberg.org/files/580/580-h/580-h.htm.

93. Gustave Courbet, *Hunt Picnic*, aka *Le repas des chasse* (1858), oil on canvas. Cologne: Wallraf- Richartz-Museum, http://www.gettyimages.com/detail/news-photo/ the-hallali-by-gustave-courbet-cologne-wallraf-richartz-news-photo/148274417.

94. Jean Anthelme Brillat-Savarin, "Meditation 15, Haltes de Chasse," in *The Physiology of Taste, or Meditations on Transcendental Gastronomy*, translated by Fayette Robinson, http://www.gutenberg.org/cache/epub/5434/pg5434.html.

95. Robert Altman, *Gosford Park* (2001). Directed by Robert Altman. Screen-play by Julian Fellowes. Produced by Robert Altman, Bob Balaban, and David Levy; Brian Percival and Andy Goddard, "A Journey to the Highlands," Season 3, Episode 9, in *Downton Abbey*. Screenplay by Julian Fellowes, 2013, www/youtube.com/ watch?v=nYiSXUpJLEs.

96. John Harris, *The Courtship, Merry Marriage, and Pic-Nic Dinner of Cock Robin and Jenny Wren. To Which Is Added, Alas! The Doleful Death of the Bridegroom*, volume 2 (London: J. Harris, 1806), http://www.archive.org/details/happycourtshipme02londiala.

97. Mary Belson Elliot, *The Mice and Their Pic Nic: A Good Moral Tale, &c. by a Looking-Glass Maker* (London: W. and T. Darnton, 1809), 24.

98. Barbara Cooney, *The Courtship, Merry Marriage, and Feast of Cock Robin and Jenny Wren, to Which Is Added the Doleful Death of Cock Robin* (New York: Charles Scribner's Sons, 1965).

99. Elliot, "Further Disasters and General Muster," *The Mice and Their Pic Nic*, 24–26.

100. Aesop, "The City Mouse and the Country Mouse," in *Aesop's Fables*, edited and translated by Laura Gibbs (New York: Oxford University Press, 2002), http://myth-folklore.net/aesopica/perry/352.htm; Also, Horace tells the story in "Satires 1, Book 2, satire 6," in *The Complete Odes and Satires of Horace*, translated by Sidney Alexander (Princeton: Princeton University Press, 1999).

101. Walt Disney, *The Picnic*. Director. Burt Gillette: Columbia Pictures, 1930, http://www.youtube.com/watch?v=ZwdpO5YHEQo.

102. Kenneth Grahame, chapter 1, "The River Bank," *The Wind in the Willows* (London: Methuen and Company, 1908), http://www.gutenberg.org/files/289/289-h/289-h.htm.

103. Grahame, chapter 9, "Wayfarers All," http://www.gutenberg.org/files/289/289-h/289-h.htm.

104. Arabella Boxer, *The Wind in the Willows Country Cookbook: Inspired by* The Wind in the Willows *by Kenneth Grahame*, illustrated by Ernest H. Shepard (New York: Charles Scribner's Sons, 1983).

105. Virginia Ellison, *The Pooh Cook Book*, illustrated by Ernest H. Shepard (New York Dutton, 1969, 2010).

106. Lewis Carroll, chapter 7, "A Mad Tea-Party," *Alice's Adventures in Wonderland* (London: Macmillan, 1864), http://www.gutenberg.org/files/11/11-h/11-h.htm.

107. Lewis Carroll, "The Walrus and the Carpenter," in *Through the Looking-Glass and What Alice Found There*, illustrated by John Tenniel (London: Macmillan, 1871), http://www.gutenberg.org/files/12/12-h/12-h.htm.

108. Lewis Carroll, "Bruno's Picnic and the Little Foxes," in *Sylvie and Bruno Concluded*, illustrated by Harry Furness (London: Macmillan & Co., 1893). *Little Foxes* is an allusion to Song of Solomon, 2:15, http://www.hoboes.com/html/FireBlade/Carroll/Sylvie/Concluded/; for discussion see Marah Gubar, "Lewis in Wonderland: The Looking-Glass World of *Sylvie and Bruno*," *Texas Studies in Literature and Language* 48, no. 4 (2006): 372–94.

109. August Imholtz and Alison Tannenbaum, *Alice Eats Wonderland* (Carlisle, MA: Applewood Books, 2009).

110. Francis Hodgson Burnett, *The Secret Garden* (New York: Stokes, 1911).

111. Amy Colter, *The Secret Garden Cookbook: Recipes Inspired by Frances Hodgson Burnett's* The Secret Garden, illustrated by Prudence See (New York: HarperCollins, 1999).

112. Ian Fleming, *Chitty Chitty Bang Bang: The Magical Car*, illustrated by John Burningham (New York: Random House, Inc., 1964).

113. Laurent de Brunhoff, *Babar's Picnic*, translated by Merle Haas (New York: Random House, 1949).

114. Laurent de Brunhoff, *Babar Visits Another Planet* (New York: Harry N. Abrams, Inc., 1972).

115. Stella Austin, *Stumps, a Story for Children*, illustrated by W. H. C. Groome (London: Joseph Masters, 1873), www.archive.org/stream/stumps00austgoog/stumps00austgoog_djv.

116. Mark Twain, chapter 31, *The Adventures of Tom Sawyer* (Hartford, CT: American Publishing Co., 1876). See illustrations by True Williams, *The Adventures of Tom Sawyer* (Hartford, CT: The American Publishing Co., 1884), http://www.gutenberg.org/files/74/74-h/74-h.htm.

117. Edward Knapp, *What—No Spinach?* (Racine, WI: Western Publishing Company, 1981).

118. *Sesame Street*, "The King's Picnic," 1978, http://muppet.wikia.com/wiki/The_King's_Picnic.

119. James L. Brooks, Matt Groening, and Sam Simon, "The Simpsons: There Is No Disgrace Like Home," 1990, http://simpsons.wikia.com/wiki/There's_No_Disgrace_Like_Home.

120. Margaret Gordon, *Wilberforce Goes on a Picnic* (New York: William Morrow and Co., 1982).

121. Ronda Armitage and David Armitage, *The Lighthouse Keeper's Picnic* (New York: Scholastic Inc., 1993).

122. Pat Tornborg, *The Sesame Street Cookbook* (New York: Platt & Munk, 1978).

123. *Sesame Street "C" Is for Cooking* (New York: Houghton Mifflin Harcourt, 2009).

124. Linda White, *Cooking on a Stick: Campfire Recipes for Kids* (Layton, UT: Gibbs Smith, 1996).

125. Sunset, *Sunset Best Kids Cookbook* (Menlo Park, CA: Sunset Books, 1992).

126. *Winnie-the-Pooh's Teatime Cookbook, Inspired by A. A. Milne*, illustrated by Ernest H. Shepard (New York: Dutton Children's Books, 1993).

127. Jane Werner and the Walt Disney Studio, *Walt Disney's Mickey Mouse's Picnic*, illustrated by Walt Disney Studios (Racine, WI: Western Publishing Company, 1950).

128. Walt Disney Productions, *Walt Disney's Mickey Mouse Cookbook* (Racine, WI: A Golden Book/Western Publishing Company, Inc., 1975).

129. Walt Disney, *Walt Disney's Mickey Mouse Book*, illustrated by Al White (Racine. WI: Western Publishing Company, 1965). This is Mickey's dog Pluto's debut. http://www.youtube.com/watch?v=nCwevopGQvA.

130. Laurence Yep, *Dragonwings* (New York: HarperCollins, 1975).

131. Faith Ringgold, *Tar Beach* (New York: Crown, 1991), unpaginated. See Faith Ringgold, *Tar Beach 1* (1990), silkscreen on silk. Solomon R. Guggenheim Museum, New York, http://www.guggenheim.org/new-york/collections/collection-online/artwork/3719?tmpl=component&print=1.

132. Albrecht Dürer, *Hercules at the Crossroads* (ca. 1498), engraving on paper. Birmingham, UK: The Birmingham Museums, http://www.bmagic.org.uk/objects/1955P47.

133. David Legare, *Hercules Protecting the Balance between Pleasure and Virtue* (1993), oil on canvas. Private Collection, http://www.davidligare.com/paintings.html.

134. Lorenzo Lotto, *The Allegory of Virtue and Vice* (1505), oil on panel. Washington, DC: National Gallery of Art, http://www.nga.gov/collection/gallery/gg16/gg16-297.html.

135. See Ovid, *Fasti*, translated by James George Frazer (Cambridge: Loeb Classical Library, Harvard University Press, and William Heinemann Ltd., 1931), http://www.theoi.com/Text/OvidFasti1.html.

136. Giovanni Bellini, *The Feast of the Gods* (1514), oil on canvas. National Gallery, Washington, D.C., http://www.nga.gov/collection/gallery/gg17/gg17-1138.html.

137. Carolin C. Young, *Apples of Gold in Settings of Silver: Stories of Dinner as a Work of Art* (New York: Simon & Schuster, 2003).

138. Norman Lindsay, *The Picnic Gods* (1907). Pen and ink on paper. Sidney: Art Gallery of New South Wales.

139. Thomas Hart Benton, *Persephone* (1938–1939), egg tempera and oil on canvas. Kansas City, MO: Nelson-Atkins Museum of Art, http://www.nelson-atkins.org/collections/iscroll-objectview.cfm?id=27583.

140. Eudora Welty, "Asphodel," in *Eudora Welty: Stories, Essays & Memoir* (New York: The Library of America, 1942; reprint 1998), 251.

141. James G. Davis, *Prometheus Bound, Prometheus Unbound*, Collection of the Artist (2007), oil on canvas, http://www.jamesgdavis.org/paintings.php.

142. E. M. Forster, "Other Kingdom" [1909], in *The Celestial Omnibus* (New York: Vintage, 1976), 109, 110.

143. George Warner Allen, *Picnic at Wittenham* (1947–1948), oil and tempera on canvas laid on wood support. London: Tate Britain, http://www.tate.org.uk/art/artworks/allen-picnic-at-wittenham-t06604.

144. Frederick Ashton, *Picnic at Tintagel* (1952). Commissioned by the New York City Ballet and premiered in 1952 in New York. The music is Arnold Bax's tone poem *Garden of Fand* (1916). A collection of photographs by George Platt Lynes are in the Houghton Library, Harvard College Library, Harvard University.

145. Günter Grass, *The Flounder*, translated by Ralph Mannheim (New York: Harcourt Brace Jovanovich, 1977), 545.

146. Grass, *The Flounder*, 545.

147. Jean Renoir, *Picnic on the Grass* (1959), directed and written by Jean Renoir. Produced by Ginette Courtois-Doynel.

148. Barbara Kingsolver, *Animal Dreams* (New York: HarperCollins, 1990), 160.

149. Edward T. O'Donnell, *Ship Ablaze: The Tragedy of the Steamboat* General Slocum (New York: Broadway Books, 2003).

150. William March, *The Bad Seed* (New York: Ecco/HarperCollins, 1954; 1997; 1954).

151. Piero di Cosimo, *The Fight between the Lapiths and Centaurs* (1500–1510), oil on wood. London: National Gallery of Art, www.nationalgallery.org.uk/paintings/piero-di-cosimo-the-fight-between-the-lapiths-and-the-centaurs.

152. Émile Zola, *Thérèse Raquin* [1867], translated by Edward Vizetelly (London, 1901), http://www.gutenberg.org/files/6626/6626-h/6626-h.htm.

153. Theodore Dreiser, book 2, chapter 47, *An American Tragedy* [1925] (New York: The Library of America, 2003), http://gutenberg.net.au/ebooks02/0200421.txt.

154. Giuseppe Lampedusa, *The Leopard*, translated by Archibald Colquhoun (New York: Pantheon, 1958), 68.

155. Luchino Visconti, *The Leopard* (1963). Film adaptation of Giuseppe Lampedusa's novel *The Leopard* (1958). Directed by Luchino Visconti. Written by Pasquale Festa Campanile, Enrico Medioli, Massimoa Franciosa, Luchino Visconti, and Suso

Cecchi d'Amico. Produced by Goffredo Lombardo and Pietro Notarianni. Distributed by Twentieth Century-Fox Film Corporation.

156. Sylvia Plath, "The Colossus," in *The Colossus* (New York: Alfred A. Knopf, 1967).

157. Sylvia Plath, *The Unabridged Journals of Sylvia Plath*, edited by Karen V. Kukil (New York: Random House, 2000), 128.

158. Ted Hughes, "Minotaur 2," in *Collected Poems* (London: Macmillan, 2003), 1178.

159. Ted Hughes, *The Iron Man: A Story in Five Nights*, illustrated by Andrew Davidson (London: Faber and Faber, 1968).

160. W. H. Auden, "Marginalia," "Thoughts of His Own Death" [1965–1968]," in *Collected Poems*, edited by Edward Mendelson (New York: Modern Library, 1994), 785.

161. Vladimir Nabokov, *Lolita* (New York: Random House, 1955), 12.

162. Anton Chekhov, "The Party," in *The Tales of Chekhov: "The Party" and Other Stories*, translated by Constance Garnett (New York, 1917), 36.

163. Katherine Mansfield, "The Garden Party," in *"The Garden Party" and Other Stories* (New York: Alfred A. Knopf 1922), 72, http://digital.library.upenn.edu/women/mansfield/garden/garden.html#party.

164. Katherine Mansfield, "To the Hon. Dorothy Brett, October 15, 1921," *The Collected Letters of Katherine Mansfield*, edited by John Middleton Murray (London: Constable and Co., 1929), 144, http://nzetc.victoria.ac.nz/tm/scholarly/tei-Mur-02Lett-t1-body-d119.html.

165. D. H. Lawrence, chapter 15, "The Water-Party," in *Women in Love* (1920), edited by Norman Loftis (New York: Basic Books, 2005), 154–89, http://www.gutenberg.org/files/4240/4240-h/4240-h.htm.

166. Joyce Carol Oates, *Black Water* (New York: Dutton, 1992), 136.

167. John Banville, *The Sea* (New York: Alfred A. Knopf, 2005).

168. Joan Lindsay, *Picnic at Hanging Rock* (Melbourne: Cheshire, 1967). See William Ford, http://www.cv.vic.gov.au/stories/images-of-melbourne/1793/at-the-hanging-rock-1875/.

169. Peter Weir, *Picnic at Hanging Rock* (1975). A film adaptation of Joan Lindsay's novel *Picnic at Hanging Rock* (1967). Directed by Peter Weir. Screenplay by Cliff Green. Produced by Hal McElroy and Jim McElroy.

170. Ian McEwan, *Enduring Love* (New York: Doubleday, 1998).

171. Jim Crace, *Being Dead* (New York: Farrar Straus, Giroux, 1999), 195.

172. James Baldwin, "Going to Meet the Man" (1957), in *Going to Meet the Man* (New York: Random House, 1965), 248.

173. William Trevor, "The Teddy Bears' Picnic," in *"Beyond the Pale" and Other Stories* (New York and San Francisco: Viking, 1982), 148.

174. L. Sabattier, "Picnics on the Old Front: Motor Tours on the Battlefields," *Illustrated London News*, June 14, 1919.

175. "Pictures of the Season," *Blackwood's Edinburgh Migraine* 68 (July–December 1850): 77–93. Edwin Henry Landseer, *A Dialogue at Waterloo* (1850), oil on canvas. London: Tate Collection, http://www.tate.org.uk/art/artworks/landseer-a-dialogue-at-waterloo-n00415.

176. J. G. Farrell, *The Siege of Krishnapur* [1973] (New York: New York Review of Books, 2004), 187.

177. Victor Fleming, *Gone with the Wind* (1939). Screenplay by Sidney Howard. See http://web.archive.org/web/20010806201410/http:/blake.prohosting.com/awsm/script/GWTW.txt.

178. Mary Boykin Chesnut, *A Diary from Dixie, as Written by Mary Boykin Chesnut, Wife of James Chesnut, Jr., United States Senator from South Carolina, 1859–1861, and Afterward an Aide to Jefferson Davis and a Brigadier-General in the Confederate Army*, edited by Isabella D. Martin and Myrta Lockett Avary (New York D. Appleton and Company, 1905), 92.

179. William Howard Russell, "The Union Army in Retreat: Virginia, July 1861," in *My Diary North and South* (New York, 1863), 472.

180. Herman Melville, "The March into Virginia Ending in the First Manassas (July, 1861)," in *Collected Poems of Herman Melville*, edited by Howard P. Vincent (Chicago and New York: Packard & Company and Hendricks House, 1947).

181. Alexander Gardner, *Gardner's Photographic Sketch Book of the War* (1865) (New York: Dover, 1959), http://education.eastmanhouse.org/SketchBook/sketch-Book.html. For the image of *The Pic-Nic* see Alexander Gardner, *A Pic-Nic Party at Antietam Bridge, Virginia, 22 September, 1862*, in *Photographic Incidents of the War: Gardner's Gallery* (Washington, DC: Gardner's Gallery).

182. Cita Stelzer, *Dinner with Churchill: Policy-Making at the Dinner Table* (Berkeley, CA: Pegasus, 2013).

183. Thomas P. Rossiter, *Pic-Nic on the Hudson [Constitution Island]* (1863), oil on canvas. Butterfield Library, Cold Spring, New York, 1863, http://www.corbisimages.com/stock-photo/rights-managed/MA06195A/picnic-on-the-hudson-by-thomas-prichard.

184. Arthur Conan Doyle, *The Great Boer War* (London: Smith, Elder, & Co., 1900), http://www.archive.org/stream/thegreatboerwar03069gut/gboer10.txt.

185. Eric Newby, *Love and War in the Apennines* (London: HarperCollins Publishers Ltd., 1971), 77–80.

186. Richard Attenborough, *Oh! What a Lovely War* (1969). A film directed by Richard Attenborough, an adaptation of the musical drama *Oh! What a Lovely War*, staged by Gerry Raffles and Joan Littlewood (1963). Original play by Charles Chilton, screenplay by Len Deighton, and musical play by Joan Littlewood.

187. Alberto Moravia, "Back to the Sea," in *"Bitter Honeymoon" and Other Stories*, translated by Bernard Wall (New York: Signet Books, 1945), 138.

188. Fernando Arrabal, *Picnic on the Battlefield* [1959], translated by Barbara Wright, in Guernica *and Other Plays* (New York: Evergreen 1961), 113.

189. Günter Grass, *The Tin Drum*, translated by Ralph Manheim (New York, 1961), 339.

190. Grass, *The Tin Drum*, 541.

191. *Apocalypse Now* (1979). Directed by Francis Ford Coppola. Produced by Francis Ford Coppola. Screenplay by John Milius and Francis Ford Coppola.

192. E. L. Doctorow, *City of God* (New York: Random House, 2000), 171.

193. Michel Leiris, "Prologue," in *Manhood: A Journey from Childhood into the Fierce Order of Virility*, translated by Richard Howard (Chicago: University of Chicago Press, 1992), 13.

194. Jean-Jacques Rousseau, "Book IV, 1731–1732 [Picnic with Graffenried and Galley]," in *The Confessions of Jean Jacques Rousseau* (London: Aldus Society, 1903), http://www.gutenberg.org/files/3913/3913-h/3913-h.htm.

195. Charles Dickens, chapter XXIII, "Blissful," in *David Copperfield, The Personal History and Experience of David Copperfield the Younger*, 1850, http://www.gutenberg.org/files/766/766-h/766-h.htm.

196. John Leech, *Awful Appearance of Wopps at a Picnic Party*, *Punch*, August 25, 1849, http://www.john-leech-archive.org.uk/1849/awful-appearance-of-wasps.htm.

197. E. M. Forster, "The Possibilities of a Pleasant Outing," in *A Room with a View*, 1908, http://www.gutenberg.org/files/2641/2641-h/2641-h.htm.

198. Forster, *A Room with a View*, 4.

199. Colette, *Ripening Seed*, translated by Roger Senhouse (London: Penguin Books, in association with Secker and Warburg, 1923), 32.

200. Omar Khayyam, "Rubáiyát 11," *The Rubáiyát of Omar Khayyám*, translated by Edward Fitzgerald (London: Bernard Quarich, 1859), http://www.gutenberg.org/files/246/246-h/246-h.htm.

201. Margaret Atwood, *The Blind Assassin: A Novel* (New York: Random House, 2000), 11.

202. Crispijn van de Passe, "Quæ Læta Hæc Species!" in *New Mirror for Youth*, 1617, translated by Ken Albala, http://emblems.let.uu.nl/nj1617020.html#tr.

203. Jean-Antoine Watteau, *The Collation*, aka *Imbiss Im Freien* (ca 1721), oil on canvas. Winterthur, Germany: The Oskar Reinhart Collection "Am Römerholz," http://www.insecula.com/oeuvre/O0026754.html.

204. Bernard Fleetwood-Walker, *Amity* (ca. 1933), oil on canvas. Liverpool: Walker Art Gallery, National Museums of Liverpool, http://www.liverpoolmuseums.org.uk/walker/collections/brief_enc/encounters7.aspx.

205. E. M. Forster, "The Story of a Panic (1904)," in *The Celestial Omnibus and Other Stories* (New York: Alfred A. Knopf, 1947), http://archive.org/details/celestialomnibus00forsuoft.

206. E. M. Forster, "The Curate's Friend" (1907), in *The Celestial Omnibus*, 129–42.

207. Evelyn Waugh, *Brideshead Revisited* (Boston: Little, Brown and company, 1945), 24.

208. A. S. Byatt, *Possession, a Romance* (New York: Random House, 1990), 295–96.

209. Thomas Trevelyon, *The Trevelyon Miscellany of 1608: A Facsimile Edition of the Folger Shakespeare Library Ms V.B.232*, edited by Heather Wolfe (Washington, DC: Folger Shakespeare Library, 2007), http://luna.folger.edu/luna/servlet/view/search?os= 0&q=trevelyon&pgs=250&sort=Call_Number%2CAuthor%2CCD_Title%2CImprint.

210. Trevelyon, *The Trevelyon Miscellany*.

211. W. Somerset Maugham, *The Razor's Edge* (1944) (New York: Vintage, 1972), 36–37.

212. Auguste Barthélémy Glaize, *Souvenir of the Pyrenees* or *The Picnic* [*Souvenir Des Pryrénées* or *Le Goûter Champêtre*] (1851), oil on canvas. Montpellier, France: Musée Fabre, 1851, http://www.the-athenaeum.org/art/detail.php?ID=21714. For discussion see Stephen Kern, *Eyes of Love: The Gaze in English and French Paintings and Novels 1840–1900* (London: Reaktion Books, 1996).

213. Édouard Manet, *Luncheon on the Grass* [*Le déjeuner sur l'herbe*]. Paris: Musée D'Orsay, 1863, oil on canvas, http://www.musee-orsay.fr/index.php?id=851&L=1&tx_ commentaire_pi1%5BshowUid%5D=7123.

214. Paul Hayes Tucker, ed., *Manet's* Le dejeuner sur l'herbe (New York: Cambridge University Press, 1998).

215. Paul Cezanne, *Luncheon on the Grass*, aka *Déjeuner sur l'herbe* (1870/1871), oil on canvas. Paris: Musée de l'Orangerie, http://www.paul-cezanne.org/Luncheon-On-The-Grass.html.

216. See Mary Tompkins Lewis, *Cezanne's Early Imagery* (Berkeley: University of California Press, 1989).

217. See Robert Lethbridge, *Looking at Manet: Writings on Manet by Émile Zola* (London: Pallas Athena, 2013).

218. Émile Zola, *Madeleine Férat: A Realistic Novel*, translated by Edward Vizetelly (London: Vizetelly & Co., 1886), http://www.archive.org/stream/cu31924027383037/ cu31924027383037_djvu.txt.

219. Carson McCullers, *The Heart Is a Lonely Hunter* (Boston: Houghton Mifflin, 1940, 229–30).

220. Vladimir Nabokov, *Ada or Ardor: A Family Chronicle* (1969) (New York: Vintage International, 1990). See *Ada Online*, with annotations by Brian Boyd, 2012, http:// www.ada.auckland.ac.nz/.

221. D. H. Lawrence, *Sons and Lovers* (London: Duckworth, 1913), http://www. gutenberg.org/files/217/217-h/217-h.htm.

222. DuBose Heyward, *Porgy* (New York: George H. Doran Company, 1926), 121.

223. George Orwell, *1984* (New York: Secker and Warburg, 1948), http://gutenberg.net.au/ebooks01/0100021.txt.

224. William Inge, *Picnic: A Summer Romance in Three Acts* (New York: Random House, 1953), 118–19.

225. Joshua Logan. *Picnic* (1955). A film adaptation of William Inge's drama *Picnic* (1953). Directed by Joshua Logan. Screenplay by Daniel Taradash. Distributed by Columbia Pictures.

226. John O'Hara, "A Few Trips and Some Poetry," in *And Other Stories* (New York: Random House, 1968), 120.

227. Richard Rodgers and Oscar Hammerstein II. *Oklahoma!* (New York: Applause Books, 100).

228. Martin Amis, *Dead Babies* [1975] (New York: Vintage International, 1991), 47–52.

229. Émile Zola, *L'Assommoir*, translated by Edward Vizetelly (London, 1877), http://www.gutenberg.org/files/8558/8558-h/8558-h.htm.

230. John Galsworthy, "The Apple Tree," in *Five Tales* (New York: Scribner's, 1918).

231. Guy de Maupassant, "A Day in the Country" (1881), in *"A Day in the Country" and other Stories*, translated by David Coward (New York: Oxford University Press, 1990), http://www.gutenberg.org/files/3090/3090-h/3090-h.htm.

232. Jean Renoir, *A Day in the Country* (1946). Directed and written by Jean Renoir. http://www.imdb.com/video/hulu/vi2021368601/?ref_=tt_wb_hulu.

233. Jean Renoir, *Picnic on the Grass* (1959). Directed and written by Jean Renoir. http://www.imdb.com/title/tt0052765/.

234. Thomas Hardy, "Where the Picnic Was," in *Satires of Circumstances: Lyrics and Reveries with Miscellaneous Pieces* (London: Macmillan, 1914).

235. Bo Widerberg, *Elvira Madigan* (1967). A film directed and written by Bo Widerberg.

INDEX

Please note: Page numbers in *italics* indicate illustrations.

Aeschylus: *Prometheus Bound,* 108;
  Prometheus Fire-Bringer, 108;
  Prometheus Unbound, 108
Aesop: "The Country Mouse and the
  City Mouse," 39, 96
Allen, George Warner: *Picnic at
  Wittenham,* 109–10
Allom, Thomas: *View from Langdale
  Pikes, Looking Towards Bowfell,
  Westmorland,* 76
Altman, Robert, 93
American picnics: African American,
  26, 29–30, 43, 58, 71, 104, 123,
  143–44; food at, 21–22, 26, 27, 28,
  32, 33, 59, 65; indoor, 40, 42; literary
  portrayals, 57–58, 115–16, 117–18,
  120–21, 126–27, 142–47; motoring
  and, 82, 85–87; nineteenth-century,
  17, 18–19, 51; sightseeing and, 76,
  77–78; tailgate parties, 27
Amis, Martin: *Dead Babies,* 147
Angelo, Henry: *Reminiscences,* 38
Angelou, Maya: *I Know Why the Caged
  Bird Sings,* 69, 71

Anna Perenna (Roman New Year
  celebration), 10, 106
Antarctica, picnic in, 49
Anthony, John, 11–12
Antietam, battle of, *128,* 128–29
Apocalypse Now (film), 133
Apollo (god), 110–12
Appleton's Journal, 19
Armitage, Ronda and David: *The
  Lighthouse Keeper's Picnic,* 102
Arnim, Elizabeth von: *Elizabeth and Her
  German Garden,* 78–79
Arrabal, Fernando: *Picnic on the
  Battlefield,* 56, 131, *132*
Ashton, Frederick, 61; *Picnic at
  Tintagel,* 110
assemblée, 14, 88, 89–90
Athenaeus, 10; *The Deipnosophists,* 12
Attenborough, Richard, 130
Atwood, Margaret: *The Blind Assassin,*
  137
Auden, W. H.: "New Year Letter," 118;
  "Thoughts of His Own Death," 118
Austen, Gillian, 90

ABOUT THE AUTHOR

Walter Levy is professor emeritus in English at Pace University, New York. He writes about picnics and food from a New York town with one traffic light. His selected food publications include "American Picnics," *Oxford Companion to American Food and Drink*, 2nd edition (2012); "Once Upon a Literary Sandwich," *Virginia Culinary Thymes* (2011); guest editor of *The CEA Critic (Food and Literary Imagination*, 2008); "Anti-Picnics," *Proceedings of the Oxford Symposium of Food and Cookery 2007* (2008); "American Picnics," *Oxford Companion to American Food and Drink* (2007); "American Picnics," *Oxford Book of American Food and Drink* (2004, 2012); "Picnics," *Scribner's Encyclopedia of Food and Culture* (2003); *Proceedings of the Oxford Symposium of Food and Cookery* for 2003, 2004, 2007; *Listening to Earth: American Environmental Writing*, with Christopher Hallowell (2004); *Modern Drama: An Anthology of World Drama* (1999); *Green Perspectives: Thinking and Writing about Literature and the Environment*, with Christopher Hallowell (1994); *Lives Through Literature: A Thematic Anthology*, with Helane Levine Keating, 3rd edition (2001); "American Picnics," *Oxford Companion to American Food and Drink*, 2nd edition (2012);"Once Upon a Literary Sandwich," *Virginia Culinary Thymes* (2011); guest editor of *The CEA Critic (Food and Literary Imagination,* 2008); "Anti-Picnics," *Proceedings of the Oxford Symposium of Food and Cookery 2007* (2008); "American Picnics," *Oxford Companion to American Food and Drink* (2007); "Some Like It Raw," *Proceedings of the Oxford Symposium of Food and Cookery 2004* (2005); "American Picnics," *Oxford Book of American Food and Drink* (2004); "Picnics," *Scribner's Encyclopedia of Food and Culture* (2003); "Picnics and Fairy Tales," *Proceedings of the Oxford Symposium of Food and Cookery 2003* (2004).